THE DEVIL'S PICNIC

The
DEVIL'S PICNIC

Around the World in Pursuit of Forbidden Fruit

TARAS GRESCOE

BLOOMSBURY

Published by Bloomsbury USA, New York
Distributed to the trade by Holtzbrinck Publishers

All papers used by Bloomsbury USA are natural,
recyclable products made from wood grown in well-managed
forests. The manufacturing processes conform to the
environmental regulations of the country of origin.

The Library of Congress has cataloged the hardcover
edition of this book as follows:

Grescoe, Taras.
The devil's picnic : around the world in pursuit of forbidden fruit / Taras
Grescoe.
p. cm.
ISBN-13: 978-1-58234-429-4 (hardcover)
ISBN-10: 1-58234-429-9 (hardcover)
1. Food. 2. Tourism. I. Title.

TX357.G85 2005
641.3—dc22
2005009248

First published in the United States by Bloomsbury in 2005
This paperback edition published in 2006

Paperback ISBN-10: 1-58234-615-1
ISBN-13: 978-1-58234-615-1

1 3 5 7 9 10 8 6 4 2

Typeset by Hewer Text UK Ltd, Edinburgh
Printed in the United States of America by Quebecor World Fairfield

CONTENTS

PROLOGUE 1

APERITIF
1. *Hjemmebrent*: The Viking Moonshine 9

CRACKERS
2. Savory Crackers: Poppies for Nanny 53

CHEESE
3. Époisses: Satan in a Poplar Box 87

MAIN COURSE
4. *Criadillas*: Brussels vs. the Bull's Balls 123

SMOKE
5. Cohiba Esplendido: It's the Law 155

DIGESTIF
6. Absinthe *Suisse*: One Glass and You're Dead 195

DESSERT
7. *Chocolat Mousseux*: The Exonerated Buzz 231

HERBAL TEA
8. Maté de Coca: Never Say No 259

NIGHTCAP
9. Pentobarbital Sodium: The Last Sip 307

EPILOGUE 345

Use, do not abuse; neither abstinence
nor excess ever renders man happy.

—Voltaire

PROLOGUE

I'VE SPENT THE last year flirting with the devil. It's been a risky experience, especially since he's been known to lead me astray in the past. But I seem to have survived the experience unscathed: I guzzled absinthe in the mountains of Switzerland and saw cocaine being made out of coca leaves in the Andes. I smuggled chewing gum and pornography into Singapore and puffed on Cuban cigars in San Francisco. And I've brought back wicked souvenirs.

Once the last of the snow has melted, I'm going to gather up my mementos and invite some of my closest friends to a picnic on the hilltop park in the center of my town—the one with the giant Catholic cross at its summit. We'll have to pick a spot that's out of sight of the police who patrol the mountain paths on horseback, as the blanket will be spread with things vilified, demonized, and banned by the lawmakers of the civilized world. To awaken my guests' appetites, I'll start with a shot of the 186-proof moonshine I picked up from a bootlegger in Norway. Then we'll have crackers and cheese: narcotic poppy-seed biscuits, banned in Singapore, spread with a reeking, five-week-old Époisses, the same unpasteurized cheese that allegedly caused two deaths from listeriosis in France. For the main course, a mixed plate of delicacies, made following recipes I learned in Spain: a pottery dish of baby eels, killed with an infusion of tobacco, and a stew of bulls' testicles in garlic and gravy. To clear the palate, I'll pass out air-polluting, emphysema-provoking Cohiba cigars, direct from Fidel Castro's yanqui-baiting socialist dystopia. As a digestif: a shot of cloudy blue, epileptic-fit-inducing absinthe, bought from a clandestine distiller in the Swiss valley where the active ingredient, wormwood, has been cultivated since the eighteenth century. For dessert, the purest Basque chocolate, "black inside . . . as the devil's ass is black from smoke," as the Marquis de Sade liked it, and spiked with powdered chili peppers. To stimulate the mind and soothe the soul, I'll bring a thermos of tea made from the leaves of the coca plant, one of humanity's oldest intoxicants, now uprooted in every nation of the earth by the minions of the DEA. The only souvenir I won't be able to offer—it's not the kind of thing I like to keep in my cupboard—will be a shot glass of pentobarbital sodium, the final drink for suicide tourists who fly to Zürich to put an end to their terminal diseases. I'll be curious to see who has the courage to make it to the end of this infernal *déjeuner sur l'herbe*. Every course consists of something guaranteed to offend the safety-conscious, the temperate, the holier-than-thou, the politically correct, the chickenshit.

Fortunately, there aren't too many puritans in my immediate circle of friends. In fact, most of them are pretty broad-minded. Which seems appropriate: an open mind, it's been said, is the devil's picnic.

When you can't have it, you want it.

It's simple psychology. Hold a soother, a teddy bear, or a lollipop out of any toddler's reach, and he'll throw a tantrum. Deny him something he's never seen before (a new toy, a never-before-sucked lollipop, the latest Disney DVD), and he'll become so obsessed with obtaining it he'll refuse to eat and begin to babble of nothing else.

Parents understand this phenomenon. Teenage babysitters understand it. Older brothers and sisters understand it—and exploit it. Governments, in contrast, never seem to get it. Generation in, generation out, they select certain goods and substances and tell their citizens they can't have them, on the ground they're harmful, addictive, immoral, or demotivating. Then they react with shock when their citizens start to act like naughty children, breaking the law to get at what they've been deemed too immature to handle. The whole situation is absurd. It's philosophically indefensible. Most of all, it's an immense waste of social and economic resources. Punishing and incarcerating people for their appetites and excesses costs society billions of dollars a year and increases the sum total of human misery immeasurably. It also ignores a simple truism: ban something, and it becomes stronger, costlier, and more coveted than ever before.

It's too bad, because never in history have we been in a better position to indulge our most extravagant desires. Thanks to globalization, middle-class North Americans and Europeans can click on a mouse and order saffron from Iran, pashmina scarves from Nepal, or brand-name runners from the sweatshops of China and have them appear in a FedEx box on the doorstep the next day—a command of the world's resources that was not even enjoyed by Roman nobility or nineteenth-century European aristocrats. The days of the Catholic Church's Index of Prohibited Books are long gone, and we flatter ourselves that we live in a period of unprecedented freedom, in which we can read *Ulysses* and *Lolita* in public, surf risqué Internet sites and watch Arabic satellite networks, eat bacon or take snuff without being terrorized by arcane religious prohibitions.

This freedom is an illusion. In the twenty-first century, the world is still riddled with atavistic interdictions. This is not merely a matter of the Hindu ban against eating sacred cows or the Islamic injunctions against gambling and intoxicants. The following activities are strictly prohibited in North America (with penalties, in some American states, ranging up to life imprisonment): planting hemp or tobacco seeds in one's garden; bringing a few ounces of authentic farmstead Camembert through customs; selling or drinking real absinthe; soothing a headache with a cup of poppy or coca tea. Every one of these prohibitions, born in climates of xenophobia or moral panic, offers an insight into society's phobias: foreign contamination; unchecked hedonism; the insidious undermining of the work ethic.

In an era of fear—fear of terrorism, fear of foreign ideas, fear of our fellow citizens—we seem all too willing to allow our individual liberty to be eroded in the name of increased security. Demonization is the age-old tool of power, and its buzzwords—*evildoer, taboo, zero tolerance*—attach a spurious mystique to activities that might otherwise be perceived as anodyne, pathetic, or merely banal. The ostensible targets of prohibitions are the substances that authority (in the form of the state, the imams, community standards, the Vatican, international bureaucracies) declare noxious. The real battleground is our own bodies—and the ultimate casualty is our sovereignty over ourselves.

I, for one, have always been fascinated by the forbidden. As soon as I encountered the words *absinthe, hashish,* and *opium* as a teenager, I was dreaming up ways to get my hands on them. I've never understood the incurious who draw the line at experimenting with different sensations, and different forms of consciousness, merely because they are circumscribed by the current crop of laws. In my experience, those who choose to cross the line—the born rebels, the ne'er-do-wells, the independent thinkers—also tend to be the best company. (In contrast, those *obsessed* by the line—the alcoholics, drug casualties, the sad addicts—can be torrential bores.)

I began this year as a kind of Aleister Crowley with a backpack, determined to track down and try all that was forbidden, scornful of any suggestion that my desires should be regulated. After twelve months of traveling, through seven different countries, I've encountered vastly different attitudes toward prohibitions, ranging from welfare-state tolerance to nanny-state fury, from urbane indifference to xenophobic hysteria; not to mention the perplexed patience of those in the developing world whose livelihoods are threatened by foreign prohibitions. The world changed my outlook, as it always does. If I started out as something of a libertarian, in favor of legalization, I ended up with a more nuanced view of how prohibition, and particularly drug prohibition, could be handled.

Of course, I should have known: nothing is as simple as it first appears. The devil, as always, is in the details.

·A P E R I T I F·

No nation is drunken where wine is cheap.

—*Thomas Jefferson*

HJEMMEBRENT

The Viking Moonshine

I KNEW ONLY ONE word of Norwegian, but I'd already found a way to work it into the conversation.

The word was *hjemmebrent*, Norwegian for "moonshine," and I was pretty sure the shaven-headed soccer fan sitting next to me would be able to tell me something about it. Outside, an armada of lead-bellied cumulus clouds steamed resolutely across an azure sky, off to invade Iceland. Wind-flattened wheat fields glowed golden, and red-roofed farmhouses and moose-crossing signs gave way to roundabouts and IKEA stores as our bus approached the suburbs of Oslo. My neighbor had been trying to focus on a British music magazine, and something in his demeanor—the three days of reddish stubble; the gamy stench of lager and tobacco; the squelched burps and oily sweat—screamed hangover, the kind that is better slept off, but which the excess adrenaline of passport control, baggage claim, and customs was forcing him to endure fully conscious. Across the aisle, his curly-haired friend, in shorts and wraparound sunglasses, was in even rougher shape: he rested his head on the seat-back in front of him, emitting the occasional groan and protesting loudly when the lady ahead of him tried to recline. They, like everybody else on the bus, were keeping their translucent duty-free bags from the Glasgow airport close to their heels. It was the first thing I'd noticed when I'd boarded the Ryanair flight from Prestwick to Torp. Every adult—without exception—was carrying at least one box of Scotch or a bottle of gin, vodka, or other liquor. I could just make out the bottle of ten-year-old Bushmills in an embossed cardboard tube at my neighbor's feet.

"Just back from Scotland?" I asked cheerily.

"*Ja*," he said wearily. "We went to see the Rangers play Hibernian. There were seven of us, but we lost two in the airport—they were in the toilet when the bus left. We are all a little tired today." His name was Rune, from Lillehammer. "I thought I was going to a meeting in Oslo on Friday afternoon, but when I showed up for work, all my friends were there. 'C'mon!' they said. 'We are going to Glasgow!' I got married in Copenhagen this winter, but I never had a bachelor party, so this was my big surprise. I have been wearing the same clothes all weekend." He plucked listlessly at his rancid shirt. "I only had one hour of sleep this night. I would like to call my wife, but I lost my cell phone at a nightclub."

Had there been any fights?

"No! We were there for the soccer and the beer. Drinks are half as expensive as in Norway, and the glasses are bigger. We were very happy. And the Scottish people were even happier, because Glasgow won."

So, I ventured, had he ever tried *hjemmebrent*?

Rune gave a start. "You know what is *hjemmebrent*?" He chuckled. "This is very popular where I live—but you can't find it in bars or shops. It is clear, like vodka, and very strong. But there has been a problem recently, with methanol, and it is harder to find than it used to be. We mix it with grape juice, or coffee. This is called *karsk*."

I repeated the word: he had pronounced it *kaarshk*.

"*Karsk*. *Hjemmebrent*. Now you know the two most important words." Rune chuckled again. Then he winced.

He leaned across the aisle, evidently explaining to his friend what I was looking for.

The man snorted. As we pulled into the Oslo bus station, he lifted his shades and pointedly met my gaze with bloodshot, black-rimmed eyes.

"Be careful," he croaked.

When it comes to alcohol, most of humanity is in denial. Though drinking causes us enormous problems, we persist anyway. (According to the World Health Organization, 4 percent of the global burden of disease can be attributed to alcohol; only tobacco, responsible for 4.1 percent of deaths worldwide, surpasses it as a risk factor in mortality in the developed world.) We envy, even secretly detest, those lucky few who seem to be able to drink with moderation. (Particularly the Italians, French, and Spanish, as they smugly relish another bottle of red wine with another multicourse dinner.) We miss work and get into fights because of our drinking. (The annual cost of alcoholism in the United States is estimated at $185 billion, mainly due to absentee-ism. The majority of murders, rapes, and property crimes are com-mitted under the influence, and forty percent of all fatal car accidents are alcohol-related.) We routinely decide our lives would be better off without booze and vow to swear off it. (Adopting doctrines like Islam, or undertaking such noble experiments as Prohibition.) And then, after periods of relative abstinence, we find ourselves succumbing to another debauched spree. (Like the post-Soviet vodka orgy still gripping Russia, or the post-ecstasy binge-drinking epidemic that is currently addling Britain.) Were our species to take the Alcoholics Anonymous quiz, it would be a serious candidate for a meeting in the nearest church basement.

Depending on the dose, alcohol can provoke wailing at the wake, donnybrooks down the pub, or stomach pumps at the emergency ward. Though less addictive than nicotine, it is far more dependence-inducing than marijuana. Unlike cocaine or heroin, it so changes the physiology of the brain, and the structure of every cell in the body, that its withdrawal can actually kill a hard-core addict. About 10 percent of drinkers will become dependent, whether they are "episodic heavy drinkers"—bingers—or full-blown alcoholics. The remaining 90 percent will derive pleasure and succor from their relationship with alcohol, and those who drink moderately—two or three glasses a day—may actually live longer than abstainers, thanks to alcohol's ability to diminish heart disease.

Scourge of mankind; blessing from God—contemporary cultures are deeply divided on what to do with the juice of fermenting grain, potatoes, and fruit. There are the French, for example, who are wont to deny that wine is a form of alcohol at all and are free to buy a plastic liter bottle of dirt cheap plonk at four o'clock in the morning. (And somehow they haven't all turned into rapists and murderers—though the statistics on drunk driving in France are pretty chilling.) Then there are the Iranians, who pay $200 for a bottle of smuggled Johnnie Walker and tremble lest the *komiteh*, or Islamic religious police, knock on their door, catch whiskey on their breath, and punish them with seventy lashes. (With that said, there is remarkably little cirrhosis of the liver in Iran—though there are two million Iranian heroin addicts.) Somewhere between the utter liberalism of Latin cultures and the complete prohibition of Islam lies the rest of the world, with its amusing webwork of contradictory drinking laws. In America alone, some states require that food be available when alcohol is served; others that no food be served at all. Some insist the interior of a bar be visible from the street; others that drinkers be shielded from view. In Arkansas and Alabama, a large percentage of counties are still completely dry. Until 2004, South Carolina's state constitution banned free-pouring, stipulating that spirits could only be dispensed from the kind of 1.7 ounce minibottles used on airplanes. Mormon-dominated Utah is truly extreme: clients must pay annual membership fees of at least $12 before they can order a drink at a bar, waiters can present wine lists to customers only if they are directly asked, and bartenders aren't allowed to pour doubles, though they can place a one-ounce sidecar of the same liquor next to a client's glass. In England, the Licensing Act of 1964 allows drinkers to mill in front of pubs with full pints, but forces publicans to call time at eleven P.M., creating a rush of hastily ordered and consumed ales. (The Labour government has proposed a revision of the act that would allow local authorities to set their own closing times. The hope is it will reduce the last call effect that turns London's West End and Manchester's Fallowfield into free-for-alls of public urination, vomiting, and brawling; the fear is that, in the short run at least, it will create a twenty-four-hour drinking culture.)

Then there's Norway, voted best country in the world by the United Nations for the fourth year running, on the strength of the usual array of brain-numbing statistics: a life expectancy of seventy-nine years, a literacy rate of 91 percent, long-term unemployment of only .2 percent, and a gross per capita national product—second only to Luxembourg's—of $36,600 U.S. Since oil was discovered offshore in the late 1960s, this nation of fishermen, sailors, and farmers has become very rich indeed—Oslo recently surpassed Tokyo as the most expensive city on earth. A liter of gas at state-owned Statoil stations costs ten kroner ($1.42), and a tram ride on public transportation is 30KR ($4.28); even dialing a toll-free 1–800 number at a phone booth costs 5KR (70 cents). Given the scale of the oil bonanza, one might expect a little celebration, some champagne and cocktails, to be in order. Forget it. Outside the Islamic world, no culture has a more restrictive alcohol-control regime. Norway, the first country to introduce blood-alcohol limits for drivers—in 1936—does not allow advertising of any alcoholic beverages but light beer. Wine and spirits can be purchased only in state-monopoly liquor stores, most of which are open till six on weekdays, three on Saturdays, and not at all on Sundays. Norway has the highest alcohol taxes, and consequently the highest official prices, of any nation on earth: a liter bottle of Smirnoff vodka costs $50 U.S., and a pint of domestic Ringnes beer will set you back $9 in downtown Oslo.

The Norwegians can marshal some impressive figures showing that their brand of government intervention and cradle-to-grave welfare has a positive impact on the public good. With only 60 prisoners for every 100,000 inhabitants (versus 730 per 100,000 in the United States), they have one of the lowest incarceration rates in the world—and since there are fewer than three thousand prison beds, some convicted criminals have to wait up to two years before they start serving their time. Norway is a great place to be female: women hold over a third of all seats in the Storting, or Parliament, and the state provides free medical care, public day-care centers, and a child cash-benefit scheme. There are typically only fifty murders in the country a year—contrast that with the city of Detroit, which has over 350—and few involve random violence. Like Switzerland, Norway has chosen not to use the euro—preferring to keep its indigenous kroner—nor is it part of the European Union. With a $140 billion Petroleum Fund socked away for a rainy day, the Norwegians don't *need* those peasants in Europe.

In every way, Norway is an exception. It is an egalitarian utopia where all gravestones have to be the same height, and *allemansretten*, "everyman's right," allows citizens to pitch their tents, pick fruit, or ski anywhere in the land, even on private property. It is a sexually liberated kingdom where the crown prince married a single mother who admitted to being a former cocaine addict, the finance minister tied the knot with his longtime male companion, and yet where the prime minister is a teetotaling former Lutheran priest. It is an extreme nanny state, where there is no smoking in bars and restaurants, and the national film board has banned three hundred films since 1955 (among them *Crash*, *Eyes Wide Shut*, and *Life of Brian*). And, for teetotalers, it is the poster boy of nations, since its strict drinking laws have apparently produced the lowest rates of alcohol consumption in Europe. According to official statistics, Norwegians drink only 5.9 liters of alcohol a year per adult—the equivalent of about one can of beer a day—making them mere tipplers next to the Italians (9.2 liters), the French (13.6 liters), and the current world champions, the Irish, who, at 14.2 liters of pure alcohol, are going through the equivalent of two and a half cans of beer per adult a day.

So, as my suitcase clattered over the paving stones in front of the neoclassical façade of the Oslo train station, I was a little surprised to find so many obviously wasted vagrants milling around the tidy streets of the world's most expensive welfare state. On Fred Olsens Gate, I almost ran into two thin, young men in black hoodies sitting cross-legged in the gutter between luxury cars, doing something elaborate with spoons and a lighter. As I crossed a parking lot, the wheels of my suitcase got tangled in little drift-piles of syringes and pressed-out blister packs of pills. From a spindly pedestrian overpass that traversed a harborfront highway, I looked back to see that the men in the hoodies had been accosted by two mounted policewomen, blond ponytails poking out of their black helmets, their towering sorrel horses pacing nervously as the young men rose stiffly to their feet.

I continued trundling my bag toward the water's edge. In Oslo, my hotel was going to be a ship. The MS *Innvik*, formerly a fjord-cruiser, was now home to a theater troupe that paid the bills by renting out its cramped upper cabins to tourists. After checking in, I ordered a tuna fish sandwich on the upper deck and tried to forget the depressing harborfront squalor.

From the starboard side, the view improved. Across the Oslo Fjord, orange and blue building-block stacks of shipping containers were piled before an evergreen promontory, and farther up the pier, a ferry pulled away from the turrets of the Akershus Castle. The illumination was ethereal, the sky as pale blue as Scandinavian eyes. Then I noticed a couple of seated figures closer to the ship, face-to-face in the shadow of a concrete barrier. It was a strangely tender scene: using a syringe, the woman patiently probed her shirtless companion's skinny forearm for a vein. After a few minutes of patting and prodding, she gave up and injected the drugs directly into the side of his neck.

I pushed aside my sandwich. My first exposure to Norwegians, those paragons of probity, was in the form of grievously hungover soccer fans and emaciated junkies shooting up in public. Something was rotten in the kingdom of Norway, and it wasn't the tuna fish.

"We were just discussing the latest chess move by the police," said Alto Braveboy, between sips of Aass beer.

It was almost ten P.M., the sun had finally set over the fjord, and I'd joined some of the theater's stagehands at a table on the upper deck of the *Innvik*. Alto, the most voluble of them, was a striking-looking character: an old punk and longtime snowboarder, he favored a black neck bandanna. The gold rings that encircled his thumbs and pierced his upper lip contrasted nicely with his creamy-coffee complexion. His family was from Grenada, but he'd lived in Oslo most of his life and spoke English with an accent cadged from a lifetime of listening to the BBC.

"The junkies used to buy their drugs on the *plata*," he continued, "the square south of the train station. But the richest man in Oslo—he owns the Hotel Opera, the one you see over there"—Alto nodded to an orange neon sign on a façade looming over the railway station—"decided he didn't want them upsetting the tourists, so the police have been ordered to move them along. Now the dealers are in twenty different squares and schoolyards around the city. In the *plata*, at least there were surveillance cameras, and people looked out for each other. If there were thirteen-year-olds trying to buy heroin, the police would do something about it. Now there's no accountability. And some of those dealers—well, let's just say they're not the most ethical people. They'll sell to anybody."

Norway is no Switzerland or Holland, whose notoriously liberal drug policies also produce some of the lowest rates of drug-related violence and health problems in the world. Like Sweden, Norway officially subscribes to the paradigm of the worldwide War on Drugs. There are at least five thousand heroin addicts in Oslo, and in 2001 alone, 338 people died of overdoses—seven times more Norwegians than were murdered—making Norway the drug-death capital of Europe. Heroin, smuggled from Afghanistan, has lately become cheaper than tobacco (not that, at $10, a pack of cigarettes is all that affordable). Heroin is not cheap enough, however, that addicts can afford to snort or smoke it—as they do in Holland—which means they use syringes and tend to overdose when there's an unexpected surge in potency. A proper methadone program wasn't established until the late 1990s, and for those who want to quit, waiting periods can stretch for up to two years.

"It's a complete mess," said Alto. "There was supposed to be a safe injection site near the station, where people could get clean needles, but it never opened. Norway is one of those countries that likes to pretend it doesn't have any problems."

He looked at me appraisingly as he took a drag on his cigarette. "But what brings you here, mate? Not drugs, I hope."

Well, a kind of drug, I admitted. I told him I was looking for *hjemmebrent*.

He laughed. "We used to drink a lot of that. We call it *heimert* in Oslo. It's not the kind of thing you keep on drinking, though— maybe a few times at parties, to get drunk. If you drink it with water alone, it's so strong you get this thing called *kald kjeft*. It means 'cold mouth' —your entire mouth goes numb the next day. It's nasty." He shuddered at the memory.

"But if you want some, it shouldn't be a problem. Up north, in the Trøndelag area around Trondheim, that's all they drink. And they *really* know how to drink up there. If you live on an island, or in some remote village, and your nearest neighbor is three Norwegian miles away, you're not going to get together on Saturday night to talk about the latest developments in literature. You're going to get pissed."

Alto pulled out his cell phone, scrolled through a menu, and made a call. I could make out a few words: "*Kanadisk . . . bok . . . heimert . . .*" He hung up, looking puzzled. "My mate says he did have some *hjemmebrent*, but he's converted it all into absinthe. But I'll keep on phoning around.

"Don't worry," he said, picking up his pint and sauntering back to the hold. "We should be able to hook you up."

I found my first Vinmonopolet (Wine Monopoly) store in Grünerløkka, a riverside neighborhood of small parks, tea lounges, and Italian bistros. The first clue to its presence was the parade of women in heels and office suits carrying dark blue bags, embossed with silver, filled with cardboard boxes of wine. Since liquor stores close just one hour after work finishes on weekdays, people often find an excuse to make a quick booze run during office hours; I'd apparently hit the lunch-time rush. The three-liter format is the most economical (though at one hundred kroner, or $14, a liter, it can hardly be called cheap). Predictably, one temperance-minded politician recently called for the banning of bag-in-a-box wine for "facilitating consumption."

All that set the store apart was an ornate logo, the letter *V* nestled in curlicues, and the impressive security curtains of forged metal behind each window, presumably to prevent armored vehicles from pulling a smash-and-grab. In a country with almost three times the surface area of England, there were only 190 shops retailing liquor and wine (contrast this with Ireland, where 2,023 off-licenses sell wine, and 808 sell liquor, to a smaller population). Though lately a few experimental self-service outlets have been opened—and the Grünerløkka branch had been tarted up with a few vaguely Italianate frescoes—the design of the majority of Vinmonopolets seemed to be inspired by austere

Soviet-era department stores. I took a numbered ticket from a machine and stood in line behind a trio in their twenties who were asked for ID cards before they could get their six-pack. (Beers with less than 4.7 percent alcohol are sold in supermarkets, though these sections are locked up after six P.M.) The red LED light over the counter flashed my number, 189, and the clerk took my ticket.

"*Hei. Kan jeg hjelpe deg?*" she asked brightly.

I must have looked confused.

"You speak English, maybe?" she said. "What would you like?"

I said I wasn't sure, since it was all hidden behind a counter.

"We have a catalog." She pointed to a rack on the wall.

The eighty-page-long *Prisliste* booklet showed the current holdings of the Vinmonopolet, with three- to five-digit numbers identifying each bottle of pinot noir, Avocaat, or Baileys. A table in the back broke down where your money was going. Of a 79KR bottle of cabernet sauvignon, the manufacturer got 20KR, but fully 32.50KR was the "Alkoholavgift"—the alcohol tax. In fact, the state was taxing the ethanol; the higher the proof, the bigger the "gift" the government treated itself to. The various government taxes on a 42-proof bottle of Campari amounted to 75 percent of what the consumer paid; on a bottle of 80-proof vodka, it was an exorbitant 86 percent of the total price. Thanks to this policy, Norwegians abroad are preternaturally conscious of alcohol content, constantly amusing the French and the Italians by favoring 13.5 percent wines over superior, but lower-percentage, reds. It also fuels the Nordic pastime of visiting neighboring countries to stock up on cheaper booze. To avoid paying the equivalent of $40 for a fifth of vodka, Norwegians drive to Sweden, where the same amount costs $28. The Swedes take ferries to Denmark, where it costs $14; and the Danes cross the border to northern Germany, where the same bottle can cost as little as $7.

I got another ticket, queued up again, and returned to the counter.

This time I pointed confidently to the catalog and said, "I'll have two bottles of—uh, 20609."

She nodded, disappeared among the shelves in the back of the store, and returned a minute later with a couple of bottles of Duvel, the high-test Belgian beer. The price was 73KR ($10.40). What's more, the bottles were warm. I walked out clutching my conspicuous blue bag, feeling slightly seedy. It was as if I'd just hocked my typewriter to buy over-the-counter cough syrup.

Judging by a visit I paid to a replica of a historical liquor outlet in Oslo's Folk Museum, buying alcohol in Norway had always been about as agreeable as getting a polio shot. Up until 1960, according to the laminated information signs, there was a three-step purchasing system, in which you placed your order, paid at the cashier's desk— illustrated by a mannequin of a severe-looking woman in a glass cage, peering over her steel-rimmed glasses at the register—and received a wrapped bottle on presentation of a receipt. Brawls over queue positions became such a problem that the government once decided to ban lineups altogether. Clients took to pacing the street aimlessly, suddenly converging on the entrance when the store opened.

At least Norway didn't have to endure the indignities of the Bratt Liquor Control System, Sweden's famous rationing system, in vigor from the end of World War I until 1955. Spirits were sold only to married men with a ration book, who were permitted to buy one to four liters a month. Officials occasionally visited homes to decide whether the applicant was sufficiently respectable to be issued a large ration; if the applicant lost his job, his card was canceled. (A similar system was used in most Canadian provinces, though the rations were much larger. Canada had its own prohibition of spirits from 1919; it lasted for only two years in Quebec, but persisted until 1927 in Ontario. To this day, alcohol sales in Canada's most populous province are under the aegis of the Liquor Control Board of Ontario, and beer is purchased in the brewery-owned, but government-managed, Beer Stores, where warehouse employees slide clients their cases down roller belts from the back of the store.)

In the Folk Museum, bottles of aquavit, port, and red wine, filled with colored water, lined the shelves. Signs had been posted, apparently to prevent parched berserkers from leaping the counter:

Innholdet i flaskene skal ikke drikkes! (The contents of the bottles must not be consumed!)

Alarm bak disken! (Alarm behind the counter!)

Even in a twenty-first-century museum, whose panels invited visitors to chuckle over the quaintness of the drinking laws of bygone days, Norwegians apparently couldn't be trusted to manage their own desires.

SIRUS, the State Institute for Drug and Alcohol Research, which helps set official alcohol policy, has been investigating Nordic drinking habits since 1960. I'd set up appointments with a couple of their leading experts and on a Thursday morning was buzzed through a gated courtyard, and into a grim, blocky government building on an otherwise pleasant cobblestoned square.

Ragnar Hauge, a criminologist and author of several books on Norwegian alcohol policy, ushered me into his office. He was a big man with tired eyes, his graying hair swept back from a square brow. Behind me, shelves were piled up to the ceiling with books and monographs on alcohol and drugs. A pack of rolling tobacco sat within easy reach of his hand. I told him that I'd heard that, per capita, Norwegians don't drink more alcohol than other people; they just drink it all at once.

"Well, *ja.*" Hauge laughed. "Maybe this is true. We have very strong norms regulating drinking. You don't drink during meals at home, or at lunch at work, during the week. But then, on the weekends, you drink, and you drink a lot. If you're invited to somebody's home, it's expected you'll have a meal with wine and beer, and then afterwards, the spirits come out on the table: aquavit, vodka, whiskey—as much as you want. If you look at the statistics, Norway is the lowest in alcohol consumption, but if you walk in the streets at night, you will see a lot of very drunk people."

I asked whether there was a historical explanation for such patterns.

"Of course, in the last two hundred years, the teetotaler movement has been very strong in Norway. Our biggest alcohol problems started in 1814, when we were not any longer part of Denmark, and we entered into alliance with Sweden. We got our own parliament, and they removed the Danish prohibition on home distilling."

As farmers gleefully started producing their own moonshine, Norway went on a nationwide bender, which saw average adult consumption rising to twelve liters of spirits a head. In reaction, a temperance movement, drawing from the tenets of Lutheranism— one of the more austere branches of Protestantism, with a tradition of thunderous preaching—succeeded in reimposing the ban on home distilling in 1840. Since then, antialcohol activists, centered in the heavily populated Bible Belt of Norway's southwest, have had an enormous influence on government policy. In 1919, a nationwide vote approved prohibition of spirits and fortified wines; in 1926, after smuggling, home distilling, and abuse of medically prescribed alcohol had become widespread, a second referendum led to repeal. Even today, the temperance movement is the behind-the-scenes lobby that limits availability and keeps prices high. The result, Hauge admitted, was a large illegal market, with some unfortunate public-health consequences.

"In the last two years, we've had a big amount of illegal imported alcohol with methanol, wood alcohol, in it. It has caused about twenty deaths; just yesterday, a woman died from it. And nobody can figure out who did this, or why, because methanol is no cheaper than spirits."

Hauge allowed himself a wry chortle.

"One might wonder if it was the Vinomonopolet or the teetotaler movement that did it, because it has temporarily killed the black market." (The methanol-laced booze, it turned out, came from southern Europe; 250 Portuguese citizens were eventually charged with smuggling in the case.) "Most factories and offices used to have contacts, and they could easily get a bottle for half the price of what you paid in the liquor store. What this has done, of course, is to increase the cross-border smuggling of alcohol from Sweden."

I ventured the idea that the restrictive control policies and high taxes might not only lead to smuggling and poisoning, but also contribute to the patterns of binge drinking in Norway.

"Probably not," Hauge quickly objected. "I have written a book on alcohol legislation over the last thousand years, and drinking to excess happened before the temperance movement. Norway was for a long time a very poor country, and grain was a very valuable commodity, which should not be used for unimportant reasons. When it was being used to make beer, then one should taste the result of one's effort. So it wasn't drunk in small quantities over a long period, like wine in Italy. When we drank, we drank a lot. The first description of Nordic alcohol habits comes from Tacitus."

He showed me an excerpt from the A.D. 100 treatise, in which the Roman historian had observed of Scandinavians: "Their foodstuffs are simple and they satisfy hunger without fancy dishes. As for thirst, they lack the same restraint: if one indulges their drunkenness by supplying as much as they long for, they will soon succumb to vices as to arms . . . To drink away the day and night disgraces no one. Brawls are frequent, as is normal among the intoxicated, and seldom end in mere abuse, but more often in slaughter and bloodshed."

Here, then, was historical evidence of a continuum between berserkers and biker gangs, an explanation for the burning of stave churches by death-metal fans and charter planes of drunken Vikings laying waste to Mediterranean resorts. Surely, though, the Norwegians were now the richest people on the planet; if they wanted, they could buy all the grain in Russia, and all the beer in Milwaukee. Couldn't a change in policy—say, a decrease in taxes—have an impact on these age-old drinking habits?

"I don't think so," said Hauge. "If alcohol were available for the same price as in other parts of Europe, we would have a very big increase in drinking. I wouldn't say it was something in our Norwegian genes, necessarily, that made us drink—perhaps we could change over time. But I think our drinking habits are integrated into the Norwegian folk soul."

In other words, when it came to drinking, it was ever thus. Because Norwegians drank like Vikings, the state was justified in imposing restrictive alcohol policies.

I went upstairs to meet Hauge's colleague Ingeborg Rossow, a criminologist and alcohol researcher. A tall, blond woman, originally trained as a dentist, she professed amusement at my interest in her compatriots' reputation for binge drinking.

I started by saying the Italians had no single word for hangover; the closest they got was *postumi di sbornia*, or "aftereffects of drinking." The Finnish, on the other hand, boast the excellent word *krappola*. Was there a Norwegian equivalent?

"Yes!" she said. "There are several. It's like the Eskimos, with all their words for snow. For example, we say *fyllesyke*, which means 'drunkenness disease.' With this, you would definitely be bothered by a headache, and probably not be capable of doing your regular work. Then there is *tømmermenn*, which literally translated is 'timbermen.' This would be a severe hangover or headache, as if you had little carpenters doing heavy work in your head. We also use the English word *hangover*, and a *blåmandag* is a 'blue Monday,' when you've had a binge over the weekend and still feel it at work or school. And there are associated words, like *reparere*, which you might translate as 'hair of the dog,' when you need a couple of drinks in the morning to 'repair' yourself."

In a recent paper, Rossow had emphasized that official statistics didn't take into account illegal spirits in Norway. I asked her where she thought they were coming from.

"About twenty-five percent of all alcohol consumed in Norway comes from unregistered consumption. About half of this is tourist imports—tax-free, cross-border trade—and the other half is split between smuggled spirits, and moonshine and homemade wine and beer."

Wouldn't the fact that people consumed illegal spirits, I wondered, be related to restrictive control policies? For example, if the nearest Vinmonopolet was two hundred miles away, you might be more inclined to whip up your own batch of moonshine.

Rossow wasn't buying it. "In my view, it's hard to see it as a kind of response to control policy in any way. It seems to be more related to other home-based activities, like carpentry, or working on your garden. It's part of a rich rural tradition. *Hjemmebrent* literally means 'home-burnt,' or 'home-distilled.' Many people take pride in making their own good moonshine and sharing it with other people—they even prefer it to cognac or whiskey. Personally, I think it tastes rather awful. But then again, some people like grappa."

Interesting, I thought. Not only had Rossow tried moonshine, she also bluntly denied that its popularity had anything to do with the high price of store-bought booze. This hardly seemed logical. If Jack Daniel's and Stolichnaya were as cheap in Norway as they were in the rest of Europe, and as widely available, there'd be no need for people to take the risk of setting up stills at home. As far back as 1924, author Louis Lewin noted the disturbing Norwegian penchant for turning to stopgap intoxicants. "In Norway, the use of ether seems to have assumed large proportions," he had written in *Phantastica*, his classic survey of drugs. "On holidays, old and young, men and women, consume the drug . . . It is easy to understand that in those countries where anti-alcoholism has succeeded in attaining an outward victory, the craving for another inebriating substance leads to the discovery of substitutes. Ether is one of those."

I put it to Rossow bluntly: Did Norwegians need to be protected from themselves? And was that the rationale behind the government's control policies?

"Well, I think that, at least in the short run, we would be much damaged if we had a very liberal alcohol policy. In Scandinavia, drinking to get intoxicated is still the norm, and we have more violence for each liter of alcohol we drink than they do in southern Europe." (Though this is relative: Russia and Great Britain have far more drinking-related violence than Scandinavian countries.) "We would probably have more problems with public nuisance, accidents due to binge drinking, and chronic diseases. Though it takes twenty or thirty years to develop a cirrhotic liver or a heavy alcohol dependency, some people who were borderline heavy drinkers now would tip over into alcoholism if wine and spirits were more available."

Surely, though, cultures can change. Norwegians were increasingly opting for wine, for example.

"Yes," she admitted, "they can change in terms of their beverage preferences. But in terms of drinking to intoxication, that seems to persist. Pioneering sociologists who looked into our drinking habits in the 1850s found that Norwegians would start drinking with a couple of liters of beer in the morning, and they would continue during all working hours, and then have liquor in the evening. They almost never drank water or milk. I think it's more fair to assume that the control policies we are implementing are more a reaction to our problematic drinking than the other way around."

There it was again, a cliché that was turning into a refrain: it was ever thus. Apparently, because Norwegians had always been immoderate drinkers, they got the drinking laws they deserved. But

Norwegians had changed in one way: they were no longer primarily manual laborers and peasants who stayed lightly sozzled all day. In fact, such drinking patterns had been a common feature of many pre-industrial societies; in rural America in the eighteenth century, for example, babies' bottles were laced with rum to keep them pacified, agricultural workers drank on the job and were partly paid in liquor, and adults seldom went for more than a few hours without a drink. (Part of this was just good sense: before Pasteur and charcoal filters, it was safer to rely on germicidal alcohol than easily contaminated water or milk. As the German proverb has it, "In wine there is wisdom. In beer there is strength. In water there is bacteria.") It was apparently intellectually expedient to cite Viking debauchery and the "Norwegian folk soul" as proof of the inevitability of national binge-drinking habits.

Conveniently, this also justified the state's paternalistic control policies—and the fantastic tax revenues they raked in from their monopoly on the sale of alcohol. The same money, not coincidentally, that went to pay the salaries of the researchers at SIRUS.

I met Per Ole Johansen, author of the definitive books on prohibition in Norway, on the steps of the National Gallery. His jacket was black velour, and silver-framed glasses sat atop a slightly blotchy, bulbous nose. He had a stoop, and an endearing sideways smirk that appeared when he was savoring the arcana of the criminal underworld. Any attempt I made to answer his rhetorical questions was cut off by rapid-fire *ja-ja-ja*s.

We sat down for coffee in a university cafeteria. "You have met my colleagues at SIRUS?" he said. "*Ja, ja, ja.* I used to work there ten years ago; now I am in the criminology department at the University of Oslo. I base my research on interviews and participant analysis— they base theirs on analyzing statistics."

Johansen didn't agree with his colleagues at SIRUS about the impact of control measures in Norway. He felt that one of prohibition's chief legacies was a culture of smuggling.

"It's very popular among crusaders here to stigmatize smugglers as classic criminals, but in fact, there are three kinds. First, the generalists, smugglers with a long history in crime, holdups, armed robberies. Second, what I call the smugglers-for-life. In the 1920s, they were sailors, living by the coast, because most alcohol came to Norway by sea. These are people who have smuggling as an identity; and they are proud of it. They don't deal with drugs; maybe some cigarettes. Finally, there are the company smugglers, with a background in business, and they are quite successful, because they can use their corporation as cover. There are hundreds of examples of these."

When prohibition ended in Norway in 1927, many smugglers returned to their regular work, "but taxes were high and liquor was available in only thirteen places all over Norway, so the black market and the moonshining went on, and it kept that peculiar Norwegian mentality alive. Booze is expensive, so you have to grab it when you get the chance.

"In the 1950s, freshmen smugglers were working alongside the veterans who had got their start during prohibition. Smuggling had become a tradition. And we saw the same thing during a series of Vinmonopolet strikes, or slowdowns, in the seventies and eighties. The veterans couldn't handle the demand, so within a matter of weeks, new smugglers were supplying a huge new customer base."

Recently, he said, the government had tried to discourage the illegal market by launching a massive television and print campaign against moonshine and officially making its purchase a crime.

"What do you think happened then? *Ja, ja, ja.* Attitudes went underground. My colleagues at SIRUS were very proud of the way these campaigns worked, because they did huge interviews with the public, and afterwards fewer people told the interviewers that they were buying moonshine or smuggled alcohol. But they forgot one thing: they had stigmatized the culture. People didn't stop buying booze; they just stopped admitting they were buying it. I was out in the field at the time, and I lost some important contacts. The moonshiners and smugglers told me, 'Two years ago, we were accepted by society, but after this campaign, they label us as mafia, so we are going underground.'

"And what's typical of an illegal market like this? First, cheap alcohol; quite opposite of what the politicians wanted. Two, strong alcohol; our moonshine is usually ninety-six percent."

Johansen paused and gave me a searching look. "Have you tried *hjemmebrent*?"

Not yet, I told him.

"*Ja, ja, ja.* Don't do it. Anyway, third consequence: you have huge quantities in your home, because you are buying ten liters of pure alcohol at a time. This is where you see the seedy, dark side of the tax machine. You are drinking in secrecy, and the drinking culture is less controlled. I believe much more in the continental style, going out in the evening and drinking with friends, or with meals, where there are more rituals, more rules."

I asked him whether he thought Norwegians might have special cultural, or even genetic, problems with drinking.

"In Iceland, where beer was prohibited for eighty years—until 1989— the politicians used to say that beer was bad for the Icelandic Viking blood. Now it's true, the Norwegian national character is very strange. We like to drink, we like to fight, and do another thing I won't mention. But we believe in Jesus Christ too. We are a very ambivalent people; we swing from very happy to very hungover, with all the associated feelings of guilt. But we don't have a reputation for being particularly violent. Most of us keep smiling when we drink; we open up, because we are a shy people, and we need a boost to become more urbane."

If the laws changed, I asked, could Norwegian drinking behavior change?

"Of course it may change! It has already changed in a number of ways. In the eighties, we started to take charter planes, and we went a bit bananas—because we were in a heaven of cheap alcohol. But we left good tips too, and we didn't get into as many fights as the English. They are brutes. But now we have traveled, we are drinking more wine, our habits are becoming more continental."

His colleagues, I pointed out, seemed to think Norwegians needed to be protected from alcohol.

"At SIRUS, they are very close to the politicians in many ways. I used to ask them, why do you never talk about the pleasures of drinking? Why do you never say that drinking is bad for a minority, but good for the majority?"

I raised an inquisitive eyebrow.

"*Ja, ja, ja.*" He allowed himself a quick smirk. "Well, it's obvious. Unless they looked at alcohol as a problem, they wouldn't get the money."

"Alcohol," wrote George Bernard Shaw, "is the anesthesia by which we endure the operation of life." Woe to the sadists who demand that everybody experience every minute of the operation fully conscious. History is littered with the endlessly predictable consequences of their good intentions.

There were, for example, the gin acts of eighteenth-century England. The arrival of *genever*, a novel Dutch method of distilling malt spirits with juniper berries, overwhelmed the English, until then accustomed to beer and wine, with a tidal wave of debauchery. By the 1720s, when a drinkable local version appeared, there were twenty thousand gin shops in London alone, and drams were sold from wheelbarrows and street-corner chandlers, from garrets and cellars, from barges on the Thames and at public hangings; by 1743, annual consumption of gin had peaked at an astonishing 2.2 gallons (ten liters) per person. In a rapidly gentrifying London, Parliament—overstocked with brewers, the natural rivals of distillers—responded to upper-class sentiment that saw any form of conspicuous consumption on the part of the poor as unseemly. In a series of acts, they raised licensing fees by astronomical amounts, pricing the poorer drinking establishments out of existence, and rewarded informers with £5 a conviction (at a time when a maid's annual salary was £5). According to Jessica Warner, author of a gripping analysis of the gin craze, "The real pattern behind the gin acts was very simple: people worried about gin when very little else seemed to be happening—and when the government was flush. [They] conveniently forgot about it in times of war, or, rather, [chose] to treat it as just another source of revenue." As with recent drug crazes, such as crack and ecstasy, the English mania for gin died a natural death, as a generation came to know the consequences of heavy abuse. "The most logical explanation comes from the most recent history of drug epidemics," Warner explained in an interview. "They really do follow a leisurely curve that is completely resistant to intervention." End result of pointless state intervention: twelve thousand people convicted under the gin acts, courts clogged for decades, and hundreds of informers beaten to death by angry mobs— until a new craze came along, this one for rum.

Then there was Prohibition—the big one, America's thirteen-year-long noble experiment. Capitalizing on anti-immigrant sentiment in World War I, the Anti-Saloon League brilliantly orchestrated a campaign to demonize decadent Catholic wine-sippers and slovenly German brewers and distillers. At midnight on January 17, 1920, the Volstead Act—its passage was overseen by one Andrew J. Volstead, of Norwegian and Lutheran background—went into effect, stipulating that "no person shall manufacture, sell, barter, transport, import, export, deliver, furnish or possess any intoxicating liquor."

At first, drinking dropped by two thirds, and with it, hospital admissions for heart attacks and cirrhosis. Unfortunately, people started dying from other causes. The poor suffered the most: they drank doctored antifreeze, bay rum, and such concoctions as yack-yack bourbon, made from burnt sugar and iodine, and sweet whiskey, a mixture of nitric or sulfuric acid and alcohol. A 170-proof medicine called Jamaican ginger extract provoked a hecatomb: the victims were rendered impotent and suffered from a mysterious ailment called jake leg, a stiffening of the limbs that gave them an all-too-recognizable, and permanent, stagger; tens of thousands were affected. (The manufacturers of jake had added a toxic plasticizer that boosted solids in the solution so the Treasury Department would be forced to approve it as a medicine rather than a beverage.) In all, Prohibition-era rotgut may have killed fifty thousand people—forty-one on New Year's Day in New York City in 1927 alone—and blinded and paralyzed hundreds of thousands more.

Meanwhile, the resistance was getting organized. By 1927, there were twenty thousand speakeasies in the United States, twice as many as all legal drinking establishments before the Volstead Act passed. Women, who had eschewed the all-male saloon, felt more comfortable in jazz-era speakeasies and developed a taste for the hard stuff. Though selling alcohol was illegal, private consumption in the home was still allowed, launching a wave of sad, secretive drinking among the more propriety-obsessed upper-middle class. Five years after Prohibition was introduced, Americans were going through 200 million gallons of hard liquor annually (about 6.6 liters per person), bootleggers were pulling in $4 billion a year, and alcohol had become America's leading industry.

Prohibition not only created a huge criminal class, it also convinced Americans their leaders were hypocrites. Lucky Luciano controlled New York City, and Al Capone, in cahoots with mayor "Big Bill" Thompson, had Chicago sewn up (and after they'd cut their teeth on Prohibition, they switched to gambling, extortion, prostitution, and drugs). While official guests to the White House got fruit juice on the ground floor, President Harding served trusted insiders whiskey upstairs. Attorney General Daugherty personally pocketed millions from rumrunners buying immunity from prosecution. Meanwhile, the homicide rate and the prison population rose to record highs; in the thirteen years of Prohibition, half a million American—mostly those who couldn't afford lawyers—went to jail for offenses against the Volstead Act.

Eventually, Prohibition imploded under pressure from outside economic forces. After the stock-market crash, even the paternalistic industrialists who had forcefully lobbied to ban alcohol had to admit that the government was losing valuable tax revenue (and, worse, the state was increasingly taxing *them*). Newspaper magnate William Randolph Hearst, an early supporter, went apostate: "I am against Prohibition," he said in 1929, "because it has set the cause of temperance back twenty years; because it has substituted an ineffective campaign of force for an effective campaign of education; because it has replaced comparatively uninjurious light wines and beers with the worst kind of hard liquor and bad liquor." All told, Prohibition's successes were slight: drinking did decrease, and with it some alcohol-related diseases and violence, but by the time of repeal, consumption was creeping up to pre–Volstead Act levels. When hard liquor was legalized on December 5, 1933, at the height of the Depression, the expected nationwide drinking binge never came to pass. With four-teen million men out of work, most people were now too broke to buy a square meal, let alone a bottle of whiskey.

Prohibition, America's war on alcohol, was the prototype for the War on Drugs; the failure to extrapolate from its lessons is further proof that those who don't learn their history are condemned to repeat it. What is heartening, in the long struggle with prohibitions of all kinds, is humanity's ingenuity in circumventing arbitrary laws. When Maine became the first American state to ban the sale of alcohol in 1851, shopkeepers started charging a nickel for a soda cracker, and offering a glass of rum on the side free of charge: no sale, thus no crime. As soon as the Volstead Act was passed, fifty-seven thousand druggists in Chicago alone applied for licenses to sell "medicinal" liquor, and whiskey soon became essential medicine for everything from gout to lumbago. Perhaps the most ingenious dodge was developed by Napa Valley winemakers, who produced dried grape and raisin cakes. Demonstrators in grocery stores pointedly told clients *not* to soak them in water and then leave the liquid in a jug for three weeks with a cork in it, because fermentation might occur. For those who needed a further nudge, the cakes were labeled "Caution: will ferment and turn into wine."

It all sounded like the ingenious lengths modern Norwegians went to skirt repressive alcohol controls. Among the racks of canned reindeer meat and brown cheese (a national specialty that tastes, and looks, as if a brick of processed cheese had been spiked with Nestlé Quik powder) in the supermarkets, I found suspiciously capacious drums of sugar and bags of dried yeast, as well as a strange section of airplane-size bottles, labeled Scotch Whisky, Ouzo, and Strand's English Dry Gin. They didn't contain any actual alcohol, but were used for adding flavor to homemade booze. The lion's share of the yeast goes not into baked goods, but illegal stills: in the 1990s, enough was being purchased to supply every man, woman, and child in the country with five loaves of bread a day. Since then, smuggling alcohol across the long border with Sweden, where booze is somewhat cheaper, has become a national pastime. Many Norwegians order cheap liquor online from American-based Internet companies and drive over the border to pick it up in warehouses in Sweden, or take booze cruises on long-distance ferries that call at non-EU ports so they can get discount alcohol duty-free. The state liquor store in Stromstad, fifteen minutes by highway from the Norwegian border, is the busiest in Sweden. The official statistics that put Norway at the bottom of the list of European nations for per capita consumption fail to take into account this illegal consumption. Instead, the government uses its misleading official figures to congratulate itself on the success of its alcohol control policies.

And whom does this status quo benefit? The simple, sordid truth is that the state is loath to abandon a monopoly that generates such a huge revenue stream. In this the Norwegian government is hardly unique. In Canada, liquor in every province but Alberta is sold by state control boards, in singularly attractive and convenient stores more akin to country clubs than drug dispensaries. Which leads to the question, if alcohol is such a dangerous substance that it has to be controlled by a government monopoly, then why is the government going to such enormous lengths to promote it? The response is simple: in Norway, as in Canada, it takes huge sums to sustain a heavily unionized, bureaucracy-choked network of official government liquor stores.

(There was evidence that the Vinmonopolet had not only become an immense, money-sucking bureaucracy, but also a corrupt one. A few months after my visit, a sacked salesman accused ten store directors, as well as the managing director of the entire chain, of accepting gifts of free alcohol and sponsored trips as far afield as Australia from liquor companies eager to tie up contracts with the Norwegian monopoly.)

Back on the *Innvik*, Alto was up a ladder in the hold, hanging some lights. I lured him down with a lukewarm Duvel and asked if he'd made any progress on the *hjemmebrent*.

"I've had a call around, and nobody seems to have any in Oslo. If you'd like, I've got some mates in Trondheim, old punks and hippies who live in a squat in the center. They're pretty *harry*, they're bound to have some."

Harry? I asked.

"It means 'rednecky'—you know, long hair and beards, country types." He pulled out his cell phone, and after five minutes of guffaws and undulating Norwegian, he had news.

"Well, he's going to try to put a bottle on the train and send it down to me. But if it doesn't arrive by Friday, you might have to go up there yourself."

I didn't relish the prospect: it would mean a sixteen-hour return trip on the train. Besides, it seemed silly to leave Oslo on the weekend, exactly when the real debauchery was going to start. I'd been roaming the bars and café terraces during the week, and though I'd seen little public drunkenness, I could feel something building, a kind of sinister energy. Throughout the working week, the Norwegians maintain a fierce probity. As a people, they are healthy, energetic, lovers of the outdoors. Physically, they seem rough-hewn, as though chopped hastily from blocks of pine; tall and handsome, their astonishingly thick hair bristles brown or blond from high brows, like wheat from goodly soil. But it was their eyes that struck me most: riding the trams, caught in the cross-glances of their pale blue gazes, I sometimes felt as if I were surrounded by timber wolves. If the clichés were true—that beneath a couple of centuries of Lutheran repression flowed the blood of the Vikings—I was pretty sure that when the Norwegians started drinking, it would be an impressive sight.

Late Friday afternoon, Alto called with news about the *hjemmebrent*.

"A mate of mine has some at Teddy's Soft Bar. You better get there soon, though, before they start drinking the stuff."

He gave me a number to call. "*Ja,*" a deep voice answered. "I'll be at Teddy's in half an hour. You can't miss me: I'm wearing shorts, and my legs are on fire."

Outside Teddy's Soft Bar, stylized 1950s images of hot dogs, milk shakes, and shellfish danced on the façade. Inside, the wallpaper peeled and tattooed clients in rolled-up blue jeans—Teddy's was a favorite hangout of Oslo's hard-core rockabilly community—got serious over $10 pints of Ringnes at the bar.

I was at the Wurlitzer, trying to choose between The Outsiders and The Box Tops, when Engel walked in. He really was impossible to miss. Hot Wheels–style flames were tattooed on his hairless calves; another tattoo, of a bloodshot, winged eyeball, peeked out of his collar. Iron Crosses adorned his Converse All-Stars, and he wore vintage Ray•Bans fitted out with clear prescription lenses. A gold tooth glinted in his mouth, and his wavy blond hair was slicked back with greasy kid stuff. He was also epically proportioned, a sideburned Viking rocker dressed like Opie gone bad.

Holding up a plastic bag, he led me outside to a narrow alley. As the occasional client from the bar looked at us curiously on his way to the bathroom, I felt like a participant in a particularly conspicuous drug deal.

"This costs more than the regular stuff," said Engel, "but I figured you should get the best. My aunt makes *hjemmebrent* in her apartment here in Oslo, but it's not as good as this shit."

He pulled out a six-hundred-milliliter plastic bottle of Imsdal, the local bottled water, undid the cap, and wet his palm with the liquid. He rubbed his palms together briskly and showed me the result.

"See?"

Though I smelled rubbing alcohol, I saw nothing but the skin of his palm.

"If it's good, it evaporates clear. If it's bad, then you see a kind of gray foam on your hands. This is pure stuff. I got it from my mate, who lives in the suburbs. It's made with sugar, water, and a bit of yeast to get the fermentation started. Some people use potatoes, but sugar is faster."

I gave Engel 200KR ($28 U.S.) for a liter, split between two bottles.

"That may seem like a lot of money, but it's ninety-six percent alcohol, so it goes a long way. It's fun at parties too. You can pour some on your hand, light it on fire, and it will just burn off."

Thinking better of advising self-immolation to a tourist, he added, "Attention: don't try this at home!"

After thanking him, I hopped a taxi to a chic subdivision of condos in the west side of the city. I'd been invited to a party by a Swiss friend, who was visiting Oslo for the weekend.

"These people are *fous*," she confided, after we'd exchanged kisses on the cheek. "They carry their bottles around with them all night. In Switzerland we bring a bottle of wine, we put it on the counter, and if we don't drink it—too bad!—we leave it as a gift for the host. Look at them—that guy is walking around with a bottle under one arm, and a wineglass in the other. He hasn't put it down all night. And him—he's corked his bottle with paper towel and he's going to take it home! It's really pathetic."

A stocky, talkative man named Alex, learning I was a foreigner, decided to take me aside to give me the lowdown on life in Norway.

"For years, Norwegians were very poor," he said, between deep swallows of beer, "and we had to struggle to get by on potatoes and grain—life was mouth-to-hand. After the war, it was a real social-welfare state, with slogans like in the Soviet Union: 'Everybody Pull Together—We Can Progress!' The Norwegian mentality has always been that nobody is better than anybody else; you can't walk around with an upstuck nose. Everybody has the chance to own their own house, or go to university. The minimum wage is really high. The problem is, we are completely dependent on oil. There is no entrepreneurship, very few big companies founded by Norwegians. We import everything, and everything is taxed: the sales tax is twenty-four percent, new cars are taxed one hundred ten percent.

"Have you noticed all the slot machines in the corner stores?" he asked.

I had. Norway's gambling laws are among the most liberal in Europe.

"They accept bills of five-hundred-kroner," he continued, "and pay off in twenty-kroner coins. Every time you press a button, you can spend a krone—and you can press a button once a second! People are ruined by these machines, entire families bankrupt. Why don't they ban these, instead of blaming alcohol for everything? I tell you, the government is really greedy; they have billions and billions of kroner and don't want to touch it. They say they're saving it for a rainy day, but I think they are just like Uncle Scrooge, sitting on his money stack."

By one A.M., the liquor had been exhausted; even the bag-in-the-box wine had been emptied, eviscerated, and blown up into makeshift balloons; the fellow next to me was hoarding the final inch of Ballantine's in the bottle. The whole thing reminded me of the morose turn a teenage party takes when the liquor cabinet has been emptied. When my head was turned, my Swiss friend picked up my bottle full of moonshine and took a good-sized swig, thinking it was water.

"Oh, *mon Dieu*!" she screamed, spitting it into the air. "That's the most disgusting thing I've ever tasted! I can't feel my tongue any-more!"

When the party finally died, I walked back to the *Innvik*, down Karl Johans Gate, Oslo's main pedestrian thoroughfare. It was four in the morning, and the last drinkers were leaving the bars; empty bottles of Smirnoff vodka had been abandoned on the paving stones. A trio of big, broad-shouldered lugs in their twenties unzipped their droopy jeans, lifted their left hands in the air, and pissed on the stairs of a church while chanting and gyrating their hips in a urinary chorus line.

Then I started to come across people passed out on the street. Not the homeless—Oslo has five thousand of them, and they are eerily silent and resigned as they wait for passersby to drop a coin into their cup—but well-dressed young people, sleeping off their binges where they fell. A teenage girl sat with her head between her knees, and her back to the wall of a bank, a purse poised beside her. A tall man in a red sweater had lain down on the ground, with a huge grin on his face; his friends vaguely tried to revive him, but he just rolled over, blissfully oblivious. In the few blocks between the American embassy and the Parliament, I counted a half dozen people peacefully passed out on benches, in the gutter, next to bank machines. In a way, it was nice that downtown Oslo was so safe that you could lose consciousness without fear of losing your wallet. It was a little sad, however, that healthy young people drank so much on a Friday that they ended up toppling over like skid-row winos.

I'd seen worse in my travels: downtown Tokyo on a Saturday night was a Boschian landscape of platform pizzas and staggering salarymen, no longer in control of basic bodily functions, and nothing can beat the eerie rage, class resentment, and xenophobia that comes unbottled when large numbers of British people start partying on foreign beaches. Both Japan and the United Kingdom had liberal alcohol retailing laws, and in those hierarchy-obsessed cultures, bingeing seemed more a steam valve for social constraint than a reaction to prohibitive laws. The egalitarian Norwegians, in contrast, were relatively straightforward drunks, with a penchant for simple oblivion: here, drinking to excess was about overcoming legal, rather than psychological, constraints.

The more I talked to people, in fact, the more I realized that getting staggeringly shellacked was a cultural norm; the Norwegians themselves loved to relate tales of drunkenness, like fraternity boys constantly amazed by their own lovable excesses. The overnight ferry from Oslo to Copenhagen, I was told, was a notoriously debauched booze cruise, where adults, loading up on duty-free alcohol as soon as they hit international waters, pissed in their jeans and vomited over their sweaters, returning with trunks full of Danish spirits. Norwegians favored British Airways not because their fares were lower—they weren't—but because they were more liberal with inflight liquor than their Scandinavian competitors; it was typical for overworked BA flight attendants, besieged by requests for booze, to give up on serving altogether and throw the drink carts open to all comers. With a glint in her eye, Ingeborg Rossow at SIRUS had told me of the *russefeiring*, the two-week-long high school graduation binge that happens in May. Students wear red or blue overalls, and caps are decorated with badges awarded for feats of alcoholic prowess: a beer cap for drinking twenty-four beers in twenty-four hours, a screw-top for finishing a bottle of liquor. The system is highly organized, with administration at the high school, municipal, and federal levels; tens of thousands of dollars are spent buying buses with state-of-the-art sound systems. One of the cooks on the *Innvik* told me that during her husband's *russefeiring*, a drunken girl fell off the top of a bus and was promptly run over by a bus going in the opposite direction.

"There was also a girl passed out naked on the top of the bus," she said, with a look of disgust. "The others spent their time drawing all over her body with felt markers. Nothing to do with my husband, right? Well, it turns out the girl had alcohol poisoning—she almost died."

The *russefeiring* was so entrenched in Norwegian society, and drunkenness was so much part of it, that in 2003 students were officially given an extra two hours in bed on the days of their final exams to sleep off their hangovers.

If coming of age in Norway meant two weeks of crapulence, was it any surprise that even adults drank like desperate teenagers?

"The moral, then, is this," one of the seminal works in the field of alcohol research concludes. "Since societies, like individuals, get the sorts of drunken comportment that they allow, they deserve what they get." It applied perfectly, I thought, to Norway.

First published in 1969, psychologist Craig MacAndrew's and anthropologist Robert B. Edgerton's *Drunken Comportment* is still unsurpassed as an examination of the fieldwork on drunken behavior around the world. It challenged the received wisdom that alcohol was some kind of universal superego solvent that inevitably depressed the higher centers of the brain, removed inhibitions, and allowed people to do things they would never do when sober. On the contrary, the authors cited dozens of societies where taboos and social structures were rigidly observed—where no disinhibition occurred—even in the midst of extreme drinking bouts. In other cases, alcoholic behavior changed from occasion to occasion: a familiar example was the bawling at the Irish wake and the brawling at the Irish pub—same substance, different contexts, different behavior. "Drunken-changes-for-the-worse," as they called them, were not an inevitable corollary of alcohol consumption; the most one could say was that alcohol provided a "timeout" during which sociability and volubility were increased. Intoxication, then, was socially constructed. People learned how to be drunk by observing others.

Most interestingly, MacAndrew and Edgerton found cases where drunken behavior changed over time. The people of Tahiti, on initial contact with English sailors in 1767, showed a marked distaste for alcohol, preferring their native intoxicant kava kava. By the time Captain Vancouver put into Tahiti in 1791, the natives had gotten into the habit of drinking spirits and displayed violent behavior when drunk; but by the twentieth century, a pattern of weekend drinking, with little associated violence, had emerged. Many native North American societies, the authors pointed out, had had completely benign reactions of tipsiness and fatigue on their first exposure to alcohol. "From one coast to the other," they wrote, "the evidence points to the fact that *when the North American Indians' initial experience with alcohol was untutored by expectations to the contrary, the result was neither the development of an all-consuming craving nor an epic of drunken mayhem and debauchery*." Only in observing the way European fur traders used drunkenness as a pretext for raping women, or ax-murdering competitors, did they realize alcohol's reputation as a toxic disinhibitor could be exploited for its excuse value.

If societies' drinking patterns can change—and *Drunken Comport-*

ment cited several other examples—then the argument that Scandinavians have a cultural, or even genetic, inability to consume moderately begins to look particularly suspect. Drinking behavior is neither exclusively nature, nor solely nurture; but experts tend to concur that culture is the more significant predictor of how an individual will act when drunk. (There is only one really well-established example of an extreme genetic difference in response to alcohol. About half of all Japanese, and many Chinese, lack a gene that helps metabolize alcohol, resulting in the Asian flush, an unpleasant reddening and sensation of heat after one or two glasses. This doesn't keep the Japanese from their sake, *shochu*, and Suntory: many learn to drink through the flush.) The climatic argument, that Scandinavians drink to excess because they are all suffering from depression because of long winter nights and seasonal affective disorder, doesn't hold much water either: some of the most extreme binge drinking happens near the summer solstice, when the sun never goes down. And the historical argument is too simplistic: just because Vikings drank to excess a thousand years ago doesn't mean their descendants are bound to do the same. The Romans succumbed to debauched orgies on Falernian wine, but their ancestors seem to be able to handle their Chianti.

Unfortunately, such changes in consumption patterns tend to happen slowly; if availability increases too suddenly, a generation may be sacrificed, as when gin hit the English market in the eighteenth century. This is particularly true in cultures that have a tradition of binge drinking. While the Italians drink far more than the British per capita (and 42 percent of them drink every day), they rarely do so to drunkenness. In Ireland, in contrast, though few people are daily drinkers, 58 percent of drinking occasions can now be considered bingeing. After a decade in which British youth took ecstasy and drank bottled water, the distillers and brewers swore revenge and fought back with "alcopops"—Bacardi Breezers and Smirnoff Ice,

Vodka Jellies, Irn-Bru-and-whiskey—which are sweet, high in alco-hol, and appeal to teenagers. Megapubs have taken over town centers cleared of butchers and grocers by out-of-town supermarkets. For whatever reason, acceptable drunken behavior in Britain lately seems to involve random brutality; 1.2 million violent incidents a year can be attributed to binge drinking in England alone.

Given these statistics, it's easy for legislators to conclude that, in cultures with patterns of episodic heavy drinking, liberalization will just mean more wife-beating, more suicide, more cirrhosis—so why bother? Robin Room, an Australian who is now head of Sweden's Centre for Social Research on Alcohol and Drugs, cites what happened in the Soviet Union in the 1980s as proof that an overall reduction in the availability of alcohol can be a boon for public health.

"About a month after Gorbachev became general secretary," Room told me, "the Soviet Union started this top-down antialcohol campaign that involved reducing production in state distilleries, cutting down the hours alcohol shops were open, and tearing up vineyards. Sure, all the sugar disappeared from grocery store shelves, and you got a big increase in *samogon*, the local moonshine. But still, the best estimates say that total consumption went down by a quarter. And homicide rates among males fell by forty-seven percent, heart deaths decreased by nine percent, and the longevity of males and females increased by a couple of years. But as soon as the Soviet Union fell apart, and the alcohol controls stopped, there was a huge increase in consumption, and the death rate for Russian males skyrocketed."

The antialcohol campaign lasted only three years, though, not long enough for a widespread illegal market to get organized. If Russian Al Capones had gotten into serious bootlegging, the consequences might have been disastrous. I asked Room about the long-term conse-quences of Scandinavian "dry" policies (as opposed to "wet" societies like Italy, France, and Spain, where alcohol is freely available).

"Well, you just have to look at 'dry' drug policies; the U.S. policy is a disaster, and so is the Swedish, for that matter. If the drug in question becomes heavily entrenched in the society, then you get a big illicit market, it becomes highly profitable, and since people can't enforce contracts, they kill each other to establish jurisdiction. The police tend to get corrupted, and the illicit market gets mixed up with others: prostitution, gambling. If you want to keep down health problems and violence, then you try to discourage alcohol consumption in a way where taking a drink doesn't become a symbolic act of defiance against the state. That's the fundamental argument against prohibition. There are other ways: discouragement policies, the kind of thing they're doing with tobacco in many countries. The argument that relaxing alcohol policies will produce better behavior may be true in the very long term. The question is, how much trouble, like increased violence, are you willing to put up with in the short term? The Nordic countries are very orderly and have a strong sense of community and tend to react very strongly to any sudden change for the worse, even if it's short-term.

"Scandinavia," concluded Room, "has a fiesta drinking culture, where all the rules are temporarily relaxed. And people are very reluctant to give it up. They don't even want to talk about it from a public-health perspective, because then they might have to change their ways."

Change will of course come. In a sense, the Norwegians are the Beverly Hillbillies of Europe: the fortuitous discovery of oil allowed them to hang on to their old customs—in their case, not Jethro's shotguns and bare feet, but state-subsidized farms and a swollen welfare state—even as they bought the latest cars and moved into expensive new homes. Of late, though, their continental neighbors have been changing their ways. Sweden and Finland are part of the EU, and in those countries import limits have been raised from a couple of bottles a trip to five liters of spirits and fifty-two liters of wine. To come in line with the rest of Europe, Sweden is planning on reducing liquor taxes by up to 40 percent, a move that could cause the level of cross-border smuggling into Norway to skyrocket. As the Scandinavian nanny-state paradigm threatens to shift to free-market liberalism, challenges to alcohol policy are liable to arrive with catastrophic swiftness, with all the attendant short-term public health problems.

The question of how to mitigate the social harms caused by alcohol—through changing habits or control policies—is once again becoming urgent. Worldwide, per capita consumption increased by 12 percent over the 1990s, mostly in Latin America, India, and Eastern Europe; the World Health Organization estimates that 140 million people worldwide suffer from alcohol dependency, and 1.8 million a year now die of alcohol-related diseases. Italian teenagers are increasingly drinking beer and alcopops, adopting the binge-drinking habits of their Anglo-Saxon counterparts. Undoubtedly, some politicians will propose new forms of prohibition as a solution. Marshaling drunk-driving statistics, they will call for an increase in the legal drinking age to the American level of twenty-one years. (Which hardly seems fair. Alcohol's relationship with humanity predates that of the automobile by at least 8,900 years. If it ever comes down to a referendum, it is surely cars, not booze, that ought to be banned.) Drug historians have detected a seventy-year cycle of oscillation in America's attitude to alcohol—it takes two generations, apparently, to forget what a disaster prohibition is—and lately the United States has been setting the worldwide agenda on psychoactive substances. If this is true, then we are just about due for another wave of puritanical overreaction and interdiction.

Should the recurrent failure of alcohol prohibition come as any surprise? Humanity's relationship with alcohol goes back at least nine millennia, when our Neolithic ancestors started getting dizzy on prehistoric wine made of fermented rice, honey, and fruit in what

is now China. Alcohol predates Islam, socialism, Christian funda-
mentalism, and any other system that has aspired to regulate it.
Doctrines may come and go, but alcohol abides; it has seniority.
(Though as intoxicants go, it is a relative newcomer: cannabis, coca,
and opium poppies are more venerable familiars.) The drive to get
intoxicated—found in the wild in elephants and starlings, insects and
primates—is universal and natural, and attempts to deny it through
prohibition and other paternalistic controls inevitably backfire, bringing out the worst kind of adolescent behavior. Drunkenness, after all,
is one of human society's most well-developed steam valves: it allows
a symbolic transgression into a drunken "time-out," but the crossing
of the border is temporary. Pharmacologically, alcohol deadens and
defers pain, but with the morning-after hangover, one finds oneself on
the safe side of the line, in a karmic payback of which any Lutheran
preacher would approve. Rather than challenging the status quo, the
whole cycle tends to legitimize the authority it represents.

Unless, of course, the state makes the mistake of completely
prohibiting alcohol, or taxing it almost out of reach; then its procurement becomes an even more potent symbol of rebellion, and—
perversely—drunkenness becomes a genuinely subversive act.

It took me a long time to get up the courage to really get into the
hjemmebrent. It was essentially Everclear—the legal, 190-proof American version of moonshine—and I had grim memories of teenage
punk-rock parties fueled by purple Jesus, the notorious mix of grape
Kool-Aid and grain alcohol. On one of my last nights in Oslo, I
hopped a tram to the Vigelands Park area, where I was fed a simple
and delicious meal of *smørbrød*—hand-peeled prawns piled on white
bread, garnished with mayonnaise, avocado, and tomato—by Marianne and her Canadian husband, Jonathan, who had recently decided
to settle in Norway with their three dogs. Jonathan gave me a
disquisition on *lettøl*, Norwegian light beer.

"It has exactly half the alcohol, and costs only two and a half kroner, a quarter of the price of regular beer. *And they can't sell it.* Only pregnant women, and maybe some old ladies, drink it. We buy it because it's nice to have a cold beer on a hot day, and sometimes you don't really want to get that drunk. It's no coincidence that the label is identical to the regular beer—the only difference is the color of the foil band—because they aren't allowed to advertise anything with alcohol in it. So they show the alcohol-free versions on posters— they're totally promoting the brand."

Marianne was Norwegian, and she explained that people typically start the evening with a *vorspiel*—a "before party," which involves a few drinks at home; then around eleven thirty P.M. they go out for a few expensive pints in a bar and finally repair to somebody's apartment for a *nachspiel*, an after. That's when the strong stuff—including *hjemmebrent*—comes out. We threw convention to the wind and decided to start the evening with *karsk*, or spiked coffee. The recipe is simple: put a copper twenty-kroner coin in the bottom of a white cup and cover it with black coffee until it is no longer visible. Then add the *hjemmebrent*, until the coin reappears (no need to worry about germs: alcohol that strong would kill plague bacilli), and you've got the perfect mix.

Marianne, recalling teenage hangovers, abstained, but Jonathan and I had a few *karsks*. It took me a couple of tries to get my first one down. Every time I raised the cup to my lips, the alcohol fumes rose to my nose—a smell that signifies *Poison!* in no uncertain terms—but by the second cup I was feeling sufficiently anesthetized. Even diluted, though, the stuff was far too strong. Forget about ritual and conviviality: all of the aesthetic pleasures one might experience in sharing a good Scotch or burgundy were absent with *hjemmebrent*. You were sober, then you were drunk. It was grim, goal-oriented, and a little sad. (And the hangover was like no other: the next day the *tømmermenn* were doing detail work driving a needle-thin pick through my brow.)

On the other hand, it was great for party tricks. Jonathan and I poured some over the floor, turned off the lights, and set the hardwood on fire. Marianne freaked out, and the dogs went crazy.

Remembering alcohol's excuse value as a toxic disinhibitor, we blamed it on the liquor.

In Norway the Good, the legacy of prohibition continues. And with it, a societywide refusal to acknowledge that its binge-drinking pattern is a problem, that an illegal market thrives, or that people die from drinking methanol because alcohol is too expensive. The researchers at SIRUS told me it was impossible to establish a conclusive link between a culture of binge drinking and the high rate of drug-overdose deaths in Norway. But it wasn't much of a leap to imagine that a society that stresses consuming too much, all at once, would see such behavior mirrored in drug use. Ragnar Hauge told me that he was part of a committee that proposed decriminalizing all drugs in Norway. The minister of justice thanked him, but told him it would never be proposed by the government; no politician would put forward such an idea for fear of losing votes. So it looked as if the junkies who roamed the docks around the *Innvik* would continue to be shuffled around by police following the orders of real-estate speculators, and Norway would continue to deny it had a problem with drugs—or with binge drinking.

There is clearly no way to force a nation to drink the way Italians or Israelis do. It took Mediterranean cultures centuries of social wine-drinking to arrive at the norms and rituals that contribute to moderation; from a global perspective, they are an anomaly. However, there is a sure way to keep a population in a state of arrested adolescent development. Cite factors such as genetics, climate, and history—the "it was ever thus" arguments—to convince your citizens they are too immature to be trusted with managing their own desires. Enforce paternalistic controls limiting availability, thereby turning alcohol into forbidden fruit, and not incidentally ensuring yourself a huge and constant stream of tax revenue. In other words, lock your liquor in a cabinet and make a big show of monopolizing the key. This will pretty much guarantee a stasis in which bingeing and shameful private drinking remain the norm, producing a guzzling, adolescent culture of intoxication that will never mature into healthful moderation.

At least the Norwegians had some cultural tradition of release, if only in their weekend drinking binges. In societies where prohibitions were even more rigorously enforced, things could get somewhat more twisted. I was about to find out. I'd just booked a ticket for the world's most notorious nanny state—a place that would make Norway look like Babylon.

· CRACKERS ·

Of all tyrannies, a tyranny sincerely exercised for the good of its victims may be the most oppressive. It may be better to live under robber barons than under omnipotent moral busybodies.

—*C. S. Lewis*

· 2 ·

SAVORY CRACKERS

Poppies for Nanny

C HANGI INTERNATIONAL Airport was air-conditioned to seventy-two degrees Fahrenheit—a perfect temperature for wearing tweed—but in spite of the chill, I was sweating like
the kid with the drugs taped around his midriff in *Midnight Express*.
Already, I'd spotted a half dozen security cameras tracking my
progress; uniformed guards watched the screens of thermal scanners,
attentive for faces glowing red or yellow—sure signs of SARS, avian
fever, or guilt-induced anxiety. Marching amidst the necktie-bound
Asian businessmen on the aerobridge, I'd felt especially conspicuous:
my hair was too long, my T-shirt was too black, my backpack too
ratty. What's more, my pen had exploded somewhere over the South
China Sea, leaking a suspiciously placed Rorschach blot over the bar
code of my disembarkation card. The one that was emblazoned, in
arterial-red ink, WARNING DEATH FOR DRUG TRAFFICKERS UNDER
SINGAPORE LAW. (Countered, in classic bad-cop-good-cop style, by
WELCOME TO SINGAPORE.) But there was no turning back: I'd entered
the nation with the highest execution rate in the world, where those
caught possessing more than a couple of grams of drugs are hanged—
and I was holding.

On the Cathay Pacific flight from Hong Kong, I'd read about the rotan, the colonial-era cane that is still used in Singapore as the punishment for everything from spray-painting to sodomy.

"There was no pain at first," recalled a sixty-two-year-old survivor, "just a warm burning sensation, but slowly, as feeling returned, the heat became unbearably painful. It felt as if a red-hot iron had been pressed against my backside. I felt my flesh tingling and then came the throbbing pain. That was only the first stroke." The procedure, he'd noted, was permanently scarring.

Ordering another Carlsberg from a passing stewardess, I'd reinspected the contents of my carry-on bag. I knew that, in the world's most notorious nanny state, seeking out prohibited goods would be a waste of time; so I'd taken it upon myself to import my own forbidden fruit. Tucked into an inner pocket was *Fanny Hill*, or *Memoirs of a Woman of Pleasure*, John Cleland's robust novel of eighteenth-century porn, its cover emblazoned with the pale buttocks of a reclining Rubenesque beauty and an all-too-prominent Erica Jong endorsement: "A ray of sunshine in the gloomy world of lust!" Banned for 250 years in England, *Fanny Hill* was still forbidden in Singapore, along with *Playboy*, Henry Miller's *Sexus*, the Marquis de Sade's entire oeuvre, and 167 other books and magazines deemed morally corrupting pornography. Maximum penalty for possession of pornography: $20,000 ($12,250 U.S.). Secreted around my person were three packs of Wrigley's gum—twenty-seven sticks in all, none of them sugarless. Chewing gum was banned in 1982 after a spate of incidents in which subway car doors were jammed and is now allowed only for medical purposes; fine for importing: $10,000 ($6,125 U.S.). Worst of all was the contraband I'd nervously been gnawing on since the pilot had announced our descent: a full package of Marks & Spencer Savoury Biscuits, studded with poppy seeds. The year before, the Central Narcotics Bureau had pulled a poppy-seed-cake mixture off supermarket shelves, fining the importer $60,000 ($36,750 U.S.). This was followed by raids on Marks & Spencer stores, a pointed crackdown on the purveyors of narcotic crackers.

"Our crackers are made with poppy seeds," an M&S executive had protested at the time. "So naturally they contain extremely low levels of opiates." I'd contacted the narcs before leaving to ask what kind of penalties they imposed for possession. "Poppy seeds are classified as a prohibited good under the Misuse of Drugs Act," Dawn Sim, their media relations person had replied by e-mail. "An individual consuming the food product containing poppy seed with morphine traces may test positive for the presence of a controlled drug in the individual's urine specimen. Strict import controls for poppy seeds are instituted, as morphine is a controlled drug."

Which hadn't really answered my question. But it all sounded pretty chilling. If nothing else, I'd probably succeeded in getting my name flagged in some database.

In Singapore, I reminded myself, official policy was zero tolerance. The preferred method of execution was the gallows.

When choosing a passport inspector, one should be circumspect but decisive. Deliberately avoiding the middle-aged men examining documents with furrowed brows, I joined the queue at counter 14. The inspector, a young Malay woman, waved me to her desk. Her thick black hair was long and wavy, her uniform trimly tailored, her epaulets stiff; she glanced at me, deftly scanned my landing card in spite of the ink blot, stamped my passport, handed it back, and gestured to the family behind me.

That was easy—too easy. But a passport stamp doesn't mean you're home free; one still has to run the gauntlet of customs. Following the walkways to the luggage carousels, I picked up my suitcase, which had beaten me through passport control—no surprise, in this famously high-tech airport. (Most cities aspire to distinguish themselves through their airports. Singapore aspires to be indistinguishable from its airport.) Trundling my trolley in the direction of the green NOTHING TO DECLARE sign, I adopted the blank-eyed gaze of the jet-lagged tourist as I passed the guards in front of the baggage-search tables, all the while steeling myself for a tap on the shoulder. But it never came. The glass doors slid open. No interrogation room for me; only the comforting realm of currency exchange and taxi stand. Endorphins of relief flooded my body.

At the Tourist Board counter, I asked for a subway map. "Welcome to Singapore," the Chinese woman at the desk said with a rigid professional smile, sweeping a hand toward the bowl before her. "Have a mint."

Singapore shouldn't really have let me in at all. I was, after all, a devil, pure spawn of the decadent West, that amoral zone of shiftlessness, welfarism, and incivility, where love is free and rebellion is an end in itself. Unshaven, reeking of twenty hours of inflight meals and recirculated air, I strode through the double, suicide-foiling doors of an impeccable Mass Rapid Transit (MRT) train and celebrated my arrival by unwrapping a stick of Wrigley's gum and demonstratively crimping it into my mouth. Over the loudspeaker, a British-accented woman's voice urged, "Please move to the center of the car." The Chinese man next to me silently watched my performance, raised an eyebrow, and edged two straps toward the exit.

Which left me with a better view of modern Singapore. The elevated MRT line was slipping through a pristine tropical suburbia, where frangipani trees, orchids, and stegosaurus-backed palms pullulated between carnation-white corporate headquarters and cloverleaf overpasses. Seventy years before, this island had been mostly fetid swamp, a colonial backwater notorious for its transvestites, opium dens, and recurring outbreaks of yellow fever. Today, it is one of Asia's great success stories, a city-state of 4.6 million, where fully half of a highly literate population of Chinese, Malays, and Indians has home Internet access, and the ubiquitous air-conditioning makes its position one degree north of the equator an easily overlooked detail. If the name Singapore resonates with Westerners at all, besides as a piece of exotica in a Tom Waits song, it's as a stopover on the way to Sydney or Tokyo, the source of cheap electronics and the occasional bizarre news item about the caning of graffiti artists. Only a little bigger in surface area than Montreal, my own island city, Singapore boasts an army of fifty thousand (with three hundred thousand reservists) and the largest air force in Southeast Asia, whose F-16s give it dominance over its much more populous neighbors, Malaysia and Indonesia. According to its apologists, it is a technocratic meritocracy with an incorruptible leadership, a Southeast Asian superpower with a standard of living higher than that of its former colonizer, Britain.

Its detractors call it Princessland, a bizarre cross between a Confucian Chinese mandarinate and a British boarding school, the ne plus ultra of the nanny state. In Singapore, life is micromanaged by a Government (invariably spelled with a capital G: here, state and ruling party are one) whose video cameras and computer networks extend far into public housing complexes. The stories I'd heard were chilling: elevators were equipped with urine detectors, and weak-bladdered debauchees caught on camera have had their photos published in the pages of the state-owned *Straits Times*. Every Singaporean is issued a number at birth, and from the age of fifteen all carry a National Registration Identity Card, which they must use to make doctors' appointments, apply for a job, open a bank account, and even reserve concert tickets or hotel rooms, giving the state a one-stop database to check up on the life history and proclivities of all of its citizen-digits. The following are banned in Singapore: firecrackers (might start fires); gold-foil-wrapped chocolate coins (could be mistaken for the real thing); walking around one's apartment naked (an outrage against public decency). The punishments are Draconian. A durian husk tossed off a balcony gets the offender a Corrective Work Order, which can mean cleaning the streets wearing a sign that says I AM A LITTERER; repeat offenders can lose their apartments. Under the drift-net Miscellaneous Offences Act, giving somebody the finger in traffic is punishable by a $1,000 fine ($615 U.S.). And consensual gay or oral sex (that is, "carnal intercourse against the course of nature") can lead to two years' imprisonment. Here, the road of excess is not only barricaded; the boys in the Palace of Wisdom have also strewn it with land mines from curb to curb.

But this was why I'd come in the first place: I wanted to take a look at a society where just about everything that could be construed as titillating, mind-altering, or even vaguely pleasurable was fenced off by rigid bans. If it wasn't hard to imagine what a libertarian utopia might look like—all I had to do was envision Las Vegas or Tijuana taken to the extremes—I was having more trouble picturing its opposite. What happens when a nation rules its citizens the way a disciplinarian patriarch rules his household? Is the resulting society a paragon of social unity, or a populace of giggling adolescent trans-gressors and sneaking tattletales? Perhaps, I thought, people here had such fulfilling lives the issue of forbidden fruit never even arose. It was just possible that the Singaporeans were a new kind of human: ones that actually had no eccentric impulses to be controlled.

I still wasn't exactly sure what the penalty for possessing poppy-seed crackers was. But according to the sign above me, which showed a red slash through a hamburger and a pop can, eating anything on an MRT train would net you a $500 fine ($305 U.S.). I noticed the Chinese man next to me staring in consternation as the crumbs from my cracker fell to the floor. When I proferred the open pack, he flushed red and abruptly turned away and made for the doors. Noticing that it was Bugis Station—my stop too—I followed him onto the platform, provoking a worried glance over his shoulder and a comical dash for the escalator.

Good God. Shocking Singaporeans was as easy as scandalizing Mormons. I was going to have fun in this town—or get arrested trying.

"So," I said, grimacing as another tequila-and-tonic effervesced down my throat, "where do you go to have a good time in Singapore?" Pam and Kevin were my blind dates for the night: two hard-drinking Singaporean travel-agency employees in their late twenties, to whom I'd been introduced after sending a frantic round of "Does anybody know anybody in Singapore?" e-mails to friends and acquaintances. Pam had boasted she would take me to the most happening place in town—"And it was voted one of the ten best clubs in the world by a London paper!"—so I'd willingly paid the $35 ($21 U.S.) cover charge. But now that we were inside, perched on stools at a small, round table, I couldn't help wondering aloud where all the action was. A labyrinthine complex of three interconnected riverside warehouses, Zouk could have been a slick hipsters' space in any metropolis, all plush-sofa chill spaces and underlit bars, but at midnight on a Friday the dance floor was empty; the only people moving were the waitresses.

"It will get going later on!" Kev shouted over the techno. "Singaporeans need to drink a lot before they're relaxed enough to dance or have sex."

Ah, much like the British, I said, just as a shiver of Englishmen in their thirties cruised past our table, sizing up Pam.

"They're looking for SPGs," Kev explained. "That's sarong party girls! They're girls who go with Westerners, mostly for the money and status." I'd noticed a few of the breed already: overly made-up, tanned shoulders exposed, teetering on high heels, often sloppily drunk. They were tailor-made for their prey, the notorious Western zero-to-hero, men beset with male-pattern balding and early onset misogyny, who come to Asia to find the girlfriends their personality disorders prevented them from scoring at home.

"Dude, you know what I do for fun?" said Kev, putting another two pitchers of crantinis on his credit card. "I go to the Night Zoo and get mellow with a bottle of wine. Chill with the rhino, check out the bats. Don't laugh—it's totally rad!"

It was Kev's vocabulary, not his idea of a good time, that had made me chuckle. He was of Peranakan descent—a quintessentially Singaporean mix of Malay and Chinese—but his speech was peppered with Californian slang, gleaned from his years as a programmer in San Francisco, and he was wearing a baseball cap and a nametag-stitched baby-blue shirt cadged from a stint as a pitboy in an Australian garage. Like Pam, he attributed his impressive tolerance for alcohol to his mixed background.

"Most Chinese people get totally tipsy after one drink. They turn red, get real loud, and end up puking. We Peranakans can knock it back!"

This was one of the reasons that alcohol prohibition—unlike every other kind of prohibition—had never been an issue in Singapore; the absence of a gene that aided in the metabolism of alcohol tended to put a self-limiting cap on abuse. Kev and Pam's Malay genetic heritage spared them the embarrassment of the notorious Asian flush.

"I'm a lush!" seconded Pam, whacking her coaster-topped tequila tonic on the table and draining it in a single gulp. "I judge the civilization and livability of a country by the price of a can of beer in a 7-Eleven. It's freaking three dollars and thirty cents here! Tooooo much!"

I told them about the poppy-seed contraband I'd brought into the country.

"Oh, man," groaned Kev. "They banned poppy seeds too? Sometimes I'm just so embarrassed about Singapore."

Midnight had passed, and the two-for-one happy hour was over, so we maneuvered through ropes and bodies to another club in the complex, this one an Ibiza-themed room decorated with Moroccan adobe and mosaics. The crowd was stylishly but conservatively dressed, in black, short-sleeved T-shirts and tight jeans; international labels predominated. There was no sartorial individuality, however, no ecstasy-dilated pupils, no suspicious snorting from the stalls in the bathrooms; just the vaguely aggressive and competitive vibe of too many alcohol-lubed guys competing for too few women.

Pam and Kev told me they'd need to be a lot drunker to hit the dance floor, so we hopped a cab to an area called Emerald Hill, a laneway of plush, mostly expat-frequented bars off Orchard Road, the main shopping drag. Over lychee martinis in the Alley Bar, conversation turned to the Government's Social Development Unit, which was trying to foster dating by organizing social dances, barbecues, and singles' cruises. I told them I'd read the unspoken goal was to encourage the Chinese majority to have more children, to counterbalance the population explosion of the more fecund Malays.

Kev reared back, startled, and said, "Whoa, dude! That's totally OB!" He peeked from beneath his baseball cap to check if anybody had overheard me.

I raised an inquisitive eyebrow.

"Like, *out of bounds*! That's the term we use in Singapore. There are three things we don't talk about in public: race, religion, and politics. You just know when something is too extreme—it's instinctive."

Was he really worried the wrong person would hear him?

"Sometimes you have the feeling that there are spies all around. It's probably not true. But people don't talk a lot in public here; they're suspicious. It's definitely not normal to start up a conversation with a stranger."

We walked down Orchard Road and hit a couple more bars, but the scene always seemed to be the same: crowds of milling single men, balefully checking out the barmaids and the few remaining female clients.

Kevin was apologetic about the lameness of it all. "Dude, people are probably just burned out after the holidays. Are you up for trying again later in the week?"

I'd definitely give Singapore's nightlife a second chance. Pam said she wouldn't be able to make it, as she was off on a business trip to Taipei.

"I'll take you to the Mitre Hotel," Kev promised. "That's a slice of old Singapore. I guarantee you'll love it!"

The first thing a visitor to Singapore notices—apart from his clothes wilting in the humidity—is all the exhortations. The city is talking to you, and the tone is anxious.

DONT LOSE YOUR FESTIVE JOY TO CRIME, entreats a passing Toyota Crown taxi.

PLEASE DRAW TOILET PAPER HERE . . . USE WISELY! the Male Toilet at the Tekka Food Centre implores its patrons.

INCONSIDERATE BEHAVIOUR HAS CONSEQUENCES, a poster in the MRT cautions, showing a blithely chatting couple, caught in the sights of a security camera, blocking traffic on a moving walkway.

Off the curb on Orchard Road, even the pavement at your feet carries a health warning. Painted in white, streaked gray with tire marks, is the neatly lettered sentence ARE YOU A SMOKER? THIS IS THE AMOUNT OF TAR IN YOUR LUNGS AFTER 1 YEAR. (Some advertisers played with the ambient authoritarianism. At a food court, I noticed the Coca-Cola napkin dispenser on my table commanded DRINK UP! BY ORDER OF MINISTRY OF ENJOYMENT!) If Tokyo and Hong Kong are shimmering vertical billboards of consumer capitalism, then Singapore is a bulletin board in a Midwestern high school, thumbtacked with a totalitarian glee club's unironic calls to good citizenship.

In this school, however, the student council can have you put to death. Singapore, according to Amnesty International, has the highest rate of capital punishment in the world. Lately, stung by a fierce economic downturn, the SARS epidemic, record-high unemployment, and a diaspora of its brightest citizens to Australia and the United States, Singapore has made a concerted effort to lighten its image. Before my arrival, headlines worldwide heralded the changes: the prohibition on chewing gum was to be lifted; the long-banned *Sex and the City* would be aired; the arts would be encouraged to flourish; bungee jumping and bartop dancing would cautiously be deregulated.

Looking at the fine print, though, it was two steps forward, two steps back. Pressure from American trade lobbyists had forced Singapore to back down on the chewing-gum issue; henceforth, medically approved brands like Nicorette would be sold, but only by pharmacists and dentists, who would also be required to take down the names of buyers. *Sex and the City* would indeed air, but Samantha's allusions to blow jobs and rimming would be scissored by the Censorship Review Committee. A massive arts center was built on the Esplanade, but the auditoriums were too big to import anything but innocuous megamusicals like *Singin' in the Rain*. Local theater companies would still have to submit potentially subversive original plays to the ominously named Ministry of Information, Communication and the Arts before they could be staged, or face having their licenses pulled. And the concessions to bartop dancing, critics argued, were just cynical attempts at social engineering. Singapore's birthrate was stuck at 1.25, well below the 2.1 children per woman necessary to renew the population, and a survey by the condom company Durex showed that adult Singaporeans had the least sex of any nationality in the world—at 110 acts per year, ranking below even Belgians (130) and Indians (116). If Singapore's Confucian culture wasn't to disappear in a sea of Malays, clearly its workaholic ethnic Chinese population would have to be allowed a few opportunities to meet and mate.

Sex, in fact, was the only area where the Government had loosened the reins. When it came to individual liberty, freedom of speech, and democracy, the ruling party was still very much calling the shots. Since

1959, Singapore has been tightly governed by the PAP, or People's Action Party. Founded as a socialist party by "Harry" Lee Kuan Yew, a Cambridge-educated lawyer, it offered independence to a people weary of British colonial rule and the brutal war years of Japanese occupation. After a brief drama that brought union with a newly formed Federation of Malaysia, Singapore was expelled in 1965, whereupon it became a fully independent microstate. Though the PAP claims to have made Singapore a democracy—one where the ruling party just happens to sweep every election, apparently out of sheer merit—it holds on to power using tactics that are Machiavellian and duplicitous. The Newspaper and Printing Presses Act of 1974 ended private ownership of the press and put papers and magazines under the direct surveillance of the state. Opposition members (there are currently two in parliament, versus eighty-two PAP members) are routinely sued, bankrupted, and even jailed if they too pointedly criticize the ruling party; Lee Kuan Yew holds the title as the most successful individual defamation litigant in history. Detention without trial is common, and the Government has acknowledged using torture as a routine interrogation technique. Districts that vote for the opposition find themselves at the bottom of the list for public spending. Lee, who liked to refer to citizens as "digits," said in 1987:

"I am often accused of interfering in the private lives of citizens. Yet, if I did not, had I not done that, we wouldn't be here today. And I say without the slightest remorse that we . . . would not have made economic progress, if we had not intervened on very personal matters—who your neighbour is, how you live, the noise you make, how you spit, or what language you use. We decided what's right. Never mind what the people think." It was as revealing as a villain's aside in an Elizabethan drama.

Though he has retired as prime minister, Lee Kuan Yew still lurks backstage, very much the God in the Machine. In 1971, he told a crowd of polytechnic students, "My son has no hope of inheriting my position. He knows it and you know it." Today, the prime minister of Singapore is Lee Hsien Loong—B.G. "Brigadier General" Lee, for short—Lee Kuan Yew's oldest child. His wife is the director of a holding company that controls virtually every large corporation on the island. Singapore, which cloaks itself in the robes of a Westminster-style parliamentary democracy, is a self-perpetuating dynastic technocracy, where the abyss between the rulers and the ruled is utterly unfilled by unions, associations, nongovernmental organizations, or any other manifestation of civil society.

Wandering the streets, overpasses, and malls of the Central Business District, I looked in vain for signs of individuality or rebelliousness. Even at one o'clock in the morning, when there were no Mazdas or Hyundais as far as the eye could see, pedestrians at street corners would wait for the light to turn green before setting foot on the pavement (and the lights stayed red in Singapore for up to three minutes, enough to make you forget why you were crossing the street in the first place). One afternoon I went to Speakers' Corner, introduced with great fanfare at the dawn of the millennium as proof of Singapore's new democratic spirit, and located in a park near the Victorian shophouses of Chinatown. (This was surely the saddest sign of Singapore's psychological colonization: a place whose population was 77 percent Chinese still had its own Chinatown.) Though it was modeled on the long-running institution in Hyde Park—where soapbox orators call for torching of the Parliament building or an end to fox hunting—the Singaporean version required prospective speakers to register with the police and barred them from discussing race or religion. Not surprisingly, there had been no great rush to sign up.

Approaching the neatly lettered brown sign with its posts planted in shrubs, I cast a curious gaze around me. Apart from a man in shorts, silently reading a Chinese newspaper on a bench, I was the only living soul at Speakers' Corner.

★　　★　　★

Hwee Hwee Tan suggested we meet in the bistro at the Borders bookshop on Orchard Road. I walked beneath huge banyan trees hung with holiday lights like creepers, past the Burger Kings and Dairy Queens and Starbucks (where the bagels sat sad and naked, unstudded with poppy seeds), and briefly popped into a Marks & Spencer (whose shelves were filled with mint humbugs, potted tuna, and high-fiber digestives, but no narcotic savoury crackers).

Borders in Singapore looked identical to its counterparts in other English-speaking cities. There were the usual piles of fluorescent-covered British chick lit, far too many cookbooks, and that bizarre expatriate subgenre, found from Bangkok to Bombay, of Asian thrillers and lubricious intercultural confessionals. What was lacking were any works critical of Singapore; there was stack upon stack, however, of the latest multivolume autohagiography of Lee Kuan Yew ("They threatened to shut down any bookstore that didn't stock his memoirs," an expat editor quipped to me).

Tan was the author of two novels, the first of which, *Foreign Bodies*, she'd written at the age of twenty-three. I'd immediately been intrigued by its opening scene, in which a shirtless English youth in the Singapore subway is caught spilling an Ovaltine-and-vodka cocktail over a spotless MRT platform; it neatly captured some of the culture shock between Western and Asian values. A Chinese Christian, Tan had studied law at Oxford and lived in the United States after winning a *New York Times* writing scholarship; but she was back in Singapore, doing freelance work, feeling stifled by the low pay and pusillanimity of the local media. Now thirty, diminutive and slim-shouldered, Tan wore a sleeveless black blouse and thick-rimmed black glasses and spoke with a nervous loquacity and quiet intensity.

The waitress brought a vegetarian pizza, and Tan dug in with gusto. Between bites of my smoked-salmon sandwich, I asked whether all the prohibitions—of chewing gum, erotic literature, and any kinds of drugs—affected her day-to-day life.

"I'm a very clean-living person," said Tan. "I've never been fined for anything in my life. But it's true, there are a lot of prohibitions in Singapore. When the chewing gum ban came in, there was hardly a ripple of protest. The Government can get away with a lot more than they ever could in the United States, just because the values are so different. In the U.S., people value freedom so highly. For people here, having freedom—freedom of expression in particular—is not a high priority. For me, the chewing gum thing is not a big deal—if you want things like gum, banned books, or vibrators, there's always ways to get them. What really bothers me is the lack of freedom of speech."

Tan, who had been eyeing my sandwich covetously, interrupted to exclaim, "I've never seen such big bread!" I cut her off a chunk and passed it across the table.

"You love food, don't you?" I observed, as she chewed.

"I'm a Singaporean, after all!" she said. "The problem with Singapore is that none of these prohibitions matter to people. Because Singapore is a very secure country, and this security becomes a cocoon. A lot of my friends don't have any kind of rebellious spirit whatsoever. They're just starting to have kids, and they don't care about censorship; they just want to know if they'll be able to send their children to music school. I know a lot of my colleagues are really unhappy and frustrated with the system, but they don't think it's going to change. These prohibitions were set up by the existing power structure, and until the people at the top die out, it's always going to be the same."

I told her that such a status quo would drive me either crazy, or abroad. I imagined it would also be maddening for anybody with a streak of individuality—like Tan herself. But she considered herself an anomaly, attributing her creative urges to bipolar disorder, an attitude I found depressingly deterministic. ("I think I'm just a freak," she told me. "When you're bipolar, you have certain artistic gifts. There's nothing in my family environment that would actually be conducive to writing.")

"You know how frustration really manifests itself?" she said. "By people not giving a shit about their jobs. Creativity is not really rewarded in Singapore, because it involves rocking the boat, being a little bit rebellious, which is actually frowned upon in society. I have a lot of friends who hate their jobs, their colleagues, their work environment. So people just shut down and succumb to ennui; there's this kind of middle-class death of the spirit."

So where did that leave Tan, riddled with the creative impulses that made her a misfit in her own land?

"I'm hoping to move back to the United States," she admitted. "I'd like to live in New York or Los Angeles and work in filmmaking. Eventually I want to direct."

I pulled my Marks & Spencer savoury crackers out of my backpack.

Tan's face lit up, and she said, "Oh! These are the ones that are banned? Can I try one?"

We chewed in silence, each of the tiny seeds offering an infinitesimal resistance before satisfyingly succumbing between our teeth. I told her she would have to consume more than six hundred packs to feel the slightest narcotic effect.

Tan looked down contemplatively, her small jaws working quickly. "They're good," said the food-loving Singaporean, a little wistfully. "I love poppy seeds."

In Singapore, joining a diaspora was increasingly the solution for the ambitious, the individualistic, and the creative. As the local quip had it, "The Government wants Singapore to open up to the world? Sure, I'll help Singapore go global: I'll leave!" In a perfectly ordered surveillance state, where creativity's affinity with deviance was rigorously denied, the sovereign mood could only be a toxic mix of ennui and stress.

Realizing I was going to have to make my own fun, I woke up in my hotel room one morning determined to go on a one-man crime spree. I started by opening my curtains, slipping out of my underwear, and making a cup of instant coffee stark naked. (Fine: $20,000— $12,250 U.S.—and up to three months in prison, for appearing nude and exposed to the public view in one's own home.) I had high hopes I'd be spotted; my hotel was in the middle of Little India, and my room overlooked a mosque, whose recorded muezzin's prayer awoke me every morning at sunrise. After doing some stretching exercises standing on my bed, I paced back and forth (inasmuch as one can pace in ten square feet of floor space) and waited for a knock on my door, or a crowd to form on the pavement below. But only the white-rimmed eyes of the mynah birds squabbling beneath the eaves outside the window beheld my nakedness.

I got dressed, stuffed my poppy-seed crackers, copy of *Fanny Hill*, and two packs of Wrigley's into my day bag, grabbed my pocket watch and a notepad, and prepared for a day on the town.

Bugis Station, 9:05 A.M. A fine morning, already sweat-inducingly humid. I buy a bottle of the sticky glucose drink Lucozade on the way to subway. Place myself within sight of a security camera on MRT platform, directly in front of sign warning of $500 fine ($305 U.S.) for eating and drinking. Remembering Ovaltine-and-vodka incident in Hwee Hwee Tan's novel, I upend my drink, pouring it slowly over shiny, spotless floor. A pool, the color of multivitamin urine, spreads across the tiles. Wait. Voice coos over the loudspeaker, "For your own safety, please stand behind the yellow line." Repeated in Hindi, Malay, and Mandarin.

9:20 A.M. MRT train, bound for City Hall station. Catch the eyes of an Indian couple sitting across from me, she in a sari and high heels, he in starched shirt. Slowly, deliberately unwrap three sticks of Juicy Fruit. Chew audibly. He gives her a nudge; her eyes widen as I blow bubble. I wink. They look away, wearing embarrassed grins. I scan the faces of the other passengers, trying to gauge reactions, if any. Most are texting messages into their hand phones. The rest are sleeping.

9:50 A.M. Internet café in Stamford House. Choose computer near window. Read sign taped to monitor: NO VIEWING OF ADULT SITES. NO DOWNLOADING ANY PROGRAM. PLEASE OBSERVE SILENCE. (Fine for downloading pornography: up to $10,000 [$6,100 U.S.] under the Computer Misuse Act. While the Government has blocked one hundred high-profile sites, they recognize this can only be a symbolic act: the Internet is too vast and anarchic for them to ever fully control.) Type in *www.playboy.com*. Site refuses to load. Type in *www.penthouse.com*. Same result. Type in the more obscure *www.suicidegirls.com*. Bingo! Given a slide show of tattooed and pierced punk-rock girls, fully naked. A Chinese man pauses outside the window, apparently taken by a pale waif with a spike through her nipple. When I look over my shoulder and catch his eye, he rushes off.

10:10 A.M. Kicked off my computer by red-faced café owner. She tells me to get out of her shop.

11:30 A.M. Orchard Road, outside the Hilton. Tubby, pink-calfed expat on Yamaha with slender Singaporean woman riding pillion roars down sidewalk and then cuts off a jeep full of policemen, wearing park-ranger-style hats with chin straps. They are forced to brake; driver grimaces. In spite of the flagrant violation, he doesn't pursue the lawbreakers.

4:05–4:30 P.M. Toilet inspections. Signs in the Chinatown MRT station Male Toilet: LET'S WORK TO KEEP THIS TOILET CLEAN AND DRY, A BETTER ENVIRONMENT FOR ALL. Illustrated with a yellow happy face. Next to it: KEEP THE FLOOR DRY (with picture of little puddle beneath urinal). Wait for stall. Short, old Chinese man shuffles out; I enter; he hasn't flushed toilet! (Fine for failure to flush: $150, or $92 U.S.) Wads of paper still float in bowl. I flush, but it won't go down at first—have to press and keep it pressed. Is this a subtle test of civic-mindedness? In the corridor, skinny attendant in yellow overalls watches the scene through an open door. Go to McDonald's toilets, with firm intention not to flush. Turn my back on toilet and hear it flush automatically. Infrared sensor has done the job for me.

6:35 P.M. Take the MRT to Police Cantonment Complex, Singapore's main police station. Imposing, brand-new building, with curving glass façade, on the edge of Chinatown. At the security check outside the door, I empty my day bag into a tray, walk through metal detector. On the other side, my belongings—*Fanny Hill*, savoury crackers, and two packs of Wrigley's—are handed back to me. I approach desk. Notice huge emblem mounted on wall: Central Narcotics Bureau. Hastily hide poppy-seed crackers in my bag. Woman at desk asks, "Do you want to see a police officer?" I nod my head. Fill out a card with passport number, am given nametag to clip to shirt.

7:10 P.M. One of the two officers on duty, a woman, waves me to the desk. "Yes?" she says, leaning on the desk. Explain I'm a foreign visitor and want to know about the status of a law. Is it legal to have chewing gum in Singapore? I lift the Wrigley's pack out of my shirt pocket and show her. Immediately regret it.

"No, it's illegal." She looks at her bulky, broad-shouldered partner, who's filling out a report about stolen luggage. "Right?"

"That's right."

Well, I say, I was hoping tourists could bring in some for personal use.

"No," he repeats. "It's still illegal."

Well, what if you needed it to relieve the pressure in your ears in the plane? Could you bring in some then?

"Maybe if you chewed them on the plane and then threw them out before you got to Singapore . . . ," she says.

So—will I get arrested?

"No, there's a fine. Five hundred dollars, I think."

I pull the gum out again. Did she want to confiscate it?

"If you brought in two or three pounds of it, then we might, because you'd be suspected of wanting to sell it. But if you only have two or three sticks . . ."

I make a contrite face: "But I have fourteen sticks!"

She checks her partner for confirmation. "This time it's okay." He nods. "Just make sure you throw it out before you go through the airport." She reconsiders. "But not on the ground."

I thank her and make for the exit. Suddenly, she darts from behind the desk and runs ahead of me toward the front. Damn, I think, it was a ruse: she's going to set off an alarm. Then, with an embarrassed smile backward, she ducks into the Female Toilet.

8:30 P.M. Celebrate the end of my crime spree with a sickly sweet, $19 ($11.60 U.S.) Singapore sling at the Long Bar of Raffles Hotel. The bar floor is covered with peanut shells, which crunch underfoot. (The ads in local magazines boast of Raffles: "Quite possibly the one place in Singapore where littering is actually encouraged.") The stout, middle-aged Englishman next to me gets off his barstool, plants his feet wide, takes a series of flash photos of the wicker-and-rattan-and-bamboo décor, and then starts abusing the Malay barman in a flowered sarong about the price of beer.

Conclude that, short of spray painting the Mercedes of the wrong politician, it's almost impossible for a white foreigner to get arrested in Singapore.

For a certain breed of expat—particularly Brits nostalgic for the good ol' days of corporal punishment and a clearly defined social hier-archy—Singapore is a paradise of easy living. The double-decker buses and MRT trains are fast and run on time, and expat privileges include Indonesian maids and air-conditioned company cars. The food served at the outdoor hawker centers—the local term for food courts—is cheap, varied, and exuberantly named: Cuttlefish Kang Kong, Fried La-La, Ice Kacang, Buddha Jump over the Wall,

Drunken Bull Frog. Even if, as author William Gibson observed, in Singapore everything is infrastructure, at least it is tropical infrastructure: the pedestrian overpasses teem with orchids, and the Stalinist-style housing projects are overhung with pink bougainvillea. Only when you imagined daily life as a Singaporean did claustrophobia start to set in. Reading the broadsheet *Straits Times* every morning was a bizarre experience. A front-page article on Wednesday detailed the crime of a former television host, who had met an inebriated thirty-year-old woman at a party. He invited her to his apartment, removed her clothes, slept naked beside her, and when she woke up, in the words of the judge, kissed her "most intimate parts." What struck me was severity of the sentence: sixteen months' jail and four strokes of the cane for "outraging the modesty of a woman."

On Thursday, one of the *Times'* lead stories dealt with senior engineer Chow Peng Wah, who, after being reprimanded by e-mail for asking his boss for a transfer, leapt to his death from the eleventh floor of a housing project. Before killing himself, Chow strangled his eleven-year-old son with a nylon cord. He left a note saying his favorite child "would not be able to adapt to environment changes" after he was gone and so he had "to be with him." The talk of the town was the case of Steve Chia, an opposition member found with topless photos of his Indonesian maid in the trash can of his computer desktop. Though the PAP had been known to hack into the hard drives of Internet subscribers, in this case it wasn't a Government snitch that had called the police: it was Chia's wife.

Over and over again, I heard stories of petty and perverse behavior that bespoke deep alienation: tattletaling, shunning, harassment. Foreign domestic workers in particular had a hard time. The Ministry of Manpower was preparing orientation courses for first-time employers, after a series of shocking cases in which Chinese employers brutalized Filipina or Indonesian domestic workers: a certain Tong Lai

Chun had abused her maid with a meat tenderizer and clothes-pegs and grabbed her hair and slammed her head against the toilet wall; Chow Yen Ping repeatedly bit her young maid's breasts until a nipple fell off; Ong Ting Ting shoved ice cubes down her Filipina maid's shorts and bra because she had left a window open while ironing. Of the ninety Indonesian maids that had died since 1999, fifty-two had perished in accidents, twenty-five by their own hand. In a setting where social solidarity was absent, and everyone was isolated from his neighbor, anomic behavior seemed to take the form of the victimization of the powerless.

I hoped that Cherian George, a postdoctoral fellow at the Asia Research Institute, recently back from the United States after teaching at Stanford, could help me make sense of some of these strange news items. We met in an open-air café at the National University of Singapore, whose lush campus was a long MRT and bus ride from the center of town. George, whose parents had emigrated from Kerala in India, was the author of *Singapore: The Air-Conditioned Nation*, a study of the island state that was easily the most provocative book I'd been able to find on local shelves. In a context where one was constantly reminded of what one couldn't do, I asked, did perverse behavior patterns emerge?

"Definitely," George replied. "Let me give you an example of something that happened in my condo complex. My car was deliberately scratched, with a metal brush, which left multiple lines. I made the mistake of parking in a space that obviously that particular resident thought was still his—ever since then, I've only seen his car in that space. And so the next morning the police came, and there were four neighbors who said, 'Oh, yeah, this block is famous for that. It happened to me, it's happened to so and so. Now you'll know not to park there.'

"What outraged me is they felt the sensible response was to learn your lesson and not park there. In the United States or Britain, the reaction would be, 'We should get together and do something about this guy, solve what is a public problem.' Here, the attitude is, 'Mind your own business.' I frankly think it's cultural. Even my Chinese friends agree that it's particularly Chinese to not think of the public, or society, as something real. It's more like me, my family, my clan, with the Government symbolizing an authority best kept at a distance. Rather than it being a repository of some sort of public will, an institution we would want to make use of for valid public reasons."

I mentioned my recent crimes against public decency and expressed my surprise at having gotten away with it all.

"Foreigners can get away with little things like jaywalking and littering," George explained. "But people here, as in most Asian countries, are very resistant to the idea that whites could be treated specially."

He reminded me of the Michael Fay case. In 1994, a teenaged American had been caned after going on a spree in which he graffitied several expensive cars—albeit with removable paint. Fay got four, permanently scarring, whacks from the rotan.

"Most Singaporeans thought, 'Who does this young white punk think he is that he can break the law?' When the case first broke, Singaporeans didn't really know that a property crime, vandalism, was a caneable offense, and there was the beginning of a quite substantive discussion on corporal punishment. But then the American diplomats got involved, and there was this very visceral reaction: 'They think they're special! It's just another example of neocolonialism!' "

Maybe my sins had been too slight. I pulled out the package of poppy crackers. Unlike Hwee Hwee Tan, George, perhaps mindful of his university position, declined to partake. I asked if he had to be careful about what he did and said in public.

"This is a city where surveillance is of an order that is much higher than in most other cities. I would say that, when sensitive topics are broached, a lot of Singaporeans look over their shoulder. Sometimes it's an inside joke; but it has become so much of a joke that they forget to question whether Big Brother is really watching them with a camera."

For George, the Government had engineered social control directly into the urban geography. Disorder was ghettoized into Designated Red Light Areas and ethnic communities such as Kampong Glam, Geylang, and Little India. Bugis Street, home of Singapore's notorious transvestites until the 1970s, had been razed and repackaged as sanitized heritage. The university where we were talking was a good example, George pointed out.

"Quite deliberately, there's no central square on the campus; no place for students to rally; it's very decentralized. Another factor is, you go through your national service at exactly the time when you might be tempted to get involved in student activism." At age eighteen, every male Singaporean was required to do two and a half years of military service, then was kept on reserve till the age of forty. "It's a way of disciplining them just when they might be getting unruly and independent-minded."

George was troubled by how successful the Government's tactics had been. "Any sort of civic action is a resource that becomes part of a society's cultural memory. In most normal societies, people know that if you come across a particular problem, you can write a petition, organize a boycott, a sit-in, a demonstration, or in extreme cases, a strike. It's a cultural resource that we draw on when we need to engage the state or corporations. In Singapore, these technologies of protest have been absent for so long that Singaporeans have just forgotten how to do it."

Even in the conservative nations of Southeast Asia, Singapore was an anomaly. On the day before I'd flown in, one hundred thousand people had rallied in the streets of notoriously materialistic Hong Kong to protest for greater democracy.

Surely, I ventured, there were signs of change. The old guard was giving way to a new generation; the new prime minister, Lee Hsien Loong, had called for the construction of a "vibrant civic society." (A fond hope, only slightly undermined when he continued by saying that, though the opposition was entitled to criticize the ruling party, "the Government has to rebut or even demolish them, or lose its moral authority.") George confessed he wasn't particularly optimistic about the future.

"The bottom line is that the Government still has at its fingertips a number of discretionary powers that it can use the moment it feels like it. It can close down a newspaper; it can lock up somebody arbitrarily on national security grounds—literally too many ways to name. Until the Government is willing to give up some of those powers, we won't really be taking a concrete two steps forward."

One thing I had to concede: Singapore seemed an efficient and orderly place, unusually unbeset by crime and drug addiction.

George fixed a severe gaze on me. "But there would be major problems if you allowed those damn poppy-seed cookies in!" he said, banging the table in mock outrage. Then, startled by his own outburst, he looked over his shoulder, as if checking whether he'd been overheard.

It may have been intended as a gesture of self-mockery. Then again, it may have been reflex. I suspected that, after years of self-surveillance, even George himself didn't know for sure.

I met Kevin, my guide to Singapore's nightlife, for a final attempt at barhopping. Once again, things were quiet, even though it was a Friday, and we were virtually alone in the first two bars we visited.

"Don't worry, dude, I'll take you to the Mitre Hotel. Though it's a place I hesitate to go after dark!"

We walked down a dark lane between high-rises and came to a two-story, colonial-style building with green-and-white shutters, set in a lot filled with towering shade trees. Electrical wires dangled from the flaking whitewash of the façade; piles of plastic containers full of beer bottles were stacked on a patio filled with junk. In a desert of shopping malls, we'd found an oasis of derelict grunge.

Inside, a laconic barman spoke French to a mustachioed Brazilian who could have passed for Gérard Depardieu. Old luggage was piled around the room; moisture darkened the white walls like sweat stains under the armpits of a dress shirt. We took a seat on a sofa spilling its stuffing like a slit Thanksgiving turkey and sipped on Tiger beers.

"Don't look behind you, dude." Kev gestured with a beringed pinkie. I wheeled around to see a naked tail scurrying into the darkness. "A rat the size of a small cat just ran past your ankle."

Kev sighed. "I love this place. It reminds me of my grandfather's house before it got expropriated to build a highway." A not un-common experience, apparently: the Government had uprooted thousands of farmers and rehoused them in faceless housing estates to build the modern city-state.

I asked Kev about the thick rings on his fingers.

"I used to be a goth. I was probably only one of ten in all of Singapore in the 1980s. We wore black lipstick, painted our nails black, listened to The Cure. People thought I was a freak! Later I wrote for a magazine called *Big O*, which was Singapore's only real alternative paper. I even wrote a play about Singapore, *The Plastic Factory*. But that was a while ago."

I wondered if, when he was younger, he'd ever experimented with drugs.

"I used to smoke a lot of pot in Australia and the United States, but it's hard to find here. It's too risky, too expensive. It's just not worth the trouble in Singapore." I mentioned they were considering decriminalizing it in Canada. "Dude, that's never going to happen here. They hang people for carrying drugs!"

It was a fact: Singapore seemed to reserve the worst punishments for those caught with drugs. Since 1991, four hundred people had been executed, most of them for trafficking. A twenty-four-year-old Malaysian day laborer with an IQ of 74 was hanged after allegedly trying to sell cannabis to an undercover narcotics officer. An eighteen-year-old shop assistant from Hong Kong, who was passing through Singapore after a vacation in Bangkok, was caught with heroin hidden in a secret compartment of a suitcase. In spite of her protests that she had been given the bag by a Chinese couple in Thailand, she too got the gallows; her seventeen-year-old friend was imprisoned for life. With its easily patrolled causeways and bridges, and famously efficient airport, it was hard to imagine smuggling could ever be enough of a threat to Singapore to justify such extreme exemplary punishments. If trafficking tends to flourish in situations where private armies, weak states, and endemic conflict rule—as with the opium growers of contemporary Afghanistan—it is relatively easy to enforce prohibitions in a totalitarian setting. Under the Nazis, cocaine trafficking was virtually eliminated, and the Taliban squashed the opium supply by prohibiting poppy growing in 2000. In Singapore, paranoia about drugs seemed to be more of an issue than drugs themselves: in local pharmacies, I'd noticed booklets of litmuslike paper next to the cash registers. "Drink Spike Detector," the packages read. "Turns dark blue if a drink has been spiked with GHB or Ketamine; 4 strips per pack."

What really stood out were the other, legal vices. Though there were no casinos—Singaporeans spent $340 million U.S. a year on gambling in neighboring Malaysia and Indonesia—the state lottery brought in $1.65 billion in U.S. tax revenue a year. While the official statistics on alcohol consumption had Singaporeans going through only 1.7 liters a year (the equivalent of two cans of beer per person a week)—making them the most abstemious nation in the developed world—alcohol was so cheap and omnipresent that any vacationing Norwegian would have thought he'd arrived in heaven. High-test beer, like Baron's Strong, 8.8 percent alcohol by volume, was everywhere, and bottles of Jack Daniel's were kept behind the tills of the ubiquitous 7-Elevens. Cigarettes—with exotic names like Texas 5's, Sahara X-Tra Slims, and Bonjour King Size—were relatively cheap, and smoking was still permitted in bars.

Surprisingly, while prostitution was technically prohibited—though actually rampant—in Bangkok, it was legal in Singapore. There were four hundred licensed brothels in six Designated Red Light Areas, and the prostitutes were required to carry a special yellow identity card with their thumbprints and submit to health exams every two weeks. I was repeatedly invited to visit the discos, massage parlors, and Chinese prostitutes of the very mainstream Orchard Towers complex, locally referred to as the Four Floors of Whores. One night I did go to the *lorongs*, or alleys, of Geylang, the Malay residential and red-light district, and strolled past the Chinese and Thai prostitutes in their short black dresses, outside a hotel, which rented rooms for a $10 ($6 U.S.) an hour "transit rate," and glimpsed the second-floor massage parlors offering "complete relaxation services."

I asked Kev whether he'd ever been in trouble with the authorities.

"I've never been arrested. It's not like they're going to take you out of your apartment at three A.M. and beat you with a hose—but there's definitely a surveillance culture here. People watch what they say. When I was in university, one of our teachers was a woman who'd been arrested for being a Marxist in the 1980s. It was all trumped-up charges, of course. We tried to get her to talk about it, but she'd always go all weird and quiet whenever we brought it up.

"Are you familiar with Michel Foucault's idea of the panopticon?" he asked.

I was. The French philosopher had used the circular prison conceived by the English utilitarian Jeremy Bentham, whose every cell could be observed by an invisible authority in a central tower, as a metaphor for surveillance in modern societies.

"It's not so much that the police are listening to everything you say.

It's more that the people of Singapore have the panopticon in their heads." Cherian George had made the same observation: since people didn't know to what extent they were actually being watched, they got into the habit of reflexively looking over their shoulders, avoiding any behavior that could be construed as being out of bounds.

After a couple more drinks, during which we watched the already thin crowd at the Mitre dwindle to nothing, Kev invited me back to his place. We taxied to an area called Paya Lebar, in the heartlands of Singapore, passing mile after mile of HDBs—short for Housing Developing Board flats—identical twelve- or thirteen-story apartment blocks set among elevated MRT lines and palm-tree-lined roads.

"You know what the number one problem in Singapore is, dude?" said Kev, as we walked up a fluorescent-lit staircase to his flat. He gestured to his front door: it was splattered with a Jackson Pollock slurry of brown and red paint.

"Debt. Everybody here lives on credit. The guy who lived here before us owed money to a loan shark. The enforcers don't seem to get the message that he's moved, so they still come by and deface our door. The first warning, they use coffee. The second, they use paint. The third, I'm pretty sure, is going to be shit. I'm not looking forward to that one." The psychology behind the intimidation was interesting: humiliate the victim by making his apartment different from everybody else's. The nail that sticks out is the one that gets hammered down.

Kev opened the door. It was a spacious flat, outfitted with high-tech appliances, the latest stereo equipment, and an aquarium full of fluorescent tropical fish. But the walls were concrete, the ceilings were low, his balcony overlooked a brilliantly lit garage, which corkscrewed like a low-rent Guggenheim toward the tropical sky.

Kev cranked Radiohead on the stereo and upended an ice-cube tray full of jiggling vodka jellies into a bowl. He'd made two hundred of them for a party last weekend, but only a handful of people had showed up.

I asked whether the music would wake up his wife.

"Ah, she'd sleep through a tsunami."

We sat sucking on the jellies, watching a man polishing his Kia in the parking lot across the street.

Kev sighed. "People my age are leaving Singapore. I mean, I understand it. But now I'm married, and I've got a mortgage. Who would want to have children where I live? Kids should be outside, running around in nature, in the parks. Not so long ago all of this was green—there were no HDBs. But Singapore has been totally built up—there's no more free land anymore. I tell you, dude, it's depressing. I'd like to go back to Australia or the States."

I suddenly got it, viscerally, in my guts: the ennui, the low fertility rates, the claustrophobia. I felt the strangeness of being on this bulge in the globe near the equator, this psychologically colonized patch of concrete, artificially cooled with Freon. Confined on a tropical island with no hinterland, ruled by paranoid control freaks and stacked in concrete rabbit pens, I'd probably lose my will to live and reproduce too. In spite of the heat, I felt myself shiver.

I'd been wondering what would happen if you eliminated all byways to deviance, when the urge, or even the possibility, to transgress was completely extirpated from a society. Well, I'd gotten my answer: *Singapore* was what happened, a society where independent thinking had been so thoroughly suppressed that creativity and innovation had to be imported from abroad. Of course, prohibitions alone weren't enough to produce such a society; they had to be accompanied by deeply embedded cultural traditions of authoritarianism and fear of power. Compliance was encouraged by Singapore's compactness, and the fact that a rigorous surveillance culture was possible in a city-state of only 4.6 million citizen-digits. In Norway, which at least boasted some traditions of egalitarianism and liberalism, the nanny state was justified by appeals to the public good and peer pressure. In Singapore, it was maintained by a kind of sinister fearmongering, by the ubiquitous No Smoking signs and the security cameras overseeing them. The result, as Cherian George had pointed out, was the disappearance of any memory of the techniques of opposition and protest. Say what you will about the current crop of forbidden substances—that some are addictive, that some make you foolish, that some expand your mind, that all can be forms of irresponsible escapism—at least they are symbolic of an impulse toward independent thinking and subversion. The most chilling thing about Singapore was the absence of the possibility of any misbehavior whatsoever, except along the socially approved lines of drinking, visiting prostitutes, or gambling—all steam-valve vices that tend to fortify the status quo, rather than challenge it.

Singapore, a dystopia of total prohibition, had provided me with a new paradigm for purgatory. I was glad I'd had the foresight to import my own forbidden fruit; no matter how innocuous crackers and chewing gum may appear to our eyes, in Singapore they have a potent symbolism. Saying good-bye to Kev, I left him with a token gesture of subversion: my copy of *Fanny Hill.* I figured some mildly stimulating reading might help him get through the long tropical nights.

The next morning, before checking out of my hotel, I ran one final errand. I took a cab to the Botanic Gardens and threaded my way between the swans and orchids. Even amidst the greenery, one was constantly walking on cement; it was forbidden to leave the paths snaking through the well-tended gardens. Finally, I found a patch of earth among a stand of ginger plants. After a quick look around for surveillance cameras, I took out my remaining savoury crackers. Crushing them between my palms, I scattered the crumbs on the moist ground.

With a little luck, the seeds might germinate, and opium poppies would again bloom in the nanny state. Given the ambient waking nightmare, I figured Singapore's citizens could use all the daydreams they could get.

· CHEESE ·

He should have a long spoon
who sups with the devil.

—Proverb

· 3 ·

ÉPOISSES

Satan in a Poplar Box

SUNDAY AFTERNOON, Eightieth and Broadway. It was a
good day to be in New York. The cherry trees were in blossom,
cyclists with industrial-strength chains looped around their necks
dodged shirtless rollerbladers, and an old man in a fedora sat on a
bench on the median strip, letting the poppy seeds from his bagel
commingle with the periods and commas on the front page of the
Sunday *Times*.

I approached the faux-Tudor façade of Zabar's, one of the world's
great delicatessens. This was no Dean & DeLuca or Marks & Spencer,
where every item seems to sit burnished, impeccable, and aloof;
Zabar's began as a family-run smoked-fish counter that had, over
seventy years, swollen into a two-story Upper West Side temple of
gourmandise. Inside, the lights were fluorescent, the staff wore
baseball caps and frayed white smocks, and the great delicacies of
the world were rudely wrapped in cellophane or plopped into plastic
tubs. I was instantly drunk on that ineffable deli smell: roasted Vienna
coffee, Indian turmeric and Norwegian smoked salmon, Russian
babkas and pickled South African Peppadew, mingling until the air
itself becomes esculent. I felt the sensory surfeit that a husky, raised on

odorless arctic winters, might feel if suddenly let loose in a Kashmir spice garden. Roaming the crowded aisles, among casual-chic Manhattanites stocking up on Israeli couscous and Caspian caviar, I recognized exotic products from past voyages—Belgian stroop! Mexican mole! Australian Vegemite!—and became lost in reveries of Central Park picnics and dinner parties at the Dakota. The next time I'm traversing a drizzly November in my soul, when I'm tempted to swat bagels out of the hands of passersby and knock old men's hats onto their newspapers, I'll remind myself to head straight for the nearest deli and inhale deeply. This is the odor the seraphim, languishing on their cumulus clouds, must strive to conjure up when they grow nostalgic for the world of the senses.

When it came to the cheese department, however, I was skeptical of Zabar's apparent abundance. They boasted of carrying over six hundred varieties, with seven tons moving through the store each week. I'd already spotted wedges of Italian kosher parmigiano-Reggiano, blue pottery jars of English Stilton, boxes of extrasharp vintage cheddar. Fat larval pods of provolone, bound in striped cords and stamped with edible ink, dangled above an electronic scale on a metal pole planted in a pile of Pont l'Evêque squares.

I'd first learned to appreciate cheese in Paris, where nothing is wrapped in Saran, and the local *fromager* takes pride in aging his product and selling regular clients only those that are *à point*—perfectly matured, a stage that often comes only a couple of days before putrescence. Besides, it was common knowledge that some of the truly great cheeses of France were prohibited in the United States. Ripe Camembert de Normandie, underaged Brie de Meaux, and pungent Valençay were as sternly repelled at the frontiers as Iraqis without visas. According to Food and Drug Administration (FDA) regulations, any cheese made with unpasteurized, or raw, milk is banned if it is aged for less than sixty days. For some reason, Canadian cheese shops, though governed by similar rules, managed to flout the law: the *affineurs* in my hometown were chockablock with forbidden foreign *fromages*. I had driven south from Montreal with one of the world's smelliest cheeses in my trunk, its poplar box wrapped in alternating layers of foil and plastic in case the sniffer dogs were out. (Those dogs are *good*. I was once pulled out of the lineup in the Cincinnati airport, after a trip to Normandy. I'd detached a couple of particularly kitschy labels from cheese boxes, on which a soupçon of veritable Camembert must have lingered. Pawing through my affairs, the Customs man held them up between rubber-gloved fingers—as though they were evidence of some shameful foreign debauch—and only grudgingly returned them when he'd determined there were no actual dairy products for him to pitch into his plastic-lined garbage can.) This time I was waved through at the border—just another pale Canadian looking for fun in the big city—and I successfully delivered my contraband to a deprived New Yorker. Nidhi, whose palate had been formed in Montreal, unwrapped the cheese in The Burp Castle, an East Village bar devoted to Belgian beers.

"God, it's beautiful!" he had exclaimed. He closed his eyes and sighed as the scent of stale Chimay was overwhelmed by something at once putrid and appetizing. "It smells like sex!" We ate it with olives and rye bread and relished the sideways glances and rude comments we got from drinkers at neighboring tables.

So, I wondered, why was the very cheese I'd smuggled across the border so conspicuously perched in a refrigerator at Zabar's, selling for far less than what I'd paid in Montreal? And why was another cheese, which by French regulation should be aged for only fifty days, prominently displayed among the tubs of mascarpone and Roquefort spread? A laser-printed card was even planted in the center of this huge wheel of Reblochon, as if taunting the inspectors: "Raw-milk semisoft cheese from the Savoie mountains. Unpasteurized cow's milk."

After buying these forbidden cheeses as evidence, I demanded to see the manager of the cheese department, but was informed she didn't work on weekends. When I finally got Olga Dominguez on the phone later in the week, she explained everything.

"We do our own importing," Dominguez told me, "and we try not to have any cheese that we're not supposed to have. Zabar's is more likely to get into trouble than the smaller, less well-known stores. In the United States, it's always been illegal to bring in raw-milk cheeses that are not aged over sixty days, but for a while, people were doing it anyway. Since the FDA introduced the Bioterrorism Act of 2003, they've really cracked down. All the exporters have to register now."

Interesting. What about that huge round of Reblochon I'd seen on the shelf, then?

"You might have noticed that it was dried out around the edges. That's because they're holding it for a little bit longer in the factory in France so they can satisfy the sixty-day aging requirement."

Fair enough. But how come they were selling the same notoriously stinky cheese I'd taken the trouble to smuggle all the way to New York? There was no way that could be legal!

"Yes, it is. The version we import is made by a different manu-facturer than the one you get in Canada. They're making cheeses for the American market, and they're pasteurizing the milk. Which is too bad, really, because even though they look the same, they don't taste the same. We used to get raw-milk Camemberts in here sometimes by accident, and when you'd open the box, the smell would just kind of overwhelm you—wrap itself around you. It's just not the same with pasteurized-milk cheeses."

Dominguez was right. I'd sampled the cheese I'd bought at Zabar's, and there was something wrong with it. Compared to the version I'd smuggled from Montreal—which, the box clearly indicated, was made from raw milk—the New York import came up short. Though equally pungent at first whiff, once you got past the rind, the innards were lacking the complexity of its raw-milk counterpart. It was insipid and gummy, an unmistakable sign of pasteurization. The cheese was dead.

In this delicatessen, which should have been a monument to a great metropolis's power to command the spice routes and ley lines of globalized commerce, the cheese being sold as genuine French was fake—a pale imitation of the real thing, being peddled at premium prices to the gourmets of Gotham. In the land of consumer freedom, an impediment to free choice had been erected. I suspected that the justification for the policy would be the same the Norwegian government used to defend their alcohol control policies: paternalistic concern for the health of the public. But scratch any prohibition and you'll find more sinister motives—including protectionism, bureaucratic inertia, and xenophobia—lurking beneath the surface. The explanation, I soon discovered, would have implications for the disappearance of gastronomic diversity from the world. Behind the superficial plenitude, all was not well on the shelves of Zabar's.

I swore to get to the bottom of this duplicity. When I got back to Montreal, I booked a ticket to France. I was going to the birthplace of Époisses.

If Satan—the horned, hoofed, brimstone-breathing Satan of the Puritans—were to make up a cheese tray for his disciples, he would certainly start with Époisses, the cheese I had found at Zabar's. He might consider a rank goat cheese from the Pyrénées, rolled in cinders, making sure a bit of manure-crusted straw was still clinging to the bottom. He'd definitely throw in a wedge of Vieux Boulogne, a soft, beer-washed cheese, redolent of manure, which was recently selected as the smelliest in the world by an "electronic nose" developed by a team of British researchers. He might also select a well-aged Stinking Bishop, from Gloucestershire, not only for the exuberant blasphemy of the name, but also for its sticky rind and aroma of old socks.

But at the center of the tray would be a wheel of Époisses, silently slumping into putrefaction. The nobility and notoriety of this cheese are well established. Perfected in the sixteenth century by the Cistercians, a particularly austere community of monks whose meat-less diet led them to seek alternative sources of protein, it was dubbed the King of Cheeses by the godfather of gastronomes, Brillat-Savarin. Originally made from raw milk, straight from the cow's teat, it is still washed in marc—a liquor distilled from grape pits and skins—until its corrugated skin achieves a glossy orangish red hue. At the summum of its maturity it oozes from its rind, as pale and sweaty as the protruding belly roll of an obese Persian satrap. It is the kind of alien foodstuff that Midwesterners have to be cajoled into eating on reality shows with the promise of large sums of money. The French, in contrast, voluntarily consume it between their *jambon persillé* and chocolate mousse.

Ultimately, Satan would favor Époisses above all others for one compelling reason: its smell. Legend has it that, like the spike-husked tropical fruit durian, which is banned in buses in Bangkok, it is illegal to carry Époisses on the Parisian métro. And if eating durian has been compared to spooning up custard in a public lavatory, then tackling an Époisses is a bit like gnawing on a urinal cake while wading through a feedlot lagoon. Once past the odor barrier of mingled ammonia and barnyard, however, one is reminded that Satan is in fact a fallen angel: the tongue is suddenly suffused with the divine essence of fresh milk, a pure distillation of salt, sugar, cream, and all the rich odors of the Burgundian countryside. Though Époisses, like most of the great cheeses of Europe, starts life as a mix of milk, rennet, salt, and mold spores, by the time it hits the market shelves it has become something considerably more complex. A recent analysis of the heady Italian cheese Gorgonzola revealed that it consisted of sixty-three discrete compounds, including fourteen forms of alcohol, twenty-one goaty esters, five fruity aldehydes, and one acrid sulfur, all of which contribute to its distinctive odor. Époisses, which makes Gorgonzola smell like Velveeta, is an even more elaborate cocktail of natural chemicals.

It can also be deadly. In 1999, an outbreak of listeriosis—a foodborne illness that typically causes fever, aching muscles, and a brief but violent stomach flu—was reported in France and traced back to a cheesemaker in Burgundy. The culprit turned out to be that most intimidating of cheeses, Époisses. A young woman died, another had a miscarriage, and a seventy-one-year-old woman was hospitalized with encephalitis, an inflammation of the brain that can be triggered by the listeria bacteria. If the French press leapt on the story (the more sensational provincial rags printed such headlines as ÉPOISSES: LE FROMAGE QUI TUE—"The Cheese That Kills"), the international media had a field day. FRANCE IN PANIC OVER KILLER SOFT CHEESE, bugled the *Independent*. LISTERIA HYSTERIA, screamed the *Wall Street Journal*, and pointedly asked, WHY DEFEND CHEESE THAT SMELLS LIKE SOCKS AND MANURE? This was proof that French cheeses—particularly the unpasteurized ones—were not only foreign and foul, but also fatal. As supermarket managers worldwide canceled orders, cheesemakers in Burgundy saw their sales fall by three quarters and were forced to destroy a half million euros' worth of stock. After at least five hundred years of dominion, it looked as if the King of Cheeses were dead.

"With all the harassment, monsieur," recalled Jean Berthaut, pulling out a pouch of pipe tobacco, "I don't mind telling you I was on the point of putting a gun to my head."

We were sitting in a sunlit office, looking out over the courtyard of the Fromagerie Berthaut, the world's leading producer of Époisses. Berthaut's was the very brand that I'd bought at Zabar's—the one I'd found lacking in flavor. It was also the best-selling Époisses in the world, and, because it was pasteurized, the only one legally allowed into North America.

I was in Époisses, the eponymous: a village of eight hundred inhabitants a three-hour drive east of Paris, whose main street—featuring a post office, a tobacconist, the mayor's office, and a restaurant called Le Relais de la Pomme—led to the moated, peak-turreted castle that is still the weekend home of a Parisian doctor descended from Burgundian nobility. The Fromagerie stands on the site of the gardens of the very cloisters where Cistercian monks had perfected the cheese. Until the late nineteenth century, it was the village market, where merchants had started daubing the rinds with alcohol-rich marc to keep the flies away.

Berthaut was a handsome middle-aged man with pale blue eyes, wavy, silvering hair, and a commanding oratorical style. When recalling some injustice, his words frothed into a mousse of indignation; I often expected him to grab me by the lapels and shake me, to emphasize just how *é-VI-dent* some folly was. Instead, he contented himself with jabbing at my chest with his pipe stem and periodically banging the desktop with the flat of his hand.

"I was forced to recall and destroy three million cheeses, monsieur, which had been shipped all around the world, as far away as Japan. I decided to declare bankruptcy. *Oui*, monsieur!" Whack! "And a representative of the very agency that had condemned me—with discriminatory and unfounded accusations—ran after me saying, 'No, please don't close!' Can you imagine?" Whack!

With a workforce of eighty-five, the Fromagerie, it turned out, was not only the largest employer in the village, but also a significant draw for tourists. Its closure would have been a minor catastrophe for the region. Although none of Berthaut's cheeses was connected to the fatal listeriosis cases, samples had come back from the labs of the local Veterinary Services showing that his Époisses was crawling with improbably high levels of bacteria. (To this day, it is whispered in the village that the samples were deliberately contaminated. Their explanation? A bureaucratic rivalry between the Health Ministry and the Veterinary Services for control of France's nascent Food Safety Association. By pouncing on a foodborne disease outbreak, government officials were apparently competing to show how incorruptible they were—and thus worthy of promotion.)

At this point, Berthaut made a crucial decision. After fifty years of working exclusively with raw milk, the family factory would switch to pasteurized production. This would at once spare them harassment from the bureaucrats Berthaut like to called the "health fundamentalists" and also clear the name of Époisses. "It would also allow us to ship to the North American market, where there is an enormous demand. And I have the pretension, monsieur, to claim that we have obtained extremely satisfying, even astonishing"—whack!—"results in terms of the architecture of the taste of our product." Berthaut isolated and preserved the original microbial strains—those indigenous to the region of Époisses—and reinjected them into the curd once it had been pasteurized. What he was making was not so much an Époisses, as an homage to the *fromage* of old: a sanitized, technically unimpeachable reproduction of an odoriferous classic for a risk-averse twenty-first century. One that, not coincidentally, would be completely acceptable to the vast American market.

When pressed, Berthaut will admit that his Époisses is not quite what it used to be. In pasteurization, milk is heated—to 145 degrees Fahrenheit for half an hour, or 161 degrees for fifteen seconds—to kill disease-causing pathogens. (Ultra-high-temperature pasteurization, in which milk is heated to 302 degrees Fahrenheit for two seconds, lengthens shelf life by months, but also nukes the very life out of milk. UHT milk doesn't go rancid; if left at room temperature long enough, it putrefies and turns black.) Critics of the process say pasteurization also kills beneficial bacteria and enzymes—the ones responsible for odor and flavor—turning cheeses into so much cello-wrapped soft plastic. (Many French cheeses exported to America are in fact *thermisé*: they are kept heated at a temperature of between 104 and 162 degrees

Fahrenheit over a long period, which is supposed to both kill pathogens and spare flavor-bearing microflora.) Pasteurization of milk may have been a smart public health move early in the last century, when unhygienic farm and transport conditions led to mass outbreaks of tuberculosis. There is little evidence, though, that raw-milk cheese ever caused significant health problems, and butterfat-rich unpasteurized milk is an excellent source of nutrition, containing numerous enzymes, all twenty-two essential amino acids, and vitamin B_{12}. It also tastes fantastic: thick, creamy, and complex. In fact, this is about as good as food gets: anybody who was breast-fed as an infant harbors formative, though subconscious, memories of the pleasures of fresh raw milk. (Bureaucrats at national health agencies, one suspects, were bottle-fed formula from day one.) If produced and shipped following stringent standards, cheeses made from raw milk should be as safe as those made with pasteurized milk—perhaps, oddly enough, even safer.

Berthaut explained, "Listeria is ubiquitous. If I took a scraping from the side of your calf"—he ran his pipe stem along my pant leg—"I'll bet you I would find listeria in the sample. *Oui*, monsieur, you are a carrier of listeria—and staphylococcus, and other germs. Thanks to pasteurization, and other forms of sterilization of our foods, we're losing our ability to cope with naturally occurring microbes; the capacity of our immune systems has been reduced. What's more, when milk is pasteurized, you remove all of the good bacteria that normally compete with and defeat the bad bacteria. Pasteurized cheese is a clean slate—and nature has a horror of a vacuum. So, if there is the least breakdown in the hygiene of the factory, pathogens like listeria—like the listeria on your leg—jump onto the cheese, and the resulting problems can be much more formidable than if the cheese was made with raw milk."

Berthaut was the first to acknowledge that his own countrymen were partly to blame for what had happened to his cheese. Louis

Pasteur, after all, was a Frenchman (as were the inventors of homogenization, the pressure cooker, and margarine), and it was the overreaction of French health authorities that had pushed Berthaut to the brink of ruin. When the topic of the United States came up, however, he couldn't help venting a little spleen.

"The Americans have to stop taking us for filthy French people, in our little berets, up to our knees in manure. When I say that our factory is like NASA, it is no exaggeration. Our internal sanitary norms are superior to any in the United States. A fraction of the American population is aware that we make safe, flavorful cheese. But the fear of disease is artificially maintained by the FDA and reinforced by restrictive economic measures. If cheese is dangerous—and humanity has been making cheese from raw milk for four thousand years—it's not the Americans"—here the whack! was so emphatic the ashtray bounced a half inch off the table—"who are going to make us discover it! Although I was forced to start working with pasteurized milk—in my case, it was a question of survival—I am thoroughly convinced that the future lies in raw-milk cheese."

I asked Berthaut whether he ate unpasteurized cheeses himself.

"Systematically, monsieur!" he replied. "Systematically! It is almost dogmatic with me. A raw-milk cheese, bought from the farm—there is zero risk involved! We, the French, ultimately decided that completely banning raw-milk cheeses was a bad thing—perhaps because we are bons vivants, and we like having strong emotions when it comes to flavor. So we've introduced Draconian regulations to guarantee sanitation and reduce risk to a minimal level. It's an approach that's a little more thoughtful—and complex, and courageous—than total prohibition."

It was a good point. Eating is an inherently risky activity: the digestive tract is the place where the outside world, with all its bacteria, viruses, and molds, actually becomes part of your body; in consuming something, you master it, but you can also simultaneously succumb to it. When it comes to food, the question of what constitutes reasonable risk varies enormously from culture to culture. The Japanese think the sensation of eating *fugu* sashimi outweighs the small but not insignificant risk of dying for your pleasure (there are still up to one hundred deaths a year from the consumption of improperly prepared puffer fish). During pregnancy, Greek women continue to consume their raw-milk feta, the Italians their espresso, the Japanese their sushi, the French their Champagne. In the United States and Canada, in contrast, pregnant woman are systematically advised to avoid chocolate mousse, coffee, raw fish, alcohol, and, of course, any soft cheeses. In spite of all the traditions of libertarian individualism and enterprise, North Americans, thanks partly to the culture of litigation, tend to be craven when it comes to flavorful but challenging foods that have safely been consumed by other cultures for centuries.

When a nation holds a food close to its collective heart, it will usually find a way to spare it from an outright ban. Though hamburger meat has brought bloody and excruciating deaths to hundreds of children in the United States, nobody ever considered a total prohibition on two-all-beef-patties. Instead—and in spite of the protests of the beef industry—the U.S. Department of Agriculture (USDA) took the sensible step of labeling supermarket ground round with cooking instructions designed to kill *E. coli* 0157:H7 and other pathogens that are ubiquitous in American ground meat. Informed consumers could then decide whether the risk of bloody diarrhea outweighed the pleasures of a summer barbecue. Given the trail of corpses it has left behind, the hamburger, had it been invented in and imported from France, would have been banned in North America long ago.

Berthaut relit his pipe and looked dreamily out the window toward his parents' house. "You know, monsieur, one day soon, I will relaunch production of our raw-milk Époisses."

There was an underlying irony to the situation. The batch of cheese that caused the outbreak—the killer Époisses that eventually forced Berthaut to switch to pasteurized milk—was itself made with pasteurized milk. It came from the Fromagerie de l'Armançon, a factory on the outskirts of the village, one that had repeatedly been accused of violating sanitary norms. On the same day the news of the listeriosis crisis broke, the factory was condemned by a court in Dijon for making a counterfeit Époisses, sold on the cheap and artificially tinted red with a colorant. (When I talked to Robert Berthaut, Jean's father and the founder of the Fromagerie Berthaut, about the whole listeriosis crisis, he observed with a chuckle of profound satisfaction, "You know what? Today, that same factory is making plastic!")

I mentioned to Berthaut that it was not widely reported in foreign newspapers that the implicated cheese was made from pasteurized milk.

Tapping his pipe into the ashtray, Berthaut allowed himself the weariest of smiles. "*Oui*, monsieur."

I toured the factory the next day. Jean Berthaut had put on a suit and tie to welcome a delegation from the Japanese Ministry of the Exterior, who were cautiously contemplating the reimportation of Époisses, four years after the listeria scare. ("*Mon Dieu*," Berthaut whispered to me between bows, "it takes them fifteen minutes just to say good-bye!") He handed me over to Nasim, an amiable expert in cheesemaking technology. From the gleaming four-thousand-liter tanks that stocked milk delivered from local farms, through the room where a dozen men in blue smocks and white rubber boots were hand-washing pale rounds of young cheese, to the warehouse where women were nestling cheeses in boxes for shipment, the Fromagerie was as gleaming and spotless as a Silicon Valley microchip factory.

Berthaut's comparison of his plant to the American space administration hadn't been mere hyperbole. The Fromagerie Berthaut, like

most French factories that export their cheeses, adheres to Hazard
Analysis and Critical Control Point (HACCP, pronounced *HASS-ip*)
standards. In 1959, NASA, concerned about the potentially messy
consequences of astronauts coming down with food poisoning in zero
gravity, asked Pillsbury to develop a series of food-safety protocols,
from "farm to rocket ship," for reducing the risk of contamination.
The HACCP norms, designed to prevent illness outbreaks in space,
proved equally effective on earth. Though expensive to implement,
they turned factories into self-policing entities, with automatic re-
cording of temperatures and regular sampling to check for microbial
contamination—records that could then be verified by government
inspectors. (This is not uncontroversial. In settings where the bottom
line rules, such as the largest slaughterhouses in North America,
shifting oversight of food safety from government inspectors to
company employees could have disastrous public health consequences.)

Touring the factory, I was required to wear rubber boots, a
comically puffy white hairnet (which the French call a *Charlotte*),
and a smock that came down to my knees. Every time Nasim and I
entered a new room, we waded through a shallow, chemical-laden
footbath intended to kill the bacteria on our boots. In a lab sealed off
from the rest of the factory by heavy doors, technicians analyzed the
milk and the cleaning solutions from every step in the production
process; Nasim told me that samples were sent to the Pasteur
Laboratories, in Lille, which conducted an independent check for
listeria and other pathogens. Though the exteriors of many of the
buildings in the Fromagerie complex were centuries old and built
from fieldstone, the inner walls were all ultrahygienic white plastic. If
I'd had any romantic visions of meeting peasants in clogs, ashes from
their corn-paper Gitanes dribbling into the curds, they were dispelled
by Berthaut's state-of-the-art facilities.

And if I'd found the idea of championing the world's most pungent cheese just a tiny bit laughable when I'd set off for France, by the time I got through talking with Georges Risoud, I was ready to mount the barricades and join the battle for Liberté, Fraternité, and Époisses. An agricultural engineer who was the head of the Syndicat de Défense de l'Époisses, Risoud had written the definitive volume on the history of the cheese. During his research, he'd found a gorgeously illustrated Spanish manuscript from 1851 proving that, even then, a cheese from Époisses had been washed with marc from Burgundy. This historical evidence allowed Époisses to be granted the coveted *appellation d'origine contrôlée* (AOC) status, making it one of thirty-four French cheeses whose names are protected by law. Since 1999, no producer can legally call his cheese Époisses unless it is 50 percent milk fat, aged for a minimum of four weeks, washed with marc, and free from all artificial coloring. Most of all, though, it has to be made with milk collected within a limited geographical area—principally the Côte d'Or, which includes the village of Époisses—the department that has been associated with the production of the cheese since at least the beginning of the sixteenth century. Like cognac from the Charente, Roquefort from the Aveyron, and Châteauneuf-du-Pape from Provence, the Époisses of Burgundy is one of six hundred products in France protected by a kind of gastronomic copyright, one that links food to the land in which it was traditionally created. Any unqualified producer who dares use the name can face prosecution in a court of law for usurpation of a trade name.

I met Risoud in the wood-paneled second-floor offices of the local town hall. Slender, with tousled, graying hair, oval gold-rimmed glasses, and a penchant for tight sweaters and tucked-in collars, Risoud was Burgundian by birth, left-leaning by instinct. His passion for Époisses was a question of both pride in his homeland and intellectual conviction in the concept of *terroir*. Originally applied to wine, *terroir*, which literally means "soil," can seem fuzzy-minded and sentimental at first glance, a contemporary version of the animism that attributes a living soul to all natural phenomena: it's the notion that the fabulous assortment of flavors that nourish the French palate are derived directly from the land. Remove the green lentils from Puy, the chickens from Bresse, the grapes from Bordeaux, and you are subtly denaturing them, robbing them of the identity—the soul—they gain from such intangibles as the richness of the soil, the exact orientation of a field or farm in relation to the sun, and, in the case of cheese, the presence of site-specific strains of mold. Risoud's work, which established that Époisses should be made from the milk of three breeds of cows—Brune, Simmental, and Montbéliard—is a kind of systematization of the concept of *terroir* to produce the perfect Époisses.

"The most important thing is that the cows are now in the fields," Risoud said, "grazing on alfalfa—which wasn't the case a few years ago. We were facing a situation in the Côte d'Or where we would have nothing but Holstein cows, kept in barns and stuffed with corn and American soy until their guts exploded! Which is a complete bastardization of the idea of a product being linked to its *terroir*. And in a case like that, I understand a cheesemaker in, for example, Australia, who says, 'My cows eat exactly the same thing as yours, I make cheese following the same techniques as you; why shouldn't I be able to call my cheese an Époisses too? You're just being protectionist!' "

In the context of modern agro-business, with its factory farms and genetically modified feed, *terroir* can seem like a laughable anachronism. It is sometimes perceived too as being an elitist European obsession; after all, champagne and prosciutto di Parma, which are protected by AOCs, tend to be far more expensive than sparkling wines and cuts of meat that don't benefit from a prestigious label. In fact, producers in the developing world are embracing the idea of geographic protection as a bulwark against the incursions of industrial agriculture. Vietnam has won from the European Union an AOC for a specific type of nuoc mam, its infamously potent fish sauce; Korea is seeking to protect its ubiquitous spicy cabbage pickle, kimchi, from Japanese imitators; Bolivia has applied for protection of the indigenous grain quinoa; and Thailand is trying to win the same for jasmine rice. And though the French were the first to develop the notion of the AOC, it doesn't always work in their favor. In 2002, thousands of angry farmers marched through the streets of Millau—the same town where Roquefort-maker José Bové had destroyed a McDonald's to protest globalization—when the European Commission granted Greek cheesemakers the exclusive right to call their sheep's-milk cheese feta.

"The idea that not everything can be delocalized—that certain things can only be created in their place of origin—is very interesting, and I think it's a good sign that countries like India are supporting it," said Risoud. Certain products, Risoud readily admitted, had been so enthusiastically exported and marketed around the world that the terms had become generic; Somerset and Normandy, for example, could no longer legitimately claim sole ownership of cheddar and Camembert, products that had long since become staples in super-markets worldwide. But as Risoud had proven, the Côte d'Or could boast an uninterrupted tradition of near-exclusive manufacture of the cheese called Époisses.

"What we're doing now is making a traditional cheese with modern methods. It took a lot of work; the Syndicat had to provide technical support and training to the farmers, but it was worth it, for both us and them: now the people who supply us with milk are better paid than those elsewhere." It was also the exact opposite of what was happening to most of the world's food supply, in which ever larger corporations were buying up smaller producers to increase their profits, and large numbers of animals were being crowded together—thus increasing the potential for severe foodborne illness outbreaks.

What was most disturbing in Risoud's study of Époisses was the evidence of a gradual decline in the number of cheese producers. In

1900, about three hundred different farms were producing Époisses; in 1939, even after the First World War had decimated the workforce, the cheese could still be found on twenty-three different farms. It was Robert and Simone Berthaut, the parents of Jean, who had snatched Époisses from the jaws of extinction; after the Second World War, Robert, nostalgic for the cheese of his childhood, had sought the recipe from a neighbor, a certain Madame Monin, and started making it with milk from his own cows. (I lunched with the Berthauts one afternoon on omelets made with local mushrooms, quiche, an excellent Savigny, and a very ripe Époisses. Looking affectionately at his wife during the meal, ruddy-cheeked Robert said, "We were both born in the village. We are pure products of the *terroir*!")

"Even in 1968, there were at least a hundred cheesemakers in the Côte d'Or," said Risoud. "Today, there are only five, of which four make Époisses." This loss of diversity—so disturbingly paralleled by the extinction of plant and animal species and the death of indigenous languages—can partly be attributed to the complexities of French and European sanitary legislation. When I visited one of the last remaining producers of farmhouse Camembert in Normandy in 1999, he complained that new European Union regulations were so expensive to implement that he was thinking of getting out of the business; two years later, he had quit altogether. Risoud said some Époisses producers had renounced cheesemaking for similar reasons.

"Bureaucrats want to eliminate every possible risk, because, confronted with the legislation of everyday life, they're afraid of being held responsible if anything goes wrong. So they open the umbrella; they protect themselves, by inspecting, by overinspecting, until the small cheesemakers say 'Okay, I'll switch to pasteurized milk if you stop harassing me.' In France, 'transparency' and 'traceability' have become obsessions, especially after mad cow and foot-and-mouth disease. Instead of risking responsibility, government officials have a tendency to ban everything."

Fortunately, the cheese course proved so close to the core of French identity that a blanket prohibition was unthinkable. In the early 1990s, when Denmark and Germany were rumored to be pushing for a ban on raw-milk cheeses in the European Union, the resulting Gallic uproar over Nordic imperialism was so intense that the EU ended up adopting the French raw-milk rules as its own in 1998. Nonetheless, the same processes that have been afflicting North America are at work in France: more people are shopping in supermarkets than in markets or small specialty shops; today, only 10 percent of the cheese sold in France is made from unpasteurized milk. Cheeses used to have their seasons: goat cheeses were best in the spring, Camembert in the early summer, Époisses in autumn (after all, who wanted to eat a cheese that pungent during a July heat wave?). But consumers now expect their cheeses to be available throughout the seasons, and pasteurization ensures year-round uniformity. The decrease in demand, coupled with more stringent regulations, has proved fatal for thousands of farmhouse raw-milk producers over the last decade.

I told Risoud I was longing to try raw-milk Époisses, and he gave me detailed directions to the last remaining producers of the real thing. The next day, I drove in the morning mist past herds of white, smooth-flanked Charolais cattle, naked as newborn gerbils, and into a forest mysteriously clotted with parked Renault panel vans—a mystery solved when I came upon a group of deer hunters, rifles dipping downward, glaring at my Parisian license plates from beneath their caps. I emerged from the pines in Gevrey-Chambertin, a town famous for its wine, which Napoléon was said to have enjoyed with an Époisses when he visited in 1804. Passing evenly spaced rows of grapevines, protected by stern warning signs—PAS DE GRAPILLAGE— "No Picking"—presumably to diminish the depredations of the German bus tourists who filled the town's wine shops and cafés, I spotted vintage Michelin direction signs still bolted to the sides of stone buildings, pointing the way to other small towns, and yet more great wines: Nuits St-Georges, Vougeot, Musigny. I finally came to Brochon, home of the Laiterie de la Côte. This was the source of the cheese I'd found in Canada—the same Époisses I'd smuggled from Montreal to New York.

In the shop on the ground floor, I examined cheeses washed in white Chablis and dusted with ashes; goat cheeses on sticks, like lollipops furred with mold; and the Laiterie's version of Époisses, which looked as lustrously vermicular as an exposed human brain. Next to the cash register hung faxes of congratulations from Paul Bocuse and Bernard Loiseau (the latter would have incriminated the celebrity chef of cheese-smuggling—"Had a great visit New York. Huge success for your Époisses . . . Brought 24 to New York"—had Loiseau not committed suicide, apparently after hearing a rumor his restaurant was scheduled to be downgraded in the Gault-Millau guide). Olivier Gaugry, with a hedgehoglike head of bristly brown hair and red cheeks darkened by bluish stubble, gave me a quick tour of his factory. It was as spick-and-span as Berthaut's and also run following HACCP standards, with its own lab; Gaugry explained that further samples were sent to Strasbourg, where they were analyzed by an independent lab. In contrast to Berthaut, Gaugry and his brother Sylvain had decided to continue working with raw milk, and his employees still hand-ladeled the curds individually into circular molds, as the Cistercian monks had done for centuries.

In the shipping room, I noticed a stack of Époisses with the name of a cheesemonger in Montreal on the side of the crate.

"We send those off when they're younger," explained Gaugry. "They're transported by ship, so it takes twelve days for them to cross the ocean."

I expressed my surprise: technically, underaged raw-milk cheeses were forbidden not only in the United States, but also in Canada.

"They're a little more flexible about importing in Quebec, though sometimes they still block shipments. I have to say, as a cheesemaker I don't agree at all with the sixty-day law; it's an aberration. It's not as if our cheeses are going to be better if they've stuck around on docks and in trucks for two months; they're actually going to be worse than if they were aged for thirty days. It's as if they're trying to make everything antiseptic. The fact is, we need certain microbes for our good health. A liter of milk is an ecosystem in itself; we shouldn't try to completely denature it. You have to keep the taste."

While Gaugry helped me pick out some cheeses that were perfectly à point, I asked whether the new European norms had caused him problems. His response surprised me.

"Not really. In fact, I think the European Union has been good for us, because globalization is also encouraging regionalization. We're becoming prouder of our own communities. We're no longer fighting for France—which is now just an entity within Europe—but for Burgundy, and as Burgundians we're proud of showing what we're capable of doing around the world. And we're realizing that the German who visits isn't just German; first and foremost, he may be a Bavarian. In that sense, the AOC designation is also a good thing, because it permits us to protect the authenticity of Époisses around the world; so that the Japanese or Brazilians can't call just any cheese an Époisses."

Winning an AOC was especially good for manufacturers who had the capital at their disposal to upgrade their facilities. Gaugry's trade was flourishing, and he proudly pointed out his office window to the much larger building—formerly a factory built by the pastis-maker Ricard—where they were planning to relocate in the near future. Glass partitions in the new facility would allow visitors to watch the entire cheesemaking process, from the arrival of the milk to the packing of the crates for shipment—utter transparency.

Driving away with a trunk full of Gaugry's finest cheeses, I reflected that, had I been touring the Burgundian countryside twenty years ago, I would have been able to pull into markets and farmhouses and sample dozens of different kinds of Époisses. The same process of globalization that Gaugry had praised—which allowed me to buy his cheese in Montreal—had also wiped out some of the gastronomic diversity that once made touring the French countryside such a pleasure.

The last remaining makers of farmhouse Époisses lived in Origny-sur-Seine, a village of only forty souls, where a silver cock pirouetted atop the steeple of a tiny church, and a butcher, baker, and grocer still made the rounds, delivering provisions in panel vans. Caroline and Alain Bartkowiez were the owners of a herd of Montbéliards and Brunes and a red-tiled farmhouse named Les Marronniers, in honor of the stately chestnut trees that shaded the village streets. Over coffee at his kitchen table, Alain explained the webwork of legislation that enmeshed anyone who wanted to make farmhouse raw-milk cheese in France. (Caroline quickly excused herself: even though she was several months pregnant—and still a daily consumer of raw milk—somebody had to look after the farm while her husband chatted with visitors.) As an adherent to the HACCP plan originally devised for NASA, they had to self-police the quality and microbial content of their milk and cheese and dispatch the results to the French Veterinary Services monthly. Samples of milk and cheese were also sent each month to an independent lab for analysis—a costly measure for farmers with a small herd. What's more, inspectors made unannounced visits, four or five times a year, to check up on sanitary conditions.

The hardest thing, Alain said, had been bringing the farm up to European norms. Touring the small cheese factory in a freestanding building next to their home, I went through the by now familiar indignity of donning foot protectors, a white smock, and a *Charlotte*, and dutifully wading through endless chemical footbaths. Les Marronniers was a miniature, LEGOLAND version of the Berthaut and Gaugry factories, with walls paneled in plastic, stacks of AOC Époisses quietly aging on stainless steel racks.

"It's too bad," said Alain. "This is a stone building dating from the beginning of the nineteenth century, and we were obliged to redo it with all this plastic. And the renovation process is incredibly expensive—at least fifty euros for every square meter of floor space. A lot of cheesemakers just gave up because transforming their farmhouses would have cost too much."

Finally, the Bartkowiezes decided the investment was worth it, as getting European certification would allow them to sell their cheese in Paris and beyond the borders of France. (Farmhouse producers without the necessary credentials are only allowed to sell within an eighty-kilometer, or fifty-mile, radius of the farm.) It had also made them the only producers of farmhouse Époisses in the world. The plan was proving to be a success.

"We're beginning to sell our Époisses in fine cheese shops in Paris, in the south of France, even in Holland. Cheese wholesalers have started to contact us, because they're interested in escaping from the routine of pasteurized cheese without any real character."

While waiting for Bartkowiez to sell yogurt and raw milk to a white-haired woman in the farm's shop, I picked out a ripe Époisses and a *flamiche burgonde*, a savory pie made with flour, eggs, milk, crème fraîche, and Époisses. I mentioned that with its walls painted white and digital-thermometer-regulated refrigerator, the shop seemed as impeccable as the factory itself—hardly what I'd expected to find on a farm.

"Astonishing, *non?*" he said. "Frankly, we believe we're forced to do a little *too* much by the authorities, especially for a farmhouse product." Farming in Europe was no longer a matter of hereditary savoir-faire, passed on from generation to generation. After completing high school, Bartkowiez was obliged to follow two years' training in a dairy or cheese factory. In all, the couple had spent five years saving their money in the north of France, Alain working in an industrial dairy that made sterilized, UHT milk, Caroline on a farm that made another of France's great raw-milk cheese, Maroilles.

Given the Bartkowiezes' credentials, it was with perfect confidence that I added their cheeses to the stock I'd picked up at the Laiterie de la Côte and set off for Paris. It was a hot day, though, and by the time I'd reached the *péripherique*, the ring road that encircles the capital, the smell in the car was downright inebriating—I was briefly afraid I'd be overcome by all the aldehydes, esters, and alcohols emanating from the trunk, lose control, and plow through four lanes of traffic and into a concrete wall. After I'd dropped off the car in a parking lot, I double-wrapped the cheese in plastic and stuffed it deep into my backpack. Even then, the odor seeped through the polyurethane. On the métro ride northward to the right bank, alighting passengers shot me looks of reproach, as if I were some new paragon of stinky-socked Eurail trash. I realized I was violating yet another prohibition—the one about not carrying Époisses on the Parisian métro. By the time I got to Châtelet, I had the entire end of the wagon to myself.

Though I was leaving France later that day, I had no intention of chucking $50 worth of perfectly good cheese into a trash can. Walking down the Rue de Rivoli, I considered buying a baguette and having a solitary picnic in the Place des Vosges, until I happened to walk past the solution: a wine bar, with a burgundy-colored awning, called La Tartine. I went up to the counter and explained my predicament to a waiter in shirtsleeves and a black vest.

"You've picked the right place," he replied, with quick good humor. "Our boss is from Burgundy. As long as you buy some wine, it should be okay."

I sat down at a window table at the end of a long bench that ran the length of the bar, and the waiter brought me a basket of spongy, thinly sliced sourdough *pain Poilâne* and a glass of Graves, from Bordeaux, quickly followed by a St-Estèphe from the Médoc; both had the requisite character to grapple with a mature Époisses. Mature was probably an understatement, as my cheeses had by then achieved meltdown. The Gaugry in particular was almost sloshing around in its box, so that it was better tackled with a spoon than a knife.

A trio of heavy drinkers, two blotchy men and a blowsy woman well into their cups (or rather, a lifetime of cups), were leaning against the zinc bar. They'd already looked my way and made a couple of appreciative grunts when gusts from the open door blew the raw-milk effluvia past their noses. Realizing there was no way I could finish both of the Époisses myself, I spooned up half of the Gaugry and carried it to them in the lid.

"Do you like cheese?" I asked.

"I like anything that's free!" snorted the woman.

They neatly dispatched it between gulps of red wine.

A beautiful, straight-backed young woman, with severely cut blond bangs, was quietly leafing through a book at the next table. It was to her credit, I thought, that she hadn't been driven from the premises by the smell.

I asked her if she would try some cheese. She gave me a suspicious look, but appeared tempted.

"They're Époisses, from Burgundy," I said. "I know they're pretty strong . . ."

That seemed enough of a challenge to her Gallic pride. She stood over my table, examined the sweating rinds.

"I love cheese!" she said. "I work in a restaurant in Geneva. When all the clients have gone for the evening, we throw ourselves on the cheese they haven't eaten."

Inviting her to sit down, I offered her a glass of wine.

"It's only four o'clock in the afternoon!" she objected. "And I've just had a cup of hot chocolate."

Nonetheless, she joined me and immediately started folding wedges of bread to slather up the cheese. Her name was Marion, she was originally from Nantes, and she was enjoying a holiday week in Paris.

After that, it didn't take much to get her to agree to a glass of wine. I reflected that I'd discovered a novel technique, new maybe even to the French. Chirting—flirting with cheese.

Marion and I were having a fine old time, wallowing in esters and aldehydes. It couldn't last, though. Finally, the waiter approached our table, a look of concern constricting his face.

"We're going to have to do something about the smell," he said, with a neigh of exasperation. "We're losing all our customers!"

I looked down the row of tables. Where once there had been a rank of chain-smoking, wine-drinking, cell-phoning Parisians, now were only empty chairs and hastily abandoned tables. I was gratified to watch the waiter seize my cheeses and wrap them in that great North American innovation, plastic cling wrap. It was like an admission of defeat. I felt personally vindicated, as though I'd discovered a cuss word that would offend an Australian, or a dance-floor gyration that would make a Brazilian blush.

Satan would have smiled at my success. I'd found—and consumed—a cheese that was too stinky even for the French.

Back in the New World, where consumers like their cheese bacon-flavored and in spray cans, I realized I'd left some questions unanswered. I called up Max McCalman, the *maître fromager* at Picholine and Artisanal, two Manhattan restaurants that specialize in cheese, to find out how new FDA measures, such as the Bioterrorism Act, were affecting business.

"It's no longer the hysteria about listeria," he said in his measured voice, which managed to be at once lugubrious and passionate. "Fear of bioterror is the thing today. It seems to be more politically driven than scientifically thought out. For years, producers were able to ship cheeses to us, no questions asked. Most recently, we've lost the Loire Valley goats' milk cheeses, because they're not aged for sixty days. And, as you've seen, it's changed the way French producers are making cheese; they're using pasteurized milk. The Époisses that we get here now"—it was from Berthaut—"is insipid." He spat the word out with disdain. "The import ban seems to be hitting France more than anywhere else. There's still this anti-French sentiment that lingers, and it is just so annoying."

The roots of the sentiment were deeper than just France's refusal to join in the invasion of Iraq. Behind the scenes, there had been a number of nasty trade skirmishes between Europe and America, which seemed to get down to fundamental differences in attitude over what constitutes decent food. In 1999, Europeans decided to ban the import of American beef fed with growth-inducing hormones, which are suspected of causing cancer. In retaliation, the United States introduced a series of crippling tariffs on Belgian chocolates, Roquefort cheese, pâté de foie gras, and Dijon mustard (some café owners in Dijon symbolically protested by raising the price of Coca-Cola to the equivalent of $100 a bottle). The profoundly conservative, even mystical, attitude toward food embodied in the idea of *terroir* was being adopted by the European Union as a whole, in the form of the precautionary principle. In contrast to the American model of risk analysis, which assesses new technologies by trying to calculate the likelihood they'll cause public harm, the precautionary principle operates on the assumption that, given uncertainity about the impact of new technology, actions should be taken to prevent possible future harm to the environment and public health. In other words, when it comes to ozone depletion, genetically engineered food, and acid rain, our species should err on the side of caution. The principle tends to favor long-standing food-production techniques, such as feeding milk-producing cows the same grains they've always grazed on, rather than innovations in biotechnology. It was deeply traditional, and deeply challenging to the American food industry, whose success had lately been predicated on patenting seeds made with fish genes and cramming cows together in vast feedlot slums and stuffing them full of antibiotics in the hopes they wouldn't succumb to disease.

In 1994, an outbreak of salmonella, from Schwan's ice cream—made with pasteurized milk—affected 224,000 people (to save time on a long run, a truck driver hadn't washed out his tank between shipments of liquid eggs and milk). *E. coli* 0157:H7–infected hamburgers hospitalized thousands of children, and killed hundreds, throughout the 1990s. The U.S. Department of Agriculture, whose twin mandate is to promote American food products and police them, and whose bosses have typically been former hog farmers and cattle ranchers, is responsible for inspecting meat and poultry—which is kind of like putting a casino owner in charge of the bunco squad. Despairing of overcoming the economies of scale of mass slaughter, the USDA long ago declared *E. coli* and other pathogens to be normally occurring constituents of meat and poultry. The result is that 80 percent of meat in American supermarkets contains antibiotic-resistant bacteria, and 40 percent of raw table poultry is contaminated with fever- and nausea-inducing campylobacter. Today, five hundred Americans die every year from listeria-contaminated hot dogs and luncheon meat. (These are statistics that make European officials shudder; Sweden, for example, began an effective program to completely eliminate salmonella from its livestock decades ago.) The burden now falls on the American consumer to cook meat at a high enough temperature to kill all the deadly contaminants swarming beneath the plastic wrap; a government Web site actually warns that "ready-to-eat" cold cuts should be thoroughly cooked by the very old, the very young, pregnant women, and anyone with a suppressed immune system.

Cheese, which is among the safest foods in existence, is also among the most ludicrously overregulated. Between 1990 and 2003, seafood caused 720 disease outbreaks in the United States, and poultry led to 355 outbreaks. Cheese, in contrast, was responsible for only 35 outbreaks, and the vast majority of these were provoked by cheese made with pasteurized milk. In fact, *no* foodborne illness outbreaks have been reported from hard aged cheeses made from raw milk. The soft, unpasteurized cheese most frequently cited in foodborne illness outbreaks is the Mexican-style *queso fresco*, which is typically made at home and sold unlabeled in farmer's markets or roadside stands. (And frankly, if you're willing to buy your dairy products from the back of a pickup truck in a parking lot in San Diego or El Paso, you should be ready for the occasional stomachache.) Professional artisanal chee-semakers are so highly regulated, and committed to their customers, that the chances of serious illness from consuming a Vermont Shepherd or a French Roquefort—if you can still afford the lat-ter—are infinitesimal.

Strangely enough, selling steak tartare is legal in the United States, as is serving Chesapeake Bay oysters, in spite of the virtual guarantee that your beef is crawling with pathogens and that one in two thousand servings of raw mollusks will make you ill. What's even more bizarre is that it is legal to buy raw milk from the farm and on store shelves in twenty-eight states (including California and Texas, the most populous in the nation). In other states, such as Wisconsin and Virginia, farmers get around the ban on raw milk by selling shares in their cows. Since it is legal for cattle owners to drink their own milk, by becoming one of hundreds of owners of a single cow, customers can come to the farm and stock up on gallons of warm milk burbling fresh from the source. The FDA is responsible for regulating interstate commerce (which they take to include imports from other countries); if a cheese moves across state lines, it has to be made with pasteurized milk or raw milk aged for more than sixty days.

The origins of this law are as obscure as its rationale is shaky. It was introduced in 1947 (coincidentally the same year that Reddi-wip, the first aerosol food product, appeared), at a time when refrigerated trucks weren't in general use. The science behind the legislation was far from sound. Samples were lost, the cheeses being investigated weren't tested for listeria, and so many were aged for completely different periods of time that meaningful comparisons were impossible. Nonetheless, this is the law that has kept North Americans from eating flavorful, healthy cheese for over half a century.

Discussing these contradictions with Max McCalman, I could hear the frustration in his voice.

"It's really not fair. Cheeses are often made on a family farm, which is one of the last forms of sustainable agriculture left to mankind, and we're seeing them banned because of all this hysterical anti-French sentiment. It's dying down a bit now, especially in New York, but it was very strong in Middle America, which is where eighty percent of the staff of our national legislative bodies come from. The allure of raw-milk cheeses in New York City ten years ago was that it was an indulgence, something risky. 'Oooh,' people would say, 'we're taking a chance by ordering this! How did they get it in?' The fact is, raw-milk cheeses *taste* better, because they *are* better. Look at the ingredients on the label: whole milk, salt, and rennet—none of these genetically modified organisms and pesticides that we really should be worried about. And I invite, I *beg*, the powers-that-be within the administration to run bacterial plate counts on these cheeses. I know what they're going to find: that there are fewer bacteria in our raw-milk cheeses than what we tolerate in our pasteurized half gallon of milk in the grocery store."

Sadly, the FDA doesn't have the budget to do any in-store testing. The safest thing for a bureaucrat to do, in such a situation, is to maintain the status quo—in the case of raw-milk cheese, a ban—therefore absolving him of official responsibility for what has become an illegal activity. And, why not throw in a little hyperbole and misinformation to guarantee the public stays well away from the stuff? The administration's consumer magazine recently warned that eating any raw-milk product was "like playing Russian roulette with your health."

After several attempts, I got through to John Sheehan, director of Dairy and Egg Safety at the FDA since 2000. He was, as McCalman had predicted, a Middle American—from Michigan—and had worked in the dairy industry for twenty years before joining the federal agency that policed dairy products. During the conference call, with the FDA's media relations man screening my questions and monitoring every word Sheehan said, there was much citing of multidigit file numbers, and referrals to other departments. After talking to the earthy, passionate lovers and makers of cheese, it was like trying to interact with 1960s-vintage IBM office equipment.

Sheehan claimed to have no bone to pick with the French: "I for one have no suspicions of France. My brother-in-law is French! I'm going to be godfather to his new child in August." (I could hear the media relations man chortling in the background, as if to say, "Good one!") "And I've been to France many times, I love going there."

(Do people still say this kind of thing? All I could think of was the clichéd retort to an accusation of bigotry: "Some of my best friends are black, Jewish, and gay!")

I told him about the cheese factories I'd visited in France, and how the standards of hygiene seemed to be very high indeed.

"Since 1986, there has been an agreement with the government of France that soft cheeses would be manufactured at facilities that are certified by the French government. If you have a small farmer in Burgundy who's making an Époisses, hopefully the producer would be registered with the government."

Unfortunately, I pointed out, farmhouse Époisses didn't satisfy the FDA's aging requirements.

"If it's a raw-milk cheese that's aged for four weeks, that would be a problem for us. Obviously that would be considered unlawful, under section 21-CFR-1240.61 of the code of federal regulations." Sheehan directed me to the FDA's Web site, whose import alert #12–03 featured a short list of all the cheeses that were completely banned—

among them Reblochon, Brie, and Camembert de Normandie—and a much longer list of those that were allowed only if they were made with pasteurized milk, including Époisses.

So, I asked, were they planning any reassessment of the original science behind the two-month aging requirement?

"That is a very good question," Sheehan allowed. "It's true, the science that supported that position has been called into question. That's why we're examining the whole issue right now. We're evaluating all the literature we can get our hands on that speaks to the issue of the safety of raw-milk cheeses. Currently we have amassed about four hundred literature references and we are proceeding to wade through them in an effort to arrive at a risk profile for raw-milk cheeses in general."

I asked whether they'd ever considered labeling raw-milk cheeses with the potential risks to pregnant women and immunodeficient individuals. (After all, the FDA had recently relaxed rules allowing just the opposite, so that foods can now be sold with labels that make all kinds of unsubstantiated and misleading health claims. Heinz, for example, claims its ketchup reduces the risk of prostate and cervical cancer, and Campbell's likes to say its V8 juice contains antioxidants that slow changes that occur in aging.) That way, responsible American consumers could make up their own minds—as they are currently allowed to do with ground beef or oysters.

"Well, for oysters, that's a different department. You'd have to talk to the Department of Seafood. But as to labeling cheese, I think we'll consider every possible option available to us when the risk profile is completed."

And when might that be? I wondered.

"Well, it was an A priority earlier this year, but it's been relegated back to a B priority. Maybe by the end of the next fiscal year, but I'm not promising anything."

I thanked Sheehan, and his sinister overseer, and hung up.

All that file-citing and buck-passing had made me a bit queasy. Not only does the FDA prevent Époisses and other amazing raw-milk cheeses from entering the country, it also ensures that Americans aren't exposed to such horrors as the cured ham from acorn-fed, free-range Spanish pigs, high-milk-fat butter encrusted in sea salt from cows that graze on the pastures of Brittany, the spicy Sichuan peppercorn, or the luscious, honeydew-melon scented mangosteen of Southeast Asia.

(Late in 2004, there were signs that things might be changing for the better. The Codex Alimentarius, a 170-country United Nations body that writes the health code for world trade in food, revised its dairy product rules, including those for cheese. The American cheese industry, headed by Kraft, had long lobbied for a zero-tolerance approach to raw-milk cheese, arguing that pasteurization was the only way to ensure product safety and uniformity. The French successfully argued that clean cheese could also be guaranteed by the kind of intense monitoring I'd seen in Burgundy, and the Codex was rewritten to allow the manufacture of unpasteurized cheeses. If American legislators continue to refuse to accept French cheese imports, France can now haul them before the World Trade Organization for creating an illegal barrier to trade. One day, real raw-milk Époisses might return to American shops and restaurants.)

Fortunately, I was living in Quebec, a part of North America dominated by the venerable Latin tradition of ignoring any rule that prevents you from fully enjoying your life. I went to the the vegetable drawer of the fridge and took out a chunk of illegally imported raw-milk Époisses from the Laiterie de la Côte. After it had come to room temperature, filling the kitchen with its pungent and intoxicating esters and aldehydes, I took a big bite and let it dissolve over my tongue.

My stomach settled immediately. Nothing like a little unpasteurized milk to wash away the taste of raw double-talk.

· MAIN COURSE ·

Listen to me and understand this:
A man is not defiled by what goes into his mouth,
but by what comes out of it.

—Matthew 15:11

· 4 ·

CRIADILLAS

Brussels vs. the Bull's Balls

ON THE ITALIAN island of Sardinia, local diners throw invitation-only get-togethers where the main attraction is *casu marzu*, a pecorino that can't be purchased in any store. It is matured in blocks the size of a human head and spread on thin slices of folded bread. The problem that faces the neophyte is not picking up the cheese but keeping it down: *casu marzu* is eaten fermented and is only considered mature enough when it is infested with thousands of transparent maggots. What's more, the fly larvae must be living, as dead maggots are a sure sign the cheese is too rotten to eat. Sardinians advise neophytes to hold a hand over the sandwich to prevent the vermin from leaping into their eyes.

In the Landes region of Gascony, aging poachers trap a protected songbird in nets, fatten it on millet in darkened cages until it is four times its original size, then drown it in Armagnac. The ortolan, also known as the bunting, is eaten at clandestine dinners by gastronomes who suck the bird's piping hot innards through its rectum. The late French president François Mitterrand, when he learned he was dying of cancer, invited thirty friends to a New Year's feast of oysters, foie gras, capon, and a plate of ortolans—a dish illegal for the hoi polloi, but, following the age-old double standard that exempts rulers from their own rulings, permissible for the elite. The tiny birds, after being roasted at high heat for five minutes, are traditionally eaten whole, bones and all, with one's head hidden beneath a white cloth napkin. Some believe the custom was conceived to prevent the grease, bone fragments, and saliva from the feeding frenzy from splattering one's fellow diners. Others say it is intended to keep what you are doing hidden from God.

Almost every European nation boasts some abstruse gastronomic tradition that its neighbors find unsanitary, incomprehensible, or just plain disgusting. Germans enjoy *Ochsenmaul-Salat*, a salad made from the thinly sliced cartilage of cow's jaws. Scandinavians have a marked penchant for putrefying seafood: Swedes enjoy *surströmming*, or rotten herring, so lightly salted that it continues to ferment on the shelf, grossly distending the cans it is packed in (the smell has been described as a cross between an unflushed toilet and a rotten egg). Icelanders are fond of *hákarl*—the poisonous Greenland shark—whose flesh is buried two meters underground for several weeks, until it has fermented and lost its toxic charge of cyanic acid; only then can it be dug up and gnawed, like ammonia-scented beef jerky, between gulps of aquavit. (The British like to believe they are above such nonsense, even as they relish another helping of spotted dick, pork scratchings, and Scotch eggs, preferably drowned in brown sauce.)

For the last ten years, I've limited my flesh intake to the occasional fish or seafood meal, but when I'm feeling adventurous, I'm willing to try an unfamiliar speciality, even a blatantly carnivorous one—though I tend to draw the line at the powdered horns of rhinos and the flesh of panda bears and other endangered species. I'm particularly open to novel meat-eating experiences in Europe, where by law livestock can't be fed genetically modified organisms, animal protein, or be injected with growth hormones. Since the 1990s, Europe has gone through a series of food scares—the mad cow disease that almost destroyed the British beef industry, the discovery of PCBs and dioxins in pigs and chickens that brought down the Belgian government, the foot-and-mouth disease that led to the destruction of six million British cattle in 2001—and from Poland to Portugal, a skittish populace has become very conscious of the potential for disaster when the food industry is left to its own devices. On a continent where the mystical link between the countryside and wholesome food is enshrined in the collective unconscious—where *nonna*'s grappa, *grand-mère*'s goat-milk cheese, and *abuela*'s pork sausage are sacred commodities—this has translated into a suspicion of large-scale agribusiness. Whatever abstract objections Europeans may have to distant authorities messing with their ancestral traditions, they have been so scarred by a decade of scares that there is an emerging consensus that the food industry needs strong oversight. In January 2002, the European Union set up the Food Safety Authority in Brussels (now headquartered in Parma, Italy), as a kind of supranational, science-based organization to oversee the safety of the food supply.

Predictably, British newspapers such as the *Sun*—the Rupert Murdoch tabloid that bashes anything to do with trade unions, refugees, homosexuals, or the European Union—attacked the European Food Safety Authority (EFSA) as another nest of "faceless" and "unaccountable" Eurocrats, unleashing poxy and politically correct inspectors on pubs and takeouts in a fiendish plot to deny honest consumers their mushy peas, prosciutto, and Bombay duck. Even the more sober *Wall Street Journal* described an uprising by Italian gourmands, worried that commissioners from Copenhagen or Helsinki would ban wood-burning pizza ovens, Tuscan pig lard, and buffalo-milk mozzarella in the name of some obscure Nordic norm. Given the size and complexity of the newly expanded European Union—in 2004, the EU incorporated ten new nations, including Poland, Hungary, and the Czech Republic—it looked as if settling on a common food-safety policy, amenable to 450 million citizens, might be a formidable challenge indeed. I feared the birth of a powerful continentwide bureaucracy might mean the days of roasted French game birds, Scandinavian whale jerky, Italian maggot cheese—and everything else that made eating in Europe an adventure—were already numbered.

Which is why I was standing at a counter in Madrid, trying to convince the bartender to give me the address of a restaurant—or a tapas bar, or even a market stall—that would sell me a plate of bull's testicles. I figured that if any country in Europe was up to resisting the ambient healthism of the EU, it would be lusty, paradoxical, devil-may-care Spain. And if there was any city in Spain that didn't give a damn about bureaucrats from Brussels, it would be proudly provincial Madrid, where you can still spew the smoke from a black-tobacco Ducado toward the ranks of dusty, fluorescent-lit hams dangling from the rafters. And if there was any bar in Madrid where they'd be able to tip me off about sketchy carnivorous delights, it would be La Torre del Oro, that slightly psychotic temple of tauromachy in the Plaza Mayor, Madrid's great central square.

I was sipping a Manzanilla at the bar, beneath the mounted head of Barbero, a bull that had, according to the plaque over my head, weighed 616 kilograms when it was in the prime of its short life. The waiters at La Torre del Oro, nattily attired in black-lapelled vests and green bow ties, had maintained the gruff good humor of their native Andalucía. I'd developed a nodding acquaintance with one of them, a proud Sevillian who squinted at the world through thick glasses, apparently always half-amused by his clientele.

"It's hard to find *criadillas* these days," he said, as he handed me a demitasse of velvety, smoky gazpacho. "The best place to look is in the markets. It's still something you only find in hidden restaurants, especially since the whole mad cow problem. But they are delicious. And because *criadillas* taste so good, people are ready to pay a lot of money for them."

Criadillas is the Spanish word for an animal's testicles—at least once they've been cooked. Downing the cojones of a freshly slaughtered bull has long been seen as a way of proving one's machismo. For years, people flocked to restaurants around bullrings in the corrida season to feast on what they believed was the dark, adrenaline-impregnated flesh of the animals they'd just seen slain. In fact, demand almost always outstripped supply, and the traditional dish *rabo de toro*, bull's tail, was more often *rabo de vaca*, the tail of a run-of-the-mill, and not-exactly-virile, cow. At the height of *la vaca loca*—the mad cow outbreak—the carcasses of bulls killed in Spanish rings were burned rather than butchered, and even the bloody ears and tails, traditionally tossed by the victorious torero into the crowd, were replaced by fakes for fear of contagion. Since 2001, the abattoir at the back of Madrid's Las Ventas bullring has officially been closed. I was beginning to think that, given the recent history of food scares, tracking down real *criadillas* might prove impossible.

"There are lots of other things to try," the bartender consoled me. "*Zarajos, entresijos, morcilla.* You still find them in certain bars. You know how to tell if a bar is good in Madrid or Seville? If the floor is dirty. If it's clean, that means they have too much time to sweep up, and it's not popular. You're better off avoiding it."

I spat a toothpick onto the floor, adding to the rich compost of olive pits, Fortuna butts, greasy napkins, and sunflower-seed shells that had already accumulated underfoot. The Spanish government had just announced that smoking would be banned in the workplace in 2006, and bars and restaurants in Spain would soon have to provide nonsmoking sections. Fat chance, I thought. Technically, smoking was *already* banned on public transportation, but, within ten minutes of getting off my train, I'd spotted three people with cigarettes in hand on the platform of the Chamartín metro station. The Latin capacity for cognitive dissonance—for a conservative Frenchman or Italian to fully endorse the institution of marriage, for example, while juggling a mistress and a wife—also explained how a naturally recalcitrant people like the Spanish could live within the strictures of the rule-obsessed European Union. Though they paid lip service to legislation, day to day they preferred to ignore it. Depending on your perspective, this was either pathetic woolly-mindedness, or worldly sophistication. (I figured it came from centuries of being forced to live with, but despairing of ever reconciling with observable reality, the strictures of Roman Catholicism.) In just measure, such laxness can make daily life quite pleasant; taken to extremes, it can also lead to the institutionalized hypocrisy of corruption. Sloppy, sophisticated, stylish, anachronistic Spain was by far my favorite country in Western Europe—at least to visit. Not the kind of place, though, I'd ever consider setting up my own business.

Looking around the walls of La Torre del Oro, I remembered something else I loved about Latin cultures: the omnipresence of death. Next to me, framed on the wall, was a *puntilla*, the same knife that had been used to bring Barbero's short life to an end. On one of the screens, a torero was being tossed headfirst over a bull's horns in slow-motion replay, so that at one point his body was actually perpendicular to the ground. A black-and-white photo showed another torero on the operating table, surrounded by orderlies, his chest bristling with scalpels and clamps.

Noticing my interest, the barman said drily, "He's the only one who's still alive. But he is also completely paralyzed."

I was enjoying my tapas and sherry in a kind of mausoleum, a temple of death. Latin cultures explicity acknowledge the heightened intensity that comes when food—or any other pleasure—is linked to transgression and risk. The frisson that comes from eating steak tartare, raw oysters, or poached game birds, if unquantifiable, is also undeniable.

It's not the kind of thing, however, a continentwide food-safety bureaucracy would find easy to write into its directives and regulations.

*   *   *

Spain came into the twenty-first century the way a bull storms into the ring: raging at its long confinement, with generations of atavistic impulses bred into its blood, proud but wary as it realized the nature and size of the stage it had been cast onto. Isolated by the forty-year-long Franco dictatorship, which almost completely sheltered the nation from immigration until 1975, Spain opted to become a full member of modern Europe, dropping its border controls and adopting the euro in 2002. It received the first picador wound of modernity with the terrorist bombings at the Atocha train station a year later—the first Western nation to be attacked since the destruction of the World Trade Center. Spain responded in a typically extreme way: by voting in a forty-two-year-old Socialist prime minister, who withdrew Spanish troops from Iraq and reestablished friendly relations with France and Germany.

I'd been to Spain a half dozen times in the last decade, and my abiding sensation was that the Spanish had never really purged themselves of the polarization of the civil war of the 1930s, which had pitted fascists against radical leftists: the conservative and progressive were still strangely, and uncomfortably, intertwined in the life of the nation. Though prostitution was legal, and the new government favored gay marriage, women still did the laundry in 84 percent of Spanish households. The trendy neighborhoods of Madrid were full of barhopping hipsters with cell phones and iPods, but 68 percent of the eighteen-to-thirty-four age group still lived with their parents. In contrast, though you might have pegged this as a nation in love with the traditional intoxicants of tobacco and alcohol—there are more bars in Spain than in all the rest of Western Europe combined—it actually boasted the highest consumption of marijuana and cocaine on the Continent. Thanks to the nonintrusive Spanish legal tradition, though, individual drug use at home was almost never prosecuted.

I, for one, found the strands of anachronism and modernity invigorating, and as I explored the backstreets in search of dodgy meals, it was a pleasure seeing transvestites share the same park benches with old men in berets and cardigans. At a deli-cum-restaurant-cum-bar called the Museo del Jamón, the Museum of Ham, I became fascinated by the ranks of hogs' legs quietly curing a couple of feet above my head. Blackhoofed, covered with green mold, and bristling with wiry hairs, this was food that had clearly been wrested from a once-living being.

I asked the barman for a plate of his finest Ibérico ham. After rolling white sleeves to the elbow, he unhitched a ham from the rafters and screwed its trotter into a wood-based vise, called a *jamonera*. Using a long, lovingly sharpened blade to carve off translucent red slices, he laid them in a circle around the edge of a white plate, explaining that they came from pigs raised in the mountains of Extremadura, free-range animals fed with acorns from the same oak trees that were cultivated for cork. I tried my first slice: marbled with amber fat, it melted at body temperature, leaving a salty, nut-flavored coating over my tongue, like the richest butter combined with the silkiest carpaccio.

I told the barman that I'd never had anything like it.

"That doesn't surprise me!" he said. "We have the best ham of anywhere in the world. But I'm happy that the Americans don't take it, because we don't have all that much for ourselves. If they tasted how good it was, we wouldn't have any left at all!"

Ibérico and all other forms of Spanish ham are completely forbidden in the United States; the maximum penalty for importing them is $10,000 and ten years in jail. (These are not just token punishments; a woman from California was recently fined $2,000 for importing a single Spanish chorizo.) The prohibition doesn't make a lot of sense. Ibérico pigs are free-run, raised in mountain forests, and classified by the Spanish version of the system that guarantees the purity of *appellation d'origine contrôlée* cheeses and wines in France. Ibérico ham is routinely rated the best in the world, beating out even Italian prosciutto di Parma.

American gourmands can't get Ibérico at home because no Spanish slaughterhouse meets Department of Agriculture standards. But why would the Spanish meat industry want to stoop so low? The USDA allows embryo splitting, cloning, and the use of antibiotics to spur growth of lifestock. Cows and pigs are fattened with an FDA-approved mix of plate waste from restaurants, out-of-date pet food, and chicken manure; cows' and pigs' blood is mixed into the cattle's drinking water to bulk them up with further cheap protein. Even though feeding animal protein to animals was likely the cause of the outbreak of bovine spongiform encephalopathy— BSE, or mad cow disease—that killed 120 people in Britain, in North America cattle remains continue to be fed to pigs and poultry, which in turn are ground up to make cattle feed. As the Bush administration (the Republican Party has been a leading benefactor of contributions from meatpackers) increasingly allowed the industry to police its own factories, the number of recalls for E. coli, salmonella, and other pathogens reached record highs: 113 in 2002 alone (all of them voluntary: the USDA has no authority to demand a recall). The besetting sin of Spanish slaughterhouses, apparently, is that, being relatively small, they sometimes handle cows as well as pigs—which is the rationale for barring Ibérico ham from the United States. (The USDA is on the verge of approving a single Spanish slaughterhouse to export its products; the first shipments might arrive as early as 2007.)

The origin of the ban apparently lies in an epidemic that affected Spanish swine in the 1970s. Or perhaps the USDA is merely nursing a grudge: in the nineteenth century, Europeans prohibited American pigs, after they'd been found to have unusually high rates of round-worm infection, provoking one of the first transatlantic trade wars. What's more likely, however, is that the influential American meat-packing lobby likes the ban just fine and would rather that smooth-as-butter Ibérico never made it into stateside butcher shops.

After all, how are you going to keep the public down on the factory farm once they've tasted Spanish ham?

Try as I might, I couldn't find much evidence that northern-European sanitary norms were particularly cramping the style of Madrid's bartenders and restaurateurs. At a restaurant whose walls were covered with old clogs and flamenco shoes, I chewed on *orejas*, or pigs ears, served on a cracked wooden plate, an ideal breeding ground for bacteria. At a bar on the Plaza de Cascorro, I ordered a plate of spicy *patatas bravas* and watched as a baby cockroach scuttled beneath my complimentary plate of green olives. A young mother came in, ordered a glass of foamy beer, and blew long plumes from her unfiltered Ducado toward the ceiling as she dandled a baby on her knee and fed coins into a video slot machine. I watched the bald barman using a dirty rag to wipe down a sneeze guard that covered plates of olive-oil-soaked anchovies, octopus, and snails, smearing a digital thermometer into translucence. In one of the only concessions to bureaucratic norms evident in Spanish bars, the electronically displayed temperatures on counters are supposed to be diligently recorded by employees every three hours. In one establishment, I'd watched a barman casually fill the chart with an entire week's worth of readings in a single sitting.

No matter how many leading questions I asked about "inspectors from Brussels," nobody really had any stories about blue-eyed Nordic types suddenly showing up to run their white-gloved fingers along their counters. When restaurateurs grumbled, it was about the boys from "Sanidad"—the local inspectors, who'd always made their lives difficult. Though Spain has a national Ministry of Health and Consumer Affairs, it is a highly decentralized nation, with seventeen autonomous communities, each with its own parliament, and each responsible for food-safety matters within its own borders. (After my visit, a Spanish Food Safety Agency, with offices in Madrid, was established to set national policy.) What's more, in municipalities with more than fifty thousand residents, it's up to the local city hall to carry out inspections. In theory, the guidelines for food handling and safety ultimately came from Brussels; but apparently there was a lot of leeway in their interpretation down the line. At Lhardy, a Frenchified restaurant off the Puerta del Sol, famous for its tripe and nineteenth-century décor, one of the managers told me he had few complaints about the new regime.

"We are inspected by the health department periodically. We have to follow European norms, but the inspectors are Spanish. Other things we have to regulate ourselves. For example, we have a sanitary register for our cheeses. We send things to a private laboratory, to have them tested, twice a month."

He pointed to a multitiered display case, a fabulous concoction of glass and metal, that was formerly used to display sandwiches.

"We've been open since 1839, and that display is two centuries old. The inspectors said we couldn't use it anymore, because they thought it couldn't be kept clean. That was unfortunate. But most of the rules are easy to follow, and logical. You have to remember, there have been problems with food in Spain in the past—with the swine epidemic, and the olive oil scandal, so people accept these rules."

Spain received its wake-up call about food safety long before most other European nations. In 1981, unlabeled bottles of olive oil being sold in weekly markets sickened twenty-five thousand people; it turned out a group of manufacturers and commodities dealers had conspired to unload stocks of cheap rapeseed oil, adulterated with a dye intended for industrial use. Six hundred people died, and thousands suffered permanent damage to their lungs and nervous system. The incident lives on in the popular memory as an object lesson in the lengths unregulated business can go to out of greed, and there were still enough foodborne illness outbreaks in Spain—3,818 in 2002—to keep people on their toes. Eggs, or *huevos*, continued to be a big problem in Spain: salmonella in eggs had led to 2,106 hospitalizations and four deaths that year. I made a mental note to think carefully before accepting any tapas with mayonnaise.

Meanwhile, my hunt for a plate of the other kind of *huevos*—which is Spanish slang for "testicles"—wasn't going so well. Following a tip, I went to Maravillas, an indoor market filled with rows of numbered counters. Madrid's traditional *castizo* cuisine was the food of the poor, the cast-off viscera of animals, often cooked up as cheap and hearty *callos*, or tripe stews, which were spiced with powdered pimentón peppers and served with chunks of blood sausage. In the butchers' section of the market, spatchcocked lamb heads, tongues lolling, lay amid bricks of kidney-bean-hued, coagulated blood (ideal for frying with onion to start a sauce, I was assured). At the Casquería Gerardo, which specialized in organ meats, I finally found them: CRIADILLAS, said a plastic sign on the end of a metal rod, for the low price of 1.8 euros a kilogram. Packed into a stainless steel tray, each oval globe looked like some incarnadine ostrich egg, covered with a crimson tracery of veins. They were definitely too big to be swallowed in a single gulp. The stallkeeper, a jolly woman with dark black hair and a white smock, looked at me a little suspiciously as I snapped pictures of my prize.

"Would you like some?" she asked.

I told her I was visiting and had nowhere to cook them. Did she know of a restaurant where I could try them?

"It's not really the right time of year to find them in restaurants," she said. "Most of my clients are housewives, buying for their family, not restaurant owners."

I was disappointed, but vowed to continue my search. In the meantime, I knew of another delicacy that could be had year-round— for a price. This one hadn't been banned, yet. (Though it probably should be, immediately.)

Along with the Japanese, the Spanish are among the world's most enthusiastic consumers of seafood. Ever since Franco's time, trucks laden with fresh oysters, hake, and lobsters had thundered from the coasts of Galicia, Andalucía, and the Basque country, making the roads leading to Madrid some of the most dangerous in the world. In my native Canada, Spanish fishing boats are widely resented as rapacious rule-breakers; a sea battle almost broke out a few years back when the Canadian coast guard fired shots over the bow of a trawler that had been poaching off Newfoundland's Grand Banks. The Spanish will eat just about anything that swims in the ocean or lurks in tide pools. Sea urchins are popular tapas in coastal towns, and lamprey eels, cooked in their own blood and served whole, are enjoyed by young and old in Galicia. When an oil tanker called the *Prestige* spilled sixty-four thousand tons of petrol off the northern coast of Spain in 2002, contaminating the ocean floor and affecting 1,250 miles of coastline, it barely put a dent in the Spanish seafood market.

At a fishmonger, the impressive Pescaderías Coruñesas, I'd already sampled *percebes*, or gooseneck barnacles, one of the most intimidating foods in the sea. When the ocean is calm off the Galician coast, fishermen set out in small boats for the rocks where the barnacles grow. Attached to each other by ropes cinched around the waist (a necessary precaution: every year, the waves claim a fisherman or two), they pry the *percebes* off the rocks with special tools and gather them in netted bags. I'd contemplated a pair the manager had scooped out of the ice for me, awed that it could ever have occurred to anybody to eat such monstrosities. Half a foot long, with blackened, leathery shafts that ended in a pink-and-white mosaic-shelled tip, they looked like the phalluses of an alien in some low-budget, sci-fi-themed porn film. The manager had beckoned me to follow him to the back of the shop and dropped two *percebes* into a huge pot of water roiling atop a stove, explaining you cook them for the time it takes to say the Lord's Prayer.

Lifting them from the pot with a meshed spoon, he'd showed me how to twist off the glanslike tip—unleashing a squirt of salty water over his shirt—which revealed the hot, pink flesh inside.

A security guard had watched me eating them with approval. "*¡Jamón del mar!*" he'd said.

"Ham of the sea." The comparison was apt: the flesh was sweet and salty, like a happy mixture of scallops and acorn-fed Ibérico.

Percebes are expensive, particularly since poachers with scuba gear have started stripping the underwater mother beds: a kilogram cost 99 euros ($129 U.S.) during my visit. But, compared to *angulas*, which were selling for 360 euros a kilo ($470 U.S.) at the seafood store, gooseneck barnacles were a steal. That night, I went to El Pescador, probably Madrid's best seafood restaurant, in search of the delicacy. On the menu, an appetizer of *angulas*, a scant 110 grams, was going for 51 euros ($67 U.S.). I swallowed hard and placed my order for the baby eels.

Eels are born in the Sargasso Sea, south of Bermuda. Each tiny, glasslike larva contains a drop of oil that allows it to float to the surface of the ocean, where it feeds on microscopic life as it is slowly buoyed toward land. Half swimming, half drifting, across forty-five hundred miles of open ocean, the baby eels—also known as elvers—can take up to three years to reach the mouths of the Duero and Ebro rivers. The males remain in the estuaries, while the females swim upstream to live in freshwater lakes—they have even been known to cross pastures to get to their goal—until they have grown to their full length of 1.5 yards and adult weight of fifteen pounds. Then they return to the river mouths, rejoin the now fully grown males, and swim back to the Sargasso Sea, where they mate and die.

It is truly an epic journey. Or it would be, if the elvers weren't scooped up in their hundreds of millions while still a few centimeters long and rushed to the fish shops and markets of Madrid. As they become more scarce, the price goes up: as high as 850 euros ($1,110 U.S.) at Christmastime, so much so that a thriving market for ersatz *angulas* has arisen. Called *gulas*, they are the flesh of Alaskan pollack pressed into elverlike strands and printed with tiny fake eyes.

Traditionally, *angulas* were delicately killed in an infusion of tobacco, but the recipe at El Pescador calls for them to be thrown into hot olive oil while still alive. The waiter brought me a fingerbowl with a lemon floating in it and a flat wooden fork with four tines. With a flourish, he laid an earthenware bowl on the table before me. I contemplated the congeries of tiny bodies. Sinuous, none longer than eight centimeters, their spines were just visible beneath colorless, ridged skin; all of them had eyes. I plunged my wooden fork into the tangle, lifted them to my mouth, and started to chew.

The first taste was of peppery, burnt garlic. I let the *angulas* slide over my tongue and then bit down: it was like velvety, saline, slightly al dente vermicelli, each strand with a tiny thread of crunchiness inside; the spine, presumably. Not bad at all. There was a certain morbid, sensuous pleasure in rolling dozens of tiny bodies around in your mouth.

But as I continued to chew, and the body count continued to rise, I started to feel very, very guilty indeed. The enormity of human decadence hit me: I was scooping up hundreds of corpses—maybe an entire generation!—every time I lifted the fork to my mouth. The eels' epic journey from tropical sea to mountain stream and back again, interrupted by human appetite, had ended on this cheap wooden fork. Though eels aren't endangered, they aren't exactly doing well, particularly in Spain. At this point, ordering *angulas* isn't quite as immoral as dining on, say, a panda steak. I could easily imagine myself, however, reading a news item a decade hence about the definitive disappearance of the freshwater eel from the rivers of Europe, and regretting I'd ever had this meal.

As much as I believed in the right to choose one's pleasures with impunity, there were clearly limits. When our consumer choices— whether it's buying ozone-depleting aerosol antiperspirant, or boots made of caiman skins—end up affecting everybody on the planet, then our elected representatives have the right, even the duty, to step in and regulate the trade. That's why the libertarian utopia of a completely free market had always seemed so shortsighted to me: the vaunted "invisible hand" that is supposed to self-regulate capitalism has never shown any evidence of being connected to a functioning brain. There is no overestimating human shortsightedness: we will scramble the last dodo egg for breakfast or chop down the last tree on Easter Island to keep the campfire going. Lately, we'd brought the Atlantic cod fishery to collapse, and it looked as if we were about to drive the sturgeon to extinction to feed the ever-more-lucrative caviar market. As a species, *Homo sapiens* has always been in need of some restraint.

I looked at my dinner; it looked back at me. That night, I was definitely part of the problem. But, hell, I'd ordered the baby eels— and at $10 a swallow, there was no way I wasn't going to clean my plate.

But take it from me: *angulas* aren't worth it. They may be tasty, but you're hungry an hour later.

If one person in Spain was in a position to tell me whether *criadillas*, *percebes*, and other traditional foods were under imminent threat from Brussels, it was Pedro Subijana, the current president of Euro-Toques, an association of four thousand chefs that was founded in 1986 to defend artisanal foods and cooking techniques from the assaults of agribusiness and bureaucracy. The owner of one of the most re-nowned restaurants in the autonomous community of Euskadi, Subijana was a television celebrity and a proud booster of new Basque cuisine. Meeting him would involve a train trip north to San Sebastián, a city of 178,000, near the French border on the Bay of Biscay.

Which wasn't exactly a hardship. San Sebastián is a bit of a belle époque bijou, its near-perfect shell-shaped bay framed by green hills and set off by a tiny island as perfectly placed as Marilyn Monroe's mole. The Parte Vieja is kind of like a French Quarter for foodies: a densely packed grid of narrow streets full of the best tapas (here called *pinchos*) bars in the world. I spent a couple of nights on a one-man *poteo*, or *pinchos*-bar crawl. In the space of a dozen square blocks, there were hundreds of bars, each with its own specialty—mushrooms, anchovies, foie gras—and in each the bartender welcomed me with a shot of Txakolí, a tart white wine whose grapes are grown in steep hillside vineyards, poured at arm's length into unstemmed glasses to increase its subtle effervescence.

It was all unrepentantly, gloriously unhygienic. Brochettes of crayfish and shrimp and sandwiches slathered with mayonnaise lay out on the counters for entire afternoons, the only measure against contagion the buzzing, blue-light fly-killers mounted on the walls. The compost on the floor was truly awesome, its layers composing a kind of archaeology of the evening; in one bar I watched as a woman on Rollerblades kept her hand on her girlfriend's shoulder as she slid to one end of the counter to snatch a pastry shell stuffed with spider-crab flesh, then to the other to snag a morsel of bacalao poised on a tangle of shredded fried potatoes. I was surprised her wheels could roll at all: with every movement she piled up drifts of sawdust, sunflower-seed shells, half-smoked Ducados, cast-off toothpicks, greasy napkins, and olive pits with the flesh still clinging to them.

I met Pedro Subijana at Akelare, his hilltop restaurant. Dressed in a white blouse, stitched with his name in blue script, sporting an exuberant salt-and-pepper mustache that stretched from cheek to cheek, Subijana was the living picture of the Michelin-starred chef.

Speaking in a mixture of French and Spanish, he pooh-poohed my surprise at the apparently lax hygienic conditions in the *pinchos* bars of San Sebastián.

"In *pinchos* bars that serve at lunch and dinnertime, there is a lot of rotation. They worry about freshness more, because they aren't stupid, and they're concerned about serving food hygienically and healthily. It's true, there are some bar owners who, when they don't sell their *pinchos* in the afternoon, try to sell them at night. But just because some bars are bad doesn't mean we should prohibit *pinchos*, interfere with the tradition. It just wouldn't be fair.

"What is happening," he continued, "is that there's a certain rebellion against sanitary norms, whether they come from Spain or Brussels. The norms can't be made for everybody. If you have a fast-food company, you have to employ teenagers who aren't qualified, who haven't studied. In that case, your employees should be made to put on plastic gloves, observe all the necessary hygiene measures. When those who are manipulating the food are professional, they know what to do and what not to do.

"Our great concern at Euro-Toques, and mine as a citizen of Europe, is that faraway administrations are going to legislate about things they know nothing about. I don't think that four bureaucrats sitting in an office in Brussels know more than all the people who have been handling food in the same way for centuries. Sincerely, I still haven't met a single sanitary inspector who knows more about food than I do."

I asked for some specific examples. Which traditions were being threatened?

"We were very involved in the campaign to require a certain percentage of cacao in chocolate before you could call it chocolate. We are in favor of the obligatory labeling of genetically modified food. And there is one thing that concerns me deeply. In Spain, it is now forbidden to crack open a fresh egg in the kitchen of a restaurant. You have to buy 'ovo-products' that come prepackaged and pasteurized in hermetically sealed containers. It's barbaric, an absurdity! The egg is the most natural product in existence. You can work on reforming the conditions in which chickens are raised. You can work on changing the fact that, to increase profits, these animals are given the lowest-quality feed, feed that is sometimes contaminated, and that that contamination can be passed on to humans. You can oblige servers to follow food-handling courses. You can even search the world over for some electronic, nuclear salmonella-detector to seek out the bad eggs. But you cannot prohibit the use of eggs!"

(Though I admired Subijana's passion, I was frankly relieved to learn the mayonnaise I'd seen sitting out for hours on bar counters was made from pasteurized eggs. A few months after our meeting, salmonellosis in Britain caused six thousand cases of food poisoning and fifteen deaths. The outbreak was linked to Spanish eggs.)

In fact, Subijana couldn't give me one example of a ban that had come directly from Brussels. The prohibition on using fresh eggs was imposed by the Spanish crown; the royal proclamation had been signed by King Juan Carlos himself in 1991 after a series of deaths linked to infected eggs. Subijana conceded he was more worried about the usual suspects—fast-food chains, supermarkets, and genetically modified food and antibiotic- and hormone-fed beef from North America—than any direct intervention from bureaucrats in Brussels. I was enjoying listening to him thunder, though.

"I believe the Spanish will be able to defend themselves better than other nationalities against the loss of traditions," he continued, "against globalization and fast food, because our culture has made us bons vivants. In general, the Spanish have a good diet, one that's varied and healthy; the quality of our products is high. And today, Spanish consumers desire more authentic products. The great challenge facing consumers is to demand the right to be informed exactly about what's in their food. Things have to be labeled—we have the right to know whether our food is genetically modified, for example."

I agreed with him completely. So far, however, I'd turned up no evidence that the infamous bureaucrats of Brussels were responsible for banning a single product—at least none that didn't deserve to be banned—or destroying one culinary tradition. True, new regulations had made life more difficult for small cheesemakers, but those that wanted to ship their product abroad had learned to adapt to the new sanitary norms.

The inspectors certainly hadn't cramped Subijana's style. In Akelaŕe's circular, glassed-in dining room overlooking the bay, I opted for a multicourse tasting menu of tapas-size servings, each course accompanied by a different Spanish wine. It was one of the better, and perhaps one of the riskier, meals I'd had in my life.

The single oyster, for example, removed from its shell and poised on a bed of icy grapes, could have given me a case of paralytic shellfish poisoning. Eating the fresh foie gras, covered with a crispy layer of fines herbes, I risked not only salmonellosis, but perhaps also attack by animal rights' protesters. The boneless, milk-fed lamb, served with amaranth and three-pepper skins, was only lightly roasted and might have given me some new variant of foot-and-mouth disease, perfectly primed to leap across the species barrier. And for all I knew, the plate of raw-milk blue cheeses, served with quince tea, could have been crawling with listeria pathogens.

But you know what? I didn't get sick. I just got *full*, exquisitely so. Pedro Subijana and his team of professionals had obviously been doing their job, protecting my health while giving me that tiny frisson that comes from flirting with the extremes of taste and texture. I lifted a glass of Navarrese muscatel in a toast to the people of Spain, and their profound knowledge that the most exquisite pleasures always come served with a dollop of risk.

Across the bay, the hilltop statue of Jesus answered my toast with a raised hand, as if offering the devil-may-care gourmands of San Sebastián his silent benediction.

Back in Madrid, I decided it was time to enlist the aid of a genuine Madrileño in my hunt for *criadillas*. I phoned up Chipi, whose number a Spanish mathematician I'd met in Montreal had given me.

"No problem!" said Chipi, after I'd explained my mission at the Bar Cervantes over a Mahou beer on a cold, wet Saturday night. "I love eating!" He even owed his name to a popular seafood dish: "Chipi" came from *chipirón*, Spanish for "small squid."

"Because I was small and ugly as a child," Chipi explained.

He'd definitely outgrown his nickname. Now in his early thirties, he worked as a lawyer for a Middle Eastern oil company. With his starched, button-down shirt, Chipi reminded me of the cartoon reporter Tintin, earnest, straight-backed, and clean-cut, as he roamed the sidewalks in search of carnivorous excess.

If we were going to find *criadillas* anywhere, Chipi told me, it would be in the working-class neighborhood of Lavapiés, whose brick streets, between ocher walls of balconied walk-ups, seemed to trickle downhill from the Plaza Tirso de Molina. Though many of the older joints catered to the crowds that came for the weekend flea market, the Rastro, the neighborhood had lately become a center of Arab immigration, where alley cats darted between *döner kebap* restaurants.

"You have to look for places where the menus are written on the walls with white paint," Chipi said. Opening the door to the Bar-Restaurante El Jamón, he peered inside and said, "This one looks pretty good." Sure enough, a hand-lettered sign on the wall above the bar read CRIADILLAS, 4€50.

We took a table in the back, where a Spanish reality show played on a flickering television set. Chipi looked at the layer of sawdust and cigarette butts on the floor appreciatively: for him, this was another good sign. ("In Denmark and Sweden, they won't even let a napkin touch the ground," he observed. "We should package up our 'compost' and export it to them. They could use it to feed their pigs.") The waitress spread paper over the tablecloth, plunked down bread, a bottle of fizzy lemonade, and a red wine called El Barrio de Lavapiés, whose label showed not a rural vineyard, but laundry hanging out to dry on a balcony.

Chipi put his palm against the bottle and grimaced. "Cold," he said. "Usually that means it's not very good."

The waitress reappeared to take our order.

"*¡Tomaré criadillas!*" I practically shouted.

"I'm sorry," she replied, "we sold out this afternoon."

I must have looked crestfallen. Chipi said, "Look, they have *entresijos* and *gallinejas*. Those are pretty extreme."

Not the same, I pouted, but agreed nonetheless. The waitress brought us a plate of oily, deep-fried organs. The *gallinejas* were lamb intestines, fatty, crispy, and bunched into tubes so they looked like the spidery-knuckled fingers of some malévolent alien. The *entresijos*—well, they came from the inside of a lamb, we knew that. Chipi was pretty sure they were parts of the respiratory tract. Glistening with grease, they bulged with strange pockets and sacs.

Like all viscera, I was discovering, they had a strong odor of the barnyard and resisted the teeth mightily. I managed to choke down most of mine by sandwiching them between hunks of bread, and washing the fatty mess down with huge gulps of Lavapiés finest red. The wine was so young it was still teething—on our tongues.

After the meal, we wandered the streets, a little stunned, each in his own bubble of grease.

Through his torpor, Chipi suddenly brightened. "We might be able to find *criadillas* here . . ."

We stopped outside the Bar Mariano, on the Plaza Tirso de Molina. The skinned head of a lamb, topped with a wreath of parsley, glared blankly at us from the window, like a figurine from some Flemish anatomist's studio.

Inside, the fluorescent lighting was maximum wattage, the sawdust was thick on the floor, and the fans following the Real Madrid soccer match were deafening. We found a small table and scanned the menu for *criadillas*, in vain.

"You're out of luck again," sighed Chipi. "But they have *zarajos!* When it comes to all this organ stuff, they're the ones I like best."

The waiter bought a plate of five, accompanied by a quarter of a lemon. Once again we were eating lambs' intestines, but these ones were artfully wrapped around two vine shoots laid crosswise, so they formed a circular mass of rubbery twine. It brought to mind some toy from the Great Depression, a homemade bouncy ball improvised by Spanky and Our Gang.

Chipi crossed his eyes as he unraveled a *zarajo* with his incisors; when he nipped off a piece, it actually rebounded against his chest like an elastic band, splattering us with grease.

I managed to get through one before pushing the plate away. I was beginning to wonder about this whole matter of eating headcheese, chitterlings, sweetbreads. No matter how you dressed it up, it was still tongues swallowing tongues, innards digesting innards, intestines slipping through intestines. The more I thought about it, the less I wanted to. But what had I expected, anyway? The name spoke for itself: it was, after all, offal.

Again we wandered the streets in a daze, checking out menus. A block toward the Plaza Mayor, Chipi looked thunderstruck. "Of course!" He led me, practically at a run, to the narrow, red-and-green façade of a restaurant.

"This is where I had *criadillas!*" he said. "The Casa Rodriguez!"

The metal curtains had already been pulled over the door for the night.

By then, Chipi had to run for the last train to his suburb, but as he trotted away, the Tintin of Tapas shouted over his shoulder, "Just go there for lunch tomorrow! They'll have your balls for sure!"

So, what, exactly, were the infamous, freedom-killing bureaucrats of the European Union responsible for, if not prohibiting *criadillas*, *angulas*, and coagulated blood? I contacted Beate Gminder, spokesperson for Health and Consumer Protection at the European Commission in Brussels. In weary tones, she dispelled a few myths about the role of the directorate.

"We are a legislative body," Gminder told me. "We are not responsible for enforcement. We are not the FDA. We have no police force. Local food controllers in the member countries are still responsible for inspecting bars, restaurants, and markets. The commission sends inspectors from the Food and Veterinary Office (FVO) to member countries every once in a while. But they are not measuring the size of oysters or smelling the cheeses. They go for a week and inspect the local inspectors, to see how the various levels of government are working together. The FVO only has one hundred and twenty inspectors; they could hardly inspect every slaughterhouse in the EU."

Why, then, had the European Food Safety Authority been founded, if not to ensure the safety of the food supply?

"Europe needed an independent, neutral authority composed of scientists and other experts to give people advice on a practical level. To tell them they needed to avoid this food, but the risk with this other food was small. Politicians can never do that, but an independent expert body can." In spite of its ominous name, the Authority merely offered risk assessment to member states, who in turn undertook the more practical, day-to-day task of risk management. In the case of a health emergency—say, an outbreak of shellfish poisoning— the commission could override member states to safeguard the health of European citizens. According to Gminder, this had only happened once, when the EU ordered Belgium to take dioxin-contaminated poultry off the shelves. (The resulting "Chickengate" brought down the Belgian government.)

I brought up some of the fears expressed by Pedro Subijana: that wood-burning pizza ovens would be banned in Italy for fear of cancer; that pâté de foie gras would disappear from restaurant menus;

that pasteurization would forever destroy the great raw-milk cheeses of Europe.

"There are no laws against foie gras," she said. "That's a matter of animal welfare, and it's up to individual member states like France to decide whether or not they want to restrict certain production methods for ethical reasons. As for wood-burning pizza ovens, that's another Euro-myth. All of the products you are referring to are still eaten and produced in Europe. The conditions under which raw-milk cheeses are made have changed, but there is a very good reason for that: our objective is to have fewer people falling sick from listeria and salmonella. If there's less variety in food choice now than twenty years ago, part of that comes from the fact that women are working more, there are more supermarkets, and people are buying more prepackaged food. But local production, for local consumption, is never affected by European regulation. Sales from the farm are always exempted. And if a hunter shoots an elk in Sweden, we have nothing to do with that. Traditional foods are almost never a problem. What we do control is novel foods which haven't been on the European market before."

Indeed, the makers of farmhouse Époisses I'd met in Burgundy had mentioned they were automatically allowed to sell their cheese within a fifty-mile radius of the farm; they'd deliberately chosen to refit their factory to European norms so they could sell beyond those limits, in Paris. While sparing traditional practices, the EU tended to be hard on producers outside its borders. Regulations stipulated that any "novel" food that wasn't part of the European diet before 1997 be rigorously tested for safety and nutrition, a rule that had prevented the import of such "novelties" as Saskatoon berries, which have safely been consumed on the Canadian prairies for generations. The main goal, however—following the precautionary principle—was to vet new biotechnology products before they were thrown onto the market.

"All these examples the chefs are giving," said Gminder, "are not coming from European regulations, but their interpretation by the member state. Politicians find it easy to blame Brussels for unpopular measures they're actually responsible for. We're an institutional scapegoat."

I believed Gminder. The scare stories in the *Wall Street Journal* and the British *Sun* had put me on the trail of the Brussels bureaucrats, but I hadn't been able to turn up any evidence in the field that the EFSA, or any other EU body, was preventing Europe's consumers from getting what they really wanted, or that they had stirred up deep resentment among producers. In a speech, Gminder's former boss, David Byrne, had reassured producers that the "EC does not intend to create European-wide standards for food quality. This is an area in which a one-size-fits-all approach would be wholly inappropriate. Europe has a rich diversity of cultures, which gives rise to a wide and wonderful range of foods. Uniformity of quality would nullify this variety to the detriment of all." Coagulated blood could still be found in the markets of Madrid, and raw-milk Époisses in the back roads of Burgundy. As for the maggot cheese of Sardinia, and the ortolans of France, they had long been illegal in their own countries anyway. Frankly, I had no problem with the fact that rotten cheese and endangered songbirds weren't available on the shelves of supermarket chains from Denmark to Malta.

In the final analysis, the food the EU was keeping off the market was stuff no sane consumer would want anyway. North Americans had never had the choice: debate about genetically modified food and hormone-fed beef had never become public. The big players in the North American food industry, given carte blanche by ever-more-complicit administrations, have long been too powerful for their—or our—own good.

When it comes to prohibiting food, the contrast in approach on either side of the Atlantic couldn't be more stark. North American legislators ban the import of, or impose huge tariffs on, the pure, traditional foods Europeans have safely consumed for generations. European lawmakers, in contrast, prohibit the import of tomatoes spliced with fish genes, milk pumped out of hormone-fed cows, and bacon that comes from pigs fed with ground-up cadavers of cows— not stuff people were clamoring to buy anyway.

It hadn't always been this way. Until the 1970s, the United States was actually in the vanguard of innovative and stringent legislation. The Endangered Species Act of 1966 was an early manifestation of the precautionary principle, limiting development if it had the potential to cause irreversible harm to a threatened species. While DDT and Red Dye No. 2 continued to be used in Europe, they were banned in the United States as potential human carcinogens, and in 1977, the United States was the first nation to ban chloro-fluorcarbons when it was learned they were depleting the ozone layer. Throughout the 1960s and '70s, a series of public health disasters—thalidomide, Love Canal, Three Mile Island—kept the need for regulation uppermost in the public mind. The change started around the time Ronald Reagan was voted into office, and subsequent Bush administrations have only deepened the gutting of public health and curtailed oversight of industry. In short, the continents have traded places: North America, and particularly the United States, is now the regulatory backwater, with no federal standards for carbon emissions, automobile and electronic recycling, or packaged wastes. Starting in 1985, when the European Council of Ministers voted to ban the use of all growth hormones in cattle, Europe started to go increasingly green; it recently introduced a blacklist of fifteen hundred chemicals in the hopes of creating a toxin-free society. Meanwhile, conservative administrations in North America have been eviscerating essential public health services that took decades to build. Though the first case of mad cow disease was discovered in a Holstein in Washington State in December 2003, the USDA continues to deny the need for systematic screening of livestock for mad cow disease, even though it would only add three to five cents to the price of a pound of beef.

Against all evidence, food safety officials in the United States continue to boast that the American food supply is the safest in the world. The World Health Organization's figures certainly don't support such smugness. There are typically 76 million cases of foodborne illness in the United States a year, or 26 cases per 100 citizens. In the United Kingdom, there are only 3.4 cases per 100 citizens, and in France, only 1.2 cases per 100 citizens (though, admittedly, in a nation where *une crise de foie*—a liver attack—is a badge of honor, there might be a little underreporting). Given the odds, I'd rather order the cheese plate in Marseille, or organ meats in Manchester, than accept an invitation to a barbecue in Minneapolis.

Finally, my scavenger hunt had come to an end. It was lunchtime at Casa Rodriguez, and sitting before me, in all its fleshy glory, was the long-sought plate of *criadillas*. I'd heard bull's balls are often baked into a pie, empanada-style, but here the dish took the form of a thick gravy, served with spicy guindilla chilis and slivers of garlic fried soft, all swimming in an earthenware bowl. A dozen suspiciously rounded lumps, each about an inch long, were distributed throughout the sauce. I took a preparatory swig of tongue-rasping red wine to lubricate my throat and dug in.

At first, what predominated was the barnyard taste I'd come to associate with all organ meats. But, after a couple more gulps of wine, my palate overcame its suspicion. The meat was soft, almost fluffy, but not at all chewy. The sauce had a bacony flavor, and eventually the irresistible blend of garlic and chilis overpowered everything, turning the suspicious lumps into just another source of protein. I ate five of them. Then ten. Then I sopped up the sauce with my bread and downed the rest of the wine.

I was cleaning my teeth with a wooden toothpick, feeling a real sense of accomplishment—perhaps even some increased virility—when the owner came up. He had jowly cheeks, beagle-folds under his brown eyes: his was the face of a sad clown. I deduced from the cries of a group of boisterous municipal street cleaners in ripped jeans and sleeveless T-shirts—"*¡José! ¡Más vino!*" "*¡José! ¡Más pan!*"—that his name was José.

José folded his arms over his green blazer and eyed me sullenly.

"We don't get many foreigners here," he said. "What did you think of our *criadillas?*"

"*¡Excelente!*" I replied. "But I didn't think they'd be so small. The ones I saw at Maravillas market were very big!" I used both hands to describe an ostrich-egg-sized oval.

"Those were *criadillas de toro*, señor. They are different. These are *criadillas de cerdo*."

In other words, pig's balls. No wonder they'd been so small. I suddenly felt quite ill.

"We usually serve the other ones during the bullfighting season." He pointed to a calendar. "It is October now. You might consider returning in April."

Well, that explained a lot. I'd missed the end of the season by a week. Trying my best to maintain my sangfroid—er, *sangre fría*—I assured him I'd do just that.

The reality was, though, that it was time for me to move on, and I'd be swearing off meat once again. It wasn't so much that I was getting fat or feeling unfit; nor had I suffered from a single bout of indigestion in Spain. It was just that, as much as I believed in my absolute freedom to choose my own poison with impunity, I also valued my freedom not to be poisoned against my knowledge or will. I was returning to North America, where I no longer had any idea what kind of pathogens were present in supermarket ground round, which now has to be labeled as if it were toxic waste. In Europe, I was happy to feast on oysters and gooseneck barnacles, lamb's intestines and bull's balls. But I had absolutely no desire to expose myself to the growth-hormone-injected, GM-grain-fed, salmonella- and *E. coli*–infested product that now passes for the American hamburger.

I may be decadent, but I'm not stupid.

· S M O K E ·

Written laws are like spider's webs;
they hold the weak and delicate who might
be caught in their meshes, but are torn
in pieces by the rich and powerful.

—*Plutarch*

5

COHIBA ESPLENDIDO

It's the Law

SORRY, SIGMUND: a cigar is never just a cigar anymore. Especially not when the cigar in question is a Cohiba Esplendido.

I was standing before the humidor at one of Montreal's leading tobacconists, inspecting a porn fest of phallic signifiers. The owner, whose great-grandfather had founded the shop in 1907, selected a single Esplendido from the varnished box and handed it to me with custodial reverence. Ramrod straight, cross hatched with veins beneath a membranous, batwinglike wrapper, the Esplendido felt firm but spongiform—indeed, almost sweaty—as I grasped its seven-inch-long shaft. It was as if some powerful shaman had sculpted vegetable matter into living tissue, pumped it into tumescence, and fettered it with a cock ring in the form of a paper band.

The owner, a soft-spoken and deferential man in glasses, cords and loafers, instructed me on the ritual. "Cut the end, just above the cap," he said, performing a pantomime circumcision with his pinkie. "Hold a butane lighter or a strip of cedar close to the other end"— here he turned his wrist, rotating the cigar—"until it's burned all around, and then light it. Don't draw on it too much. A cigar of this size should burn for about an hour and a half." A dreamy look came over his face as he said, in hushed tones, "Oh, it's a fine cigar, sir."

I stifled a smirk. For me, cigars are another generation's egregious, too obvious symbol of masculine potency, along with pendulous neckties, knotty-pine walking sticks, marlins and moose antlers mounted on varnished plaques. On a trip to Cuba in 1997, I'd tried hard to fathom the mystique of the stogie. I toured the Dickensian Pártagas cigar factory in Havana, where a *lector*—a professional reader—kept the rollers distracted by reciting a translation of *The Count of Monte Cristo* over a crackling loudspeaker. I was in the same group as two polo-shirted tourists from Philadelphia who videotaped the entire experience ("Flew in from Toronto," one of them told me with a wink). As they clowned beside a thin black woman at her workstation—hoping, perhaps, to catch her in the apocryphal act of rolling a cigar between her thighs—they didn't hear the guide tell us that the average worker took home only 180 pesos a month: not enough to buy one of the fat cigars the tourists had been sucking on since the tour had begun. On the way out, I bought a Romeo y Julieta from the factory's gift shop and smoked it on the rooftop of my guesthouse. True, there was a decadent appeal to puffing in the moist Caribbean twilight—Cuba is the world's biggest humidor—while the salsa band at the club next door rehearsed, bats swooped, and the streetlights blinked off during the third blackout of the night. But I immediately felt sick to my stomach and awoke the next day with an ashtray in my mouth, as a million cells succumbed to nicotine poisoning and coalesced in filmy layers of cheek lining on my tongue. I brought back a box of Lanceros and tried to enjoy one from time to time after a good meal. The experience—ineffable, interminable— always felt more like punishment than reward.

At the time, it was hard not to associate cigars with Arnold Schwarzenegger, Sylvester Stallone, Michael Douglas, and other paragons of self-congratulatory privilege who appeared on the covers of the five-hundred-page issues of *Cigar Aficionado* magazine. The nineteenth-century American politician Horace Greeley, I decided, had pulled a punch when he'd referred to a cigar as "a fire at one end and a fool at the other." Ever since Bill Clinton had inserted a Cuban Monte Cristo No. 2 into Monica Lewinsky, removed it, and suavely commented, "It tastes good!" even the dimmest sot had had to acknowledge the link between the phallus and the cigar. That such working-class heroes as Karl Marx, Che Guevara, and Bertolt Brecht had also been cigar lovers was just so much long-forgotten trivia. The new, more precise definition of a cigar smoker had to be, a dick sucking on a dick.

Since the salad days of the fad in the late 1990s, however, when Americans were smoking 350 million cigars a year—10 million of them smuggled Cubans—things had changed. The dot-com boom had busted, California had banned smoking in bars and restaurants in 1998, with New York following suit in 2003. Cigar smokers—far from being laughable, middle-of-the-road bandwagon-jumpers— were being transformed into outlaws and pariahs, a dwindling minority lurking twenty feet from the doorways of public buildings, where they attracted disdainful stares from well-toned passersby carrying yoga mats under their arm.

So I looked at the Esplendido in my hand with new respect. It wasn't just the $65 price tag. This was a Cohiba, after all, the first new cigar born after the Cuban Revolution. In 1967, Fidel Castro, still watchful after rumors that the CIA had tried to kill him with an exploding cigar, bummed a smoke from one of his bodyguards. Impressed by the quality of the tobacco, he made the Cohiba his private brand, and Avelino Lara, the Michelangelo of rollers, became Castro's personal supplier. Fashioned with thrice-fermented leaves harvested exclusively in the richly loamed Vuelta Abajo region, Cohibas were handed out to visiting dignitaries until 1982, when the brand was commercialized and offered to all takers. The fall of the

Soviet Union meant the disappearance of an automatic buyer for Cuba's sugar crop, and cigars became the nation's leading earner of foreign currency. At once a Communist product demonized by a capitalist embargo, an affront to every notion of clean living in an increasingly litigious and health-obsessed society, and an elite status symbol whose procurement bespeaks its acquirer's influence and position above—rather than merely outside—the law, the Cohiba had lately become immorality incarnate. As a fetish item for phallo-cratic fat cats that emitted mushroom clouds of carcinogenic gas, an Esplendido had the power to grievously offend more Americans than just about any other product in existence. A perfect offering, I thought, for the touchy citizens of California, the state that had spearheaded the ban on public smoking, and one not known for its self-restraint in imposing its vision of public health.

The owner was hardly fazed when I told him about my travel plans. Americans, after all, were among his leading clients, and he was used to offering advice on smuggling.

"You don't want the sniffer dogs to smell them, so just put them in a Ziploc bag. We'll provide one for you. I wouldn't even bother declaring them. If you were bringing down a whole box, I'd suggest you remove the bands. But they're not going to stop you for two or three cigars."

Ringing up my purchase—I threw in a couple of smaller-caliber Havanas for good measure—he allowed himself the slightest of smiles.

"You're going to make a lot of people down there jealous with these, sir," he said. "Forbidden fruit, you know."

If I expected to track down smokers in San Francisco, I was going to have to become a smoker myself.

This was a problem. I had smoked with great gusto and application for a decade, from my teens to mid-twenties. For four years, I'd lived in Paris, where my mornings had generally started with a single *express* at a zinc counter and the first of the day's many forty-centime Chesterfields. I could still remember stubbing out butts in armrest ashtrays on transatlantic flights when airplane No Smoking lights were something more than ornamentation. During a college case of strep throat, I'd even numbed my trachea with anesthestic spray so I could get the nicotine down my windpipe and into my bloodstream. But then something tipped, and the whole thing started to feel shabby. I decided I didn't want to spend the remaining mornings of my life coughing up phlegm and watching an umber-toned slug creeping toward the shower drain. So, at the age of twenty-six, I quit. Apart from my abortive flirtation with cigars in Cuba, it had been years since I'd taken anything more than a cursory puff on a passing cigarette.

So I knew I'd have to work my way up to the moment I could handle my Esplendido without turning gray, gagging, and spitting up my port. One evening, I sat down with a friend and lit up my first real cigarette in over a decade. Alex, an ex-addict himself, has convinced himself he has the willpower to enjoy a civilized puff after dinner. (And perhaps, like the late John Paul II, who, early in his papacy, was said to have smoked only three cigarettes a day—one after each meal—Alex has indeed achieved a mature command over his desires. We'll see.) Alex's smoke of choice is the refined New York brand Nat Sherman, whose glossy brown packs he keeps in his freezer-cum-humidor. He favors Nat Sherman's MCDs—made with "additive-free, natural tobacco," packaged with retro 1930s-style typefaces, each stick wrapped in brown filter paper that is subtly imbued with sugar, like Popeye candy cigarettes for the carriage trade.

The gestures of smoking were riding-a-bicycle familiar; flick of the match toward my body, flame to tip, slow but determined suction through the well-packed tube. Alex and I leaned back in our arm-chairs, and into the reverential silence of ritual. By now it is the most clichéd of aperçus, but, as I squelched a gag, it struck me with force: smoking is a strange thing to do to yourself. Human beings, scientists have noted, are the only mammals that willingly fill their lungs with burning plant matter. (The only known exceptions are lab monkeys, who will overcome their aversion to smoke when it is in the form of crack cocaine.) After ten years of smoke-free living, I felt as if I were thirteen years old again, sucking on my first filched menthol in the back alley behind my parents' house, struggling to keep my feet attached to the ground. I realized I'd just experienced a head rush; but I managed to keep my cool.

"These are smooth," I said to Alex, playing the connoisseur.

It was coming back to me, this smoking thing. First, that quick crank up the roller coaster of bodily distress. Nicotine is extremely toxic. A single full-sized cigar contains enough nicotine to kill two mice, and far fewer milligrams of nicotine are needed to murder a human being than heroin or cocaine. As I stubbed my cigarette out, well before the cone had burnt down to the filter, I remembered the relaxation that follows the stimulation. Nicotine, like alcohol, is a biphasic drug. The first few drinks or puffs stimulate, as your body wrangles with its self-inflicted poisoning; but the next few ounces or deep drags can actually depress the central nervous system. In the calm that followed, I felt as if I'd won a small victory; I'd ridden the roller coaster without white-knuckling the safety bar and returned to the asphalt euphoric, but also soothed. Kid's stuff. The second familiar sensation, though, was regret: the regret of backsliding, of deliberately overwhelming my lungs' cilia, the hardworking cell filaments that beat off irritants, with an aerosol blast of toxic particulates. Nicotine in and of itself is not carcinogenic; it's all the other crap, the thousands of irritants in the tar, that makes cells veer cancerous. The chief danger of nicotine is that it is insidiously addictive; as a drug it's far more dependence-inducing than either alcohol or heroin.

As Alex and I sipped wine and talked about relationships, I kept eyeing the open pack of MCDs on the coffee table. I was being seduced by their elegance, by the tiny silvery logo faintly visible on the brown paper, and, not incidentally, the promise of another dose of nicotine.

Alex noticed the direction of my gaze as he leaned over to refill my glass. "You want another?"

"I'd better not," I said, self-restrained as a pontiff.

The pope, God bless him, had had the right idea.

A wave of the hand from booth number 11, and I was allowed to cross the yellow line.

"Boarding card, passport."

Once again, I was standing in front of a customs official, and once again, I was bearing contraband. This agent was tanned, square-jawed, a young man with boredom in his eyes. Ennui and absolute power are a sinister combination; the wrong word could set off anything from a baggage search to a rectal probe. Though I was standing in a Canadian airport, on the island of Montreal, technically I had entered American territory, and under the 1912 Trading with the Enemy Act, I could be fined up to $250,000 and jailed for up to ten years—potentially in a nonsmoking prison—for carrying Cuban products. (Though, more realistically, they would simply snip my cigars in two on the spot and bar me entry into the United States for the next five years.) A twelve-foot-tall replica of the Statue of Liberty, Kryptonite green and golden-crowned, glared at me accusingly from the other end of the room.

"Where are you going today?" the official asked.

New York and San Francisco, I replied.

"For how long?"

Twelve days.

"What do you do for a living?"

I'm a writer, I said.

This gave him pause. "And will you be doing any journalism while you're in the United States?"

(I had four notebooks and a tape recorder in the backpack on my shoulder.)

No, I said, looking into his eyes. They were gunmetal blue.

He flared my passport at the photo page, slid it through a reader. Nothing beeped.

"Are you carrying any tobacco products today?"

Three cigars, I admitted.

"Cubans?"

Christ—the guy was asking all the right questions.

No, I said. Dominicans.

He was obviously too bored—or maybe I was too Caucasian and too blue-eyed myself—to bother ordering a search. Riffling my passport to a free page, he brought down the rubber stamp. As my luggage was loaded onto a conveyer belt—and with it my Ziploc-wrapped Cohibas—I glanced at my passport.

"U.S. Immigration," the stamp read, the red ink bleeding to the margin. "Admitted."

But I wasn't admitting to anything. Especially not to the fact that I was already smoking my third cigarette in less than half an hour. After all, the smoking lounge of the Nat Sherman shop, right across Forty-second Street from the marble flanks of the New York Public Library's lions, was built for just such indolent exhalation. What's more, it was one of the last places in the once worldly metropolis of New York where one could still legally smoke indoors. After checking into my hotel, I'd ridden the subway to Grand Central Station, pushed my way through revolving doors beneath a statue of a vigilant Indian bearing a sheath of cigars on his outstretched left palm (presumably awaiting the arrival of Christopher Columbus and his syphilitic crew), and stepped into a bygone era of socially acceptable smoking. An Asian-American clerk, with a narrow Cigaratello dangling from her lips, pulled cigarette samples out of wooden drawers:

the cork-toned Phantoms, the multicolored Fantasias, the slightly flattened Havana Ovals. After selecting ten packs of MCDs, I walked up a twisting staircase and past the vaporous confines of a room-sized humidor. The lounge was a rec room for plutocrats: stock quotes paraded across a wide-screen plasma television, wooden-rod-tethered *Wall Street Journals* dangled from a newspaper rack. I sat down in a high-backed leather chair, sipped a free coffee, and lit an MCD.

It had been just over a year since Mayor Michael Bloomberg had banned smoking in the bars and restaurants of the city's five boroughs. The bêtes noires of the previous mayor, Rudolph Giuliani, had been the bared breasts of Forty-second Street and the barely surviving of every other street, but he'd always been a man who appreciated a good smoke: rumor had it that he'd kept a stock of cigars in locker No. 66 of Nat Sherman's humidor. The current mayor, a billionaire who'd spent $72 million on his own campaign, was one of those former smokers who could no longer abide the smell of tobacco. He'd helped batter down a $6.5 billion deficit by doubling parking fines and introducing a tax of $1.50—on top of a state tax of the same amount—on every pack of cigarettes sold in the city.

"If it were up to me," Bloomberg was quoted as saying, "I would raise the cigarette tax so high the revenue from it would go to zero." The price of twenty name-brand cigarettes now averaged $7.50. In less than a year, maintaining a pack-a-day habit would cost a New Yorker the same as a round-the-world plane ticket.

A thin, middle-aged Englishman with a furrowed brow, plagued by facial tics and smoking a slender Nat Sherman cigar, had sat down, quite erect, on the metal chair next to the lounge's faux fireplace. He was talking to an ample fellow from Queens, a caricature of the fully decked fat cat: double-breasted suit, pinkie ring curlicued with illegible gold initials, stubby Honduran smoldering.

"People should be allowed to do what they want to do!" the Englishman was proclaiming stroppily. "I've just come from London.

I couldn't smoke in the plane. I couldn't smoke in the airport. I couldn't even smoke in the taxicab. Now I've just come from the Harvard Club, where I've been staying for the last twenty years. There used to be an enormous cigar bar at the entrance. It is no longer there. And this time I was informed that I would not be allowed to smoke on the premises at all. Apparently, the Nat Sherman store is one of the few places in the entire city where one can smoke indoors."

"Yeah, what are ya goin' do," said the guy from Queens, billowing a cloud in the direction of the stock prices on the plasma screen. "If ya ask me, it's just stupid. In my borough, they just put chairs outside the bars, so half the bar is sitting outside, smoking. They've got drinks in their hands, they're leaving their butts on the sidewalk. Then the neighbors start complaining. It's just trading one problem for another."

"It's more than that," replied the Englishman, straightening his striped tie. "It's a question of *civility*. In London, you would never dream of asking an adult to extinguish a cigarette in a drinking establishment intended for other adults."

Queens was unimpressed by such claims of Old World urbanity. "From what I hear, ya can't even smoke in pubs in Ireland anymore. Ehh," he repeated, "what're ya goin' do."

I lit another cigarette and asked Queens whether he thought the mayor would go down because of the smoking ban.

"The smoking ban's mostly just a tax grab. The government wants it both ways. They get forty-six percent of the price of every cigar I smoke, they also get to look good because they're supposedly taking care of the public health. Bloomberg's going to go down because business hasn't come back like it was supposed to. Unemployment's up. Taxes are up. And nobody likes him.

"Well, welcome to New York, you guys." He stood up, carelessly dismissing the ash from his sleeve, and the out-of-towners from his consciousness. "It ain't like it used to be."

★   ★   ★

I'd been trying to explain this to my French friends Guillaume and Alexandra, with whom I was sharing a hotel room. They were a Parisian couple, in their twenties, and this was their first time in the United States. By North American standards, they were chain-smokers: they smoked before coffee, they smoked before and be-tween courses, they smoked in bed. Guillaume had gone native with Canadian du Mauriers, though Alexandra quickly switched from Gauloises to taxing my stock of Nat Shermans.

I was confident we could find places to smoke indoors. Early reports of reactions to the ban had shown signs of both recalcitrance and inventiveness: an Upper East Side restaurant had permanently parked a twenty-seat limousine outside its doors to allow its patrons to smoke in comfort. An Italian chef had announced a menu that included gnocchi made with Empire English tobacco, and a filet mignon marinated in Golden Virginia. A Latin joint had started selling $12 Nicotinis, made with tobacco-infused vodka, as the "cocktail equivalent of the patch." And a bouncer at a bar called Guernica in the East Village had been fatally stabbed during an argument with two clients who refused to extinguish their cigarettes.

Alexandra was not shy about declaring our mission. On our way to the East Village, she trotted up to a pair of hipsters, asking breathily:

"You know where can we find any smoking bar?" Just in case they were having trouble with her accent, she held her smoldering MCD high.

They exchanged glances, but looked stumped.

"I think there's a place in the Village," the woman said. "But I've only seen people smoking there very late. I just smoke at home now."

All down Third Avenue, it was the same story. People remembered seeing some smokers, somewhere, but they couldn't remember the name of the bar. Finally, on St. Mark's Place, we managed a few cigarettes on the patio of an Irish pub, where most of the clients looked like off-duty cops or firemen. A yakuza-themed Japanese restaurant had a smoking back room, but we had to abandon our sake to retreat to a glassed-off concrete courtyard, filled with rickety benches and ventilation shafts. At the Knitting Factory, after an elaborate process of age verification and hand-stamping, we were permitted to leave again, so we could stand behind a rope that left one foot of sidewalk before the gutter for smokers. Over and over, we heard banished smokers repeating the same mantra: "Ah, what're ya goin' do?" It seemed to have replaced "Excelsior" as the state motto.

The nonsmoker had a new slogan too. When Alexandra approached a man sitting with a friend outside a French bistro in the West Village with her customary ingenuous request for the address of a smoke-easy, she got the response we'd heard a dozen times before.

"You can't smoke in New York City anymore," he said primly. "It's the law."

It's the law? How fucking lame. Fortunately, the guy's friend, a big redhead, was a bit cooler. "You could try the White Horse Tavern. That's the bar where Dylan Thomas drank himself to death. They got a terrace outside."

We were optimistic. Surely a place that had once served a Welsh alcoholic nineteen straight whiskeys in a row would allow a trio of foreigners to smoke outside its doors. We walked to Hudson Street, spotted the Ye Olde England–style neon sign, and chose a table separated from the sidewalk by a waist-high wrought-iron fence. Guillaume discovered that by balancing one haunch on the rail and placing his left foot on the sidewalk, he could reach for his bottle of Sam Adams, smoke his du Maurier, and continue talking to us all at the same time.

But not for long. A broad-shouldered bouncer, in sunglasses and a tan leather jacket, had spotted Guillaume's hand reaching for his beer.

"Excuse me, sir," he boomed. "You are going to have to be *off* of our property if you want to smoke. And that rail you're sitting on *is* our property. So I suggest that you either extinguish your cigarette, or you pay and leave immediately." He crossed his arms and let his mirrored sunglasses do their work. Guillaume stubbed out his cigarette. Later, when the crowd at the door had thinned, the bouncer seemed to regret his severity. He ambled over, leaned against the railing, and talked at us as he worried a toothpick.

"Look, we've just opened our patio for the spring. You gotta understand, from now until Halloween I'm going be dealing with people like you every night. I gotta watch for the underage kids. I gotta watch for the drunks. See that joker at that table over there, trying to take his drink onto the sidewalk so he can smoke? I gotta watch him. If we get ticketed three times, we don't just get a fine. We get shut down. It's no joke anymore. There was a bar round the corner. Everybody knew the guy was letting people smoke late at night. Well, you know what? That bar ain't there anymore. They pulled his license."

Right. By now, we knew the stock response. "Bloomberg, huh?" I said. "What're ya goin' do?"

Alexandra, not easily discouraged, made one last stab at finding a smoke-easy. She approached a handsome woman, in her sixties, impeccably accessorized with trim, pleated slacks, a jaded smile, and a long, thin cigarette. She looked as elegantly intelligent as Mary McCarthy, as reflexively sardonic as Dorothy Parker.

"Smoking bar?" she replied with a gravelly snicker. "Boy, have you come to the wrong town. Why do you think I'm sitting on this bench? Where you from, anyway?

"Paris? God, I've been planning to move to Europe for the last twenty years." She looked at her cigarette ruefully. "Maybe now's the time to do it."

As we walked away, we heard her mutter to the spring air, "First time I've said this, but I'm embarrassed for New York."

Alexandra shook her head. "*Mon Dieu.* It's pretty sad when you have to apologize for your own city."

★   ★   ★

When chain-smoking columnists, particularly British ones, start to rant about the creeping ban threatening to engulf the industrialized world, "California health Nazis" are fingered as the instigators of the modern equivalent of the Reichstag fire. There is some truth to this perception: the antismoking extremists in California can be very extreme indeed. As far back as 1977, the city of Berkeley passed a clean-indoor-air ordinance, and California launched the first state-wide ban on smoking in bars and restaurants in 1998. Not content with ending smoking in enclosed places, Californians turned to the great outdoors: cigarettes were first banned from Solana Beach in 2003, then Santa Monica and its celebrated pier, then from every beach in Los Angeles, creating a thirteen-mile stretch of smoke-free coastline (in spite of efficient grooming machines that removed cast-off Coke cans, broken glass, and cigarette butts from the sand). In 2005, cigarettes were banished from public parks and open spaces in San Francisco, including Golden Gate Park and Union Square. In Davis, a university town northeast of San Francisco, a kind of nadir of folly was achieved: smokers were no longer allowed to stand still on public sidewalks. Like ever-vigilant sharks, they had to be in constant motion while smoking or risk suffocating lest their gills become clogged with citations and infractions.

In New York, I'd said good-bye to Guillaume and Alexandra and hopped a westbound jet. Changing planes in Chicago, I'd realized that traveling the world with a tobacco habit has lately become a bit of a chore. I'd had to walk past dozens of gates until I'd hit an escalator that took me below and beyond the hand-luggage checkers. After sucking on my Fifth Avenue, additive-free Nat Sherman while looking out over a fluorescent-lit multileveled parking lot, across lanes of taxis and shuttle buses, I was forced to go back through security, wait in line for twenty minutes, and remove my shoes. There was nothing particu-larly glamorous about it; at this point, I was merely servicing an addiction.

My friend Maud picked me up at the San Francisco airport and she watched with amusement as I lit up as soon as I'd walked through the sliding doors.

"You know, I don't smoke anymore," she told me, as we loaded the luggage into the back of her car.

This was a shock. Maud seemed to be the least likely person to be influenced by the ambient healthism of California. She was French, outspoken, and worked in the advertising industry. What's more, we'd met on a trek in Nepal, and I seemed to remember her, even at ten thousand feet above sea level, lighting a cigarette as the first light of dawn crept down the crags of Annapurna.

"No—I have just had—how do you say it in English?—a detached lung. So, I am very sorry, but you understand, I won't be smoking with you on this trip."

Fair enough. But her husband, John, had e-mailed to tell me he still enjoyed the occasional butt—or groid, or dirt, as he called them, in his mongrel Minneapolis–West Coast slang—and had promised to accompany me on a tour of the city's smoke-easies. Unlike New York, which was still reeling from the crackdown, San Francisco had had several years to adjust to the prohibition. Though this had been the first metropolis in modern times to utterly ban smoking indoors, something funny had happened. People were still smoking and drinking, indoors, at the same time. In certain bars, at certain times, it was simply understood that you could light up, and the bartender wouldn't do a thing. The names of the bars were passed on by word of mouth; when one got too many fines, another simply took its place. In spite of the healthy West Coast vibe, it made a certain kind of sense: the Bay Area supplied the vast bulk of the attendees of the infamous Burning Man Festival. The culmination of the event was the torching of a giant human effigy, which every September choked the Nevada desert sky with fumes. From the head shops of the Haight to the year-round preparations for the annual immolation, this was a town that fetishized smoke.

"Boss," said John, when he got home from work, "Just off the top of my head, I can name a *dozen* bars where you can smoke, within a ten-block radius of our house. The smoking ban has become kind of a joke. You wanna smoke? Let's go."

We walked from John and Maud's Noe Valley Victorian to a bar on Twenty-second Street, in the Mission. There was a single palm tree outside, a wooden planter filled with butts, a white neon martini glass on the façade. Venetian blinds prevented passersby from peeking inside. The interior was gloomy, art-deco-themed, cozy as a suburban study; the tables were cloth-covered and candlelit; Dusty Springfield swooned over the son of a preacher man on the stereo. Among the half dozen clients were two guys at the far end of the bar, in Birkenstocks and plaid, enveloped in an illicit cloud. I lit an MCD.

"So," I said, when the bartender-waitress brought our Guinness, "what do I do with the ashes?"

Silently, she lifted the candle from the middle of our table and placed it next to the shallow dish it had been sitting in. Instant ashtray.

"You know what?" said John, flicking ashes. "I like to smoke sometimes, but I also like the smoking prohibition. I only have two pairs of jeans, and I hate it when I come home stinking of smoke all the time. Now I've got the choice. If I'm really in the mood for a groid, I can go to a smoking bar. But I can also pick a nonsmoking bar and forget about the laundry."

I'd hear the same sentiments even from tobacconists and hard-core cigar smokers, who conceded they didn't want somebody smoking next to them while they were eating dinner. But there was always an addendum: total prohibition was too extreme. There should be some places where adults could go if they wanted to enjoy a cigarette and a drink at the same time.

The next morning I took a long ride in the 1970s futurist BART train below the East Bay, reemerging in the back lots of Oakland.

Almost thirty years ago, radical Berkeley, birthplace of the free speech movement, had been the first muncipality to ban smoking in the workplace. On campus, signs on every door warned there was NO SMOKING WITHIN 20 FEET OF BUILDING. An insistent carillon concert began in the peak-roofed campanile at the heart of the campus, announcing lunch, and with it, an outflux of scurrying students. Out came bicycle helmets, Frisbees, guitars, muffins, Tupperwared sprouts and carrots—but no cigarettes. At the Doe Memorial Library— smokers had always congregated outside the main library of *my* university—I found a group of students on the brick plaza, a third of them Asian, most of them barefoot. A tanned woman with curly blond hair and a Polarfleece vest lifted her arms over her head, while intoning, "Open your eyes, and gather chi, while inhaling." Eventually I scented tobacco and followed the source. It was a hand-rolled number, protruding from a scraggly yellow beard. I trailed the rebel as he shuffled right into the undergraduate library. I was about to ask him for a light when I noticed he was rummaging through a garbage bin.

Right. It was a tendency I'd already noticed: California's most refractory and conspicuous smokers were the homeless. In the developed world, poverty is now one of the strongest predictors of tobacco addiction. The less money you have, the more likely you are to smoke. In New York, Mayor Bloomberg's approval ratings were lowest among blacks and Latinos—at once his poorest constituents and those most likely to smoke.

Berkeley's smokers apparently didn't show themselves until the afternoon. I walked beneath a latticework of leafless plane trees toward the Moffitt Library, where a half dozen people of all ages were now puffing. One of them was exceptionally pretty. Braided strands of hair, dyed blue, encircled the light brown skin of her oval face. A vertically placed ring pierced her lower lip; her legs, in cargo pants, were crossed as she sat on a circular bench directly beneath an upper balcony (which was clearly lettered NO SMOKING BELOW OVER-HANG).

In my decade of abstinence, I'd forgotten that smoking provides you with an instantly available icebreaker—"Gotta smoke? Gotta light?"—that, with a little imagination, can be parlayed into a full-on conversation, a pub crawl, or the beginning of a beautiful relationship. During the Cold War, spies had been encouraged to carry cigarettes— and to practice using them—even if they didn't smoke themselves: they were the perfect prop for establishing contact with strangers. Lately, bartenders in Dublin and New York had been commenting on a new phenomenon, born of prohibition. A pretty girl would leave her drink on the bartop to go to the sidewalk for a quick puff, and three guys would follow in her wake. Suddenly freed from the meat-market atmosphere, drinkers could casually beg a cigarette or proffer a light, thus starting a conversation that seemed more natural than predatory. The trend-spotters were calling it a renaissance of smirting, of smoking and flirting. (And in North America, it was definitely a safer bet than flirting with Époisses.)

Well, I was single—and, for the time being, at least, I was smoking. Sitting down next to the pretty student, I pulled out my pack of MCDs, lit one, and casually placed the pack next to her.

She glanced my way. "Nat Shermans? I haven't seen those since I left New York. They're *goooood*." Stubbing out her half-smoked American Spirit, she accepted one from the splayed pack. "I smoked for ten years, then I quit for five. I've just started again in the last few months. I guess it's the stress of studying."

Her name was Tamara, and she was finishing a doctorate in electrical engineering.

"I started smoking again in college. During final exams coffee didn't work, but for some reason cigarettes made me more alert. But they also seem to relax me. When you think about it, when you exhale deeply, none of your muscles can tense up. So for five minutes or so, you're doing a little relaxation exercise."

Forget about tai chi, I said. Nicotine yoga!

"We should start a class!" She laughed, exhaling a long plume of smoke. Just then a young Asian woman with a tiny backpack teetered by on platform-heeled rubber clogs. As she traversed Tamara's cloud, she scrunched up her face in disgust and demonstratively waved a hand in front of her face.

Tamara shook her head. "You get that a lot out here. Usually from older people. Baby boomers, people with kids, come right up to you and say, 'Smoking is bad for you, you know.' That would *not* happen out East. Especially in New York. Out there, you don't want to push your opinion on anyone else, 'cos you don't know who you're dealing with. They might be explosive."

Things had changed since Mayor Bloomberg's ban, I told her.

"I don't believe those statistics they're giving out about people quitting. I think smoking is *up* in New York. Certainly after 9/11, everybody I knew who quit started smoking again.

"You know," she continued, "there *is* a lot of self-righteousness in California. But then sometimes people are just being friendly. They say, 'What's a pretty girl like you doing smoking? Don't you know it'll make you wrinkle faster?' "

I gave her a long look in the eyes, took a drag on my cigarette, and said, "Hasn't happened yet."

She took the compliment, smiled, exhaled, looked away.

Damn, this smirting was easy. Possibly even addictive.

"You didn't get her number, boss?" John drawled. "That's lame."

I smothered a comment about professionalism with a gulp of beer. It was Friday night, and John and Maud were taking me on the long-promised smoke-easy pub crawl. We'd started at a place off Guerrero, just down Sixteenth Street from the astonishingly good *crêperie* Ty-Couz. John introduced me to his friends, survivors of the San Francisco dot-com boom-and-bust, most of them repeat Burning Man attendees. One of them was Moss, who was quitting cigarettes gradually. *Very* gradually. He was smoking one last pack of every brand he could find, and chronicling the experience on his Web site, *www.greasepig.com.*

"Yeah, turns out there are a lot of brands in the world," he snickered. "Chunghwa, for example. They weren't that great. Best thing about them was they were Chinese."

Suddenly, a vision out of the 1940s appeared: a cigarette girl, dressed in a pillbox hat and a flared skirt, topped by a Sergeant Pepper–style marching-band jacket.

"That's a Peachy's Puffs girl," explained John, noticing my widening eyes. "They make the rounds of all the bars."

"Hi, I'm Christie!" she said, flouncing up to our table. "You want cigarettes, Milk Duds, mints?" She batted long eyelashes toward the tray that was projecting from her waist. I bought a pack of Camels, thereby transgressing another prohibition. According to an old, rarely enforced law, it is illegal for non residents to buy tobacco in California; retailers are technically supposed to ask their customers for state ID.

So what about it, I asked John. Could I light up inside?

"Naw, better not. Come out back." We went past the fifty-cent-a-game pool table and into a rear courtyard. A miserable concrete no-man's-land that had formerly been used to dump garbage was now the bar's most populated area, the smoking pit. I sat on concrete steps, next to a bleach blonde with kohl-rimmed eyes who was taking quick puffs from a Camel Light. It turned out she owned the place.

Tough town to run a bar in, I observed.

"Yeah. I'm from Washington State—you can still smoke in most bars there. They make bartenders take a course so they know all the laws and their legal obligations. But here in California, where they've got way more regulations, there's no course. I don't have the time to police the whole bar, especially when it's as crowded as it is tonight.

Somebody lights up in the corner—you can't be watching every-where!"

Back inside, nonsmoking Maud was looking a little miffed at her brief abandonment; she'd been left alone at a ghost table, surrounded by pints of beer, each of them covered with coasters to prevent the waitresses from clearing the table. John gave Maud a conciliatory kiss. She sighed. "That's the thing I miss most about smoking. The special club, the bonding. I wanted to go out there with you guys just for the pause. It's like something is going on I don't know about."

Maud told us she was going to call it a night, but John and I kept up our crawl. At a bar in the Financial District, near the Stockton Street tunnel, I asked the bartender whether we could smoke.

"As long as you don't tell me, and I don't see you," he replied.

It succinctly summed up an entire worldview: specifically, the Dutch notion of *gedogen*, which, roughly translated, means "turning a blind eye." In the Netherlands itself, the concept is controversial. For some, it is simply a question of tolerance, a philosophy of "live and let live." For others, it is a symptom of a generalized indifference to the plight of others. (It depends, I suppose, whether you are a tourist smoking pot in an Amsterdam "coffee shop" and marveling at the open-mindedness of the locals, or a Jewish girl trying to survive genocide in an attic.)

On a gentrified stretch of Hayes Street, among the shopfronts of the True Sake Store and Zenzi's Cosmetology Training Center, John and I approached a dark façade. There was a No Smoking sign from the San Francisco Bureau of Environmental Health beneath the neon beer logos, but also a hand-lettered sign, with two crossed knives above the message "Keep this door closed if you know what's good for you." We soon understood the need for the warning: the place was a smokers' den.

"Wow," I said, a little disingenuously, as the bartender handed me a pint, "a place where you can smoke and drink."

"Yeah. Keep it under your hat," she said, out of the side of her mouth. "Just use your coaster as an ashtray."

At a bar called Amber, just north of Market, there wasn't even a pretext of clandestinity. A police car was parked down the street, ticketing a double-parked car, while flagrantly smoking scofflaws were planted on barstools, clearly visible through the windows. I asked the bartender, who looked to be barely past the legal drinking age, whether they'd paid off the cops.

"We're an owner-operated bar," he explained. "That means technically, if you don't have any employees, you can allow your clients to smoke."

He seemed young, I observed, to own his own bar.

"Oh, I'm not the *only* owner. There are like fourteen owners."

I had to laugh. Like the cow-share program that let the lovers of raw milk become part-owners of cows, or the buyers of the raisin cakes that magically turned into wine during Prohibition, it was another heartening example of the ingenuity used to circumvent prohibitions.

John told me there was one last place I had to see. Buried deep in the Mission, it was an Irish bar, and by one thirty in the morning it was as rambunctious as a county Cork pub overrun with tinkers.

"This is an IRA bar," said John, pushing open a door into a long room, blue with smoke. "They don't give a shit about American smoking laws."

Just in case, I offered the bartender, who was wearing a Manchester United jersey, a Nat Sherman.

"What is it, then?" he said with a thick Belfast brogue. "Heroin?"

No, I said, it's a cigarette.

"In that case"—he laughed—"I'm fine. I've got me own."

After only a couple of days of pub-crawling, I'd compiled a list of at least fifteen smoking bars, from the Financial District to the Castro. I followed up with my own inspections. Some taverns had adapted by creating smoking rooms: closed-off sections, with space heaters and sliding garage-style doors that opened directly onto the street—a year-round possibility given San Francisco's clement weather. At peak hours these rooms were inevitably more crowded with drinkers—and thus more amenable to smirting—than the bar itself.

Finally I called up the Department of Public Health to find out what they thought about all of this. I met Thomas Rivard, a senior environmental health inspector, at a carrot-juice-and banana-muffin kind of café he'd picked on Mission Street. A youthful-looking middle-aged man with blue eyes, and a well-ironed blue shirt open at the collar, Rivard was tall and clean-cut, his long fingers and slightly graying hair completely unstained by nicotine.

"Oh, sure!" Rivard said. "We know there are bars that still allow smoking. We've got twenty-five inspectors, each covering his own district. Of the eleven hundred bars in the city, there are probably between thirty and sixty where people still smoke, and that doesn't include the ten or so owner-operated bars. Usually they're smaller places, neighborhood bars."

The first version of the antismoking law, which applied to restaurants and other workplaces, had been introduced in 1995.

"When the state legislature passed the law, I get the feeling they never really thought through how it pertained to bars—it was intended for all workplaces. But you couldn't say a bartender or a cocktail waitress was less of an employee than anyone else, so bars kind of got looped in. They made an attempt to come up with a ventilation standard for bars"—which would mean installing expensive, state-of-the-art air purification systems—"but when you're dealing with a human carcinogen, it's very difficult for anybody to say what's an acceptable amount."

When the law covering bars came into effect on New Year's Day, 1998, Rivard's role—enforcement—began.

"In the beginning, we made the mistake of using the police, and we'd go into bars and give tickets, seventy-six dollars per infraction, to bar patrons. And compliance was very poor—at first, something like fifty percent of bars were still allowing people to smoke. We were being called 'smoking fascists.' In this one bar in Haight-Ashbury, a client said to me, 'If the police weren't here, I'd take this pool cue and beat the shit out of you.' All we were doing was creating sympathy for the smokers who were being issued tickets."

Finally, the Health Department started concentrating on the owners themselves. Since a tavern owner could easily write off a $500 ticket (the fine for a third offense) as a cost of doing business, the department started suing repeat offenders under the Unfair Business Practice statutes of California, saying that certain bars gained a competitive advantage by permitting clients to smoke. The stratagem worked, according to Rivard:

"Some of the settlements have been for amounts as high as ten thousand dollars, and the judge issues an injunction to prohibit smoking in any way, shape, or form. So if you're caught again, you're actually in contempt of court."

I brought up New York's zero-tolerance model, and the resentment it seemed to be creating.

"There's a point when overzealous enforcement may well yield a result that's not consistent with the greater good of society. In San Francisco, we know there are places that allow smoking late at night, for example. It's not that we're saying it's okay; but you have to look at the other problems. Do you want people drunk out on the sidewalk, smoking, in a residential neighborhood, late at night? Or if the bar's in a dangerous neighborhood, do you want people forced into the street? The compliance rate is in the eighty-to-ninety percentile range now, and we can live with that. The net effect is that most bars are pretty nice places to drink now."

I had one last question for Rivard. When I'd first called up the

Health Department, the recorded message had said, "If you are calling to request a Cannabis ID Card, press three." I'd been told that with a single doctor's approval (for complaints ranging from alcoholism to constipation), you could get a card that would allow you to obtain cheap and legal marijuana from the city's many medical cannabis dispensaries. It was a dodge straight out of Prohibition, when doctors wrote prescriptions for medicinal whiskey. But were you allowed to smoke on the premises?

Rivard chuckled. "You can smoke marijuana in those places, but not tobacco. I was born in San Francisco, and I tell you, it's a hard town to be an enforcement officer in. We're zealous about tobacco; loose on marijuana. It can be a little hard to explain to outsiders."

Nice enough guy, I thought, as Rivard left for his afternoon round of inspections. But all through the interview, I'd been fighting an irrational urge to pull out a cigarette, light it, and casually blow a cloud of smoke in his face. Picking up my notebook, I hurried to the back of the café and asked if there was anywhere I could smoke. The owner pointed to a side door, where an outdoor terrace ran the length of the café.

There was an ashtray on every table.

In Sherlock's Haven, a fine tobacconist and bastion for cigar smokers in the shadow of the Embarcadero Center, Marty Pulvers was spluttering, a stubby Arturo Fuente Rothschild Maduro in one hand. I was smoking one of my smaller Cohiba cigars and managing not to retch. The regulars, including a gray-headed fellow in a wheelchair and an older Asian woman, were all enjoying Dominican cigars next to the humidor, and looking at my genuine Havana with what, I liked to think, was well-disguised envy. In a little over a week, I'd become a grown-up smoker; I was now averaging fifteen cigarettes a day and could savor the taste of a high-quality cigar without discomfort.

Marty, emphatic, pugnacious, was definitely not Left Coast. More

Lower East Side, with an attitude to match. A hand-painted sign on his front door read, IN CONSIDERATION OF OUR CUSTOMERS SENSIBILITIES, PLEASE DO NOT BRING STINKY FAST-FOOD BURGERS AND FRIES INTO OUR STORE. I asked him whether he really had a problem with fast food.

"Yeah! That stuff is putrid!" he fumed, with the flue-cured tones of the lifelong smoker. "If we're really worried about the health of those who don't have the volitional choice to be in a nonsmoking environment, then why aren't there laws against bringing a three-year-old into a fast-food place and having that junk crammed down the little bastard's gullet? This prohibition of tobacco—and if it's priced and taxed beyond one's means, and there's no place to use it, then what else is it but a prohibition?—has nothing to do with health. It's just snotty morality, like the puritans who imposed alcohol prohibition back in the 1920s. If you let the government decide what's healthy, where does it end? They're certainly obligated to provide information, but then they might end up banning everything—including fast food."

I recognized the libertarian argument. It was founded on distrust of government, and its exponents liked to point out that the first societywide, health-based ban on smoking in public had been initiated by Adolf Hitler, who, in addition to being a mass murderer and a vegetarian, was also a nonsmoker. For many libertarians, smoking was an inalienable individual right; give an overbearing government an inch, and they'd ban chewing gum, semiautomatics, and whistling in public. There were clearly degrees, though. Most jurisdictions were merely limiting the places where people could smoke. The only nation with a prohibition worthy of the name was the tiny Himalayan kingdom of Bhutan, which, in 2003, had actually banned the sale of tobacco in any form.

Marty distractedly dribbled ashes over a file folder as he looked for the relevant fact sheet. ("Hey, Doc, how are ya? . . . Good, thanks," he said, greeting a man with a briefcase who was inspecting the jars of pipe tobacco.) "Oh, yeah, because the fact is, we *can* provide clean air inside if we so choose! We could give bar owners or restaurateurs the chance to install an air purification system that meets some kind of standards! But the government decided to impose the law, unilaterally, without ever establishing those standards. At rush hour every day there's gridlock and diesel buses running their engines outside my doors. The air in well-ventilated bars could easily be cleaner than the air outside!"

"There's a little hypocrisy going on too, isn't there?" I suggested. "I mean, there are a number of prominent politicians who like to smoke. And not just any cigars. Cubans, like the one I'm smoking."

Marty gratified me with a knowing smirk. When it came to the fetish item of plutocrats, the double standard was common knowledge. Before John F. Kennedy announced the 1962 trade embargo on Cuba, he got his press secretary to lay in a stock of twelve hundred Petit Upmanns, his favorite Havanas. Mayor Bloomberg had declined comment when, at a dinner at the St. Regis, some of New York's leading financiers pulled out cigars, flagrantly violating his own law. (As the populist *New York Post* put it, "public puffing" is okay with the nanny mayor as long as "you're a fellow gazillionaire.") *Cigar Aficionado* repeated a rumor that actor-director Rob Reiner had pushed through a proposition raising California tobacco taxes to fund public schools, saying, "It won't affect me. I smoke Cubans." And the current governor of California, Arnold Schwarzenegger, had made news because he'd had a smoking terrace installed in the capitol in Sacramento. Apparently it was exempted from legislation stipulating one must stand twenty feet from public building entrances, because the law referred to linear horizontal feet, not vertical feet—and the terrace was on the second floor.

"Yeah," said Marty, "as I understand it, it's even legal for congresspeople to bring back Cuban cigars when they go on their 'educational' trips to Havana."

"No!" said his Asian-American colleague, puckering his mouth in mock outrage.

"Yeah!" shot back Marty. "You're stunned, huh?"

In another cigar store, San Francisco's oldest, the owner had given me his card and offered to show me some vintage 1972 Monte Cristos.

Marty, seeing all this was going on the record, opted for the safest course: denial. "I simply don't touch Cubans. People are always saying, 'C'mon, sell me your Havanas, I know you got 'em!' But I don't have them! I don't need to stay awake at night, worrying I'm going to get caught."

But Jacky, a regular customer from the East Bay, with a shaved head and a diamond stud in his left year, had nothing to lose by talking about Cuba. "Sure, I went down to Havana, ended up buying fifteen thousand dollars' worth of cigars. We flew back into Canada. Paid for our whole trip—and more—selling the cigars for a nice profit when we got back. I gotta say, the United States is so far behind the rest of the world when it comes to Cuba. Maybe when Fidel Castro dies, we'll lighten up on this stupid embargo."

As I left Sherlock's Haven, leaving the cigars slumbering in their maple boxes, a quote popped into my head, muttered in a Midwestern monotone with devilish relish: "Hypocrisy is the greatest luxury."

The speaker had been William S. Burroughs, that connoisseur of disgust, and when he'd said it, his wrinkles had been overwhelmed by an impish grin. When it comes to the rarefied, the expensive, and the prohibited, it has always been one of the great pleasures of the elite to publicly profess a standard from which they privately exempt themselves. The greatest hypocrisy, of course, is that of national governments that caution against tobacco use while raking in taxes; in the United States, for example, cigarettes generate more money for local and federal administrations than any other product on the market. If most—or even some—of that money were being devoted to treating addictions of all kinds, governments might be in a better moral position. But taxing tobacco so heavily seems more self-serving than fair; after all, if you follow a strictly utilitarian calculus, tobacco is a pretty good deal for the coffers of the government. Smoking causes few health problems during the productive years of the working population, then neatly kills them off before they can collect social security and pension payments. But the ruling classes have been exploiting the double standard since at least 1604, when James I wrote his screed "A Counterblaste to Tobacco," denouncing the Stygian weed as a "filthy novelty."

Rather than banning tobacco use outright, however, he pragmatically raised taxes by 4,000 percent, ensuring a revenue stream that has been fattening national treasuries ever since.

Was the United States simply going through one of its periodic paroxysms of antitabagism? After all, this wasn't the first time tobacco had been satanized and repressed in America. Sales of the "devil's weed" were banned by the Washington State legislature in 1893, and by the turn of the last century, Lucy Gaston—a spinster schoolteacher who spiritedly argued that the poison furfural led to delinquency and the unmistakable contortions of "cigarette face"—had successfully lobbied to have cigarette sales prohibited in Tennessee, North Dakota, and Iowa.

In his matchless analysis of the semiotics of smoking, *Cigarettes Are Sublime*, author Richard Klein argues that tobacco is regularly demonized as cycles of "healthism" overtake America. But then some crisis intervenes—a world war, a depression—and smoking experiences a resurgence. For Klein, the cigarette, at once an instigator and reliever of anxiety, is also a reification of the anxiety over death that suffuses all of life. A cigarette allows one to hold an agent of mortality between stained fingers, watch it smolder to the end, and dismissively flick the butt—a memento mori, a little splinter of death—toward the sewer grate. In times of crisis, when the ambient fatalism is over-whelming and comforts are few, smoking becomes a socially accept-able way of thumbing one's nose at death. Hence the ubiquitousness of coffin nails in soldiers' rations, in prisons, as props in film noirs, and as the accessories for doomed rebels of all stamps, from Humphrey Bogart to James Dean.

Personally, I could never *not* have known that smoking was harmful. In 1966, the year I was born, the U.S. surgeon general forced cigarette manufacturers to put the first messages on packages warning that smoking was a health hazard. (In many nations, includ-ing Canada, these warning labels now splatter half the pack with graphic images of disintegrating gums and blackened bronchi. In Europe and Singapore, the message is stark and simple: SMOKING KILLS. In the developed world, one of the few throwbacks is Japan, where the government monopolizes the industry, and there are eight cigarette machines on the premises of the Health Ministry alone. In Tokyo, the labels are still politely tentative: "As smoking might injure your health," they entreat, "please be careful not to overdo it.") Frankly, I didn't need to be told smoking was a bad thing: I felt sick, intoxicated, the first time I sucked on that menthol at the age of thirteen. It was a thrilling poisoning, though, one that bore closer investigation; with some application, I overcame my initial distaste. It is smoking cigarettes, I suspect, rather than marijuana, that is the most universal gateway drug experience: daring this first illicit intoxication at an early age opens up the doors to everything from slamming tequila shots to mainlining crystal meth.

There may be something to the notion that we are merely living through another of history's hysterical cycles of "healthism." But this time around, the public-smoking ban that started in California—and now includes five other American states, three Canadian provinces, Norway, Malta, Italy, Sweden, and Ireland—is threatening to become a developed-world norm. By 2007, Scotland, Australia, and England will have similar bans in place. (Cuba, where half of all adults smoke, shocked smokers worldwide by announcing a ban on public smoking in 2005.) The spread of these restrictions is backed by a long-growing understanding that cigarettes are a product that, if used as intended, will kill one quarter of their consumers. What's more, tobacco is a substance—one of the few discussed in this book—that has the potential, through secondhand smoke, to directly affect not only the body of its consumer, but also the body of the person next to him. Given the growing evidence about the dangers of secondhand smoke, John Stuart Mill, the nineteenth-century philosopher whose defense of individual sovereignty has made him a darling of libertarians, would probably have been willing to concede that society had a right to limit tobacco's use precisely to "prevent harm to others."

Meanwhile, tobacco manufacturers don't have to pray for the next world war or a new global depression to boost sales: their market is still developing in the Philippines, where fully three quarters of adult males now smoke, and China, population 1.3 billion, where almost two thirds of all men are smokers. Today, 75 percent of the world's smokers live in developing nations.

The custom of smoking the leaves of the tobacco plant, that bizarre and compulsive behavior that both distinguishes the moderns from the ancients and man from the other animals, is particularly suscep-tible to social setting. When maintaining a habit becomes a huge pain in the ass—when you have to pay an hour's wages for a single pack or walk through a mile of airport for your Camel—then there's a chance that a certain percentage of smokers will opt to quit with antide-pressants, hypnotherapy, the patch, or a box of nicotine gum. When fewer people around you smoke, you are less likely to be tempted— and young adolescents, who, legally at least, are below the age of volition, will be less likely to start a habit that seems to be more hardwired into mind and body the earlier in life it starts. Call it peer pressure or a law of the market: when a commodity that is enjoyable and addictive is also both cheap and socially acceptable, it also tends to be widely used.

On the other hand, aggressive social engineering tends to explode in the faces of its instigators, like a cheap vaudeville cigar. If you boost taxes, then smuggling—between states, provinces, and nations—becomes rampant, turning bootleggers into millionaires. (It is estimated that a third of the 5.5 trillion cigarettes consumed in the world every year are smuggled. In Australia, smuggled tobacco from Asia, called chop-chop, is sold in corner stores, and in eastern Canada, you can buy tax-free Native, Seneca, or Omaha brand cigarettes from peddlers on the street. For much of the 1990s, Philip Morris shipped tax-free cigarettes to places like Gibraltar, Cyprus, and Malta, knowing full well they would be smuggled back into the European Union and sold on the black market.) Since Mayor Bloomberg banned smoking in New York City, a steady stream of traffic has been crossing the Hudson River to fumigate the bars of Hoboken, New Jersey, where the restrictions don't apply. In the boroughs, hole-in-the-wall neighborhood joints are handing out saucers to customers, in lieu of ashtrays. An investigation by a team of Columbia School of Journalism graduate students found that since tobacco taxes have been raised, massive bootlegging has been going on in Harlem, the Bronx, and Queens, with crack dealers switching to far-less-risky street-corner sales of cigarettes, purchased on Indian reservations or in neighboring states with less exorbitant taxes. (The report estimated that, after only a year, the city was losing $400 million annually in taxes to the bootleggers.) There was currently a war of statistics going on, with the mayor's office claiming that thanks to their unique mix of zealous enforcement, increased taxes, and antismoking educational programs, over one hundred thousand citizens had quit tobacco in a single year, and that 10,600 more bar and restaurant jobs had been created. Meanwhile, the New York Nightlife Association was claiming exactly the opposite: that there had been a 17 percent drop in waitering jobs and an 11 percent drop in the number of bartenders.

In San Francisco, I had a conversation that seemed to sum up the inherent dangers of overaggressive social engineering. I bummed a light from Lance, who was smoking a Camel Light outside Delaney's Wash & Dry on Lower Haight as his clothes dried. He was from Kansas City, where smoking was still allowed, and he was fed up with the vibe in California.

"Nobody needs to tell me smoking is going to kill me," he said. "I hear it every day in the news, on billboards; I'm constantly bombarded, even by people at work. And it only makes me want to smoke more!"

I brought up the idea of counterwill, a psychological term that describes rebelling against adult control by self-destructively reacting against the parental vision of a child's best interests.

"It's counterwill, exactly!" said Lance. "And you still have that impulse as an adult, which makes the problem very hard." Lance had tried to quit before, with the patch, but it had never worked, and he'd got little advice or support from his doctor. "They invest time and money into campaigns to prevent people from smoking, but once you're a smoker, it's like you're evil—this abandoned child, and you shouldn't come back until you've quit."

It was true: for all the sanctimonious talk I'd heard about support for quitters, I'd noticed that forty-eight Nicorettes—a two day's supply—cost up to $44 in the local drugstores.

Lance was an administrative assistant at a law firm that specialized in getting licenses for bars and restaurants. Instead of whacking the entire city with the stick of prohibition, he argued, why not dangle some kind of carrot?

"They should have implemented a tax incentive for bars to go nonsmoking or not. If the incentive was big enough, it would become known as a nonsmoking bar, and people who wanted that kind of environment could go there. Give people some kind of choice!"

It was the most sensible public policy suggestion I'd heard so far. It's a long municipal tradition to control the number of establishments that can serve alcohol by issuing a limited number of liquor licenses. Why not do the same thing with smoking bars? Lance took a last suck on his Camel, tossed it aside with disgust. "They argue that if they raise taxes, people are going to stop buying cigarettes. I remember when it cost me a buck for a pack. These days, I'm paying five dollars. And I'm not going to stop buying them until I actually decide to quit, no matter how high they raise the price."

It was counterwill at its best. I felt the same as Lance: in the context of the Californian prohibition, smoking was irresistible. Every time you lit up, you crossed an invisible line, joining a private club that snubbed its nose at the reigning healthism. Not coincidentally, you got to meet the coolest guys, the most interesting girls—like Moss, Tamara, and Lance—and distance yourself from an oppressively clean-living majority. San Francisco's smoke-easy culture was how I imagined Prohibition-era Chicago's speakeasy scene, a parallel society founded on scorn for puritanism, with killer tobacco rather than bathtub gin as the demonized substance. After only a few years, San Francisco, where the modern smoking ban had started, had eased into a state of mature prohibition. Already, citizens, bar owners, and restaurateurs had found a dozen imaginative ways around absurdly restrictive laws that the compliance officers had given up all hope of completely enforcing. In New York City, Oslo, Rome, and Dublin, it was still the early days, and the opposition was busy getting organized. Give them a few years, I thought, and those cities would have as many smoke-easies as San Francisco.

I was having fun flirting with my Nat Shermans, feeling like an outlaw. But by now I'd been smoking for a couple of weeks, and I was up to a pack a day. I noticed my teeth were yellowing, and my face was getting puffy, with a slightly gray undertone. A metal band seemed to have been permanently strapped across my chest. Worst of all, as soon as I got out of bed, I was thinking about my first cigarette; I had to force myself to defer the impulse until at least after breakfast.

Nicotine had got its claws into me again.

That was why I'd quit cigarettes in the first place. The only complete pleasures, I'd come to realize, were voluntary ones. When an infernal hankering has robbed you of your free will, when you are compelled by commingled physical and psychological need to succumb to a predictible euphoria, what you are feeling is more relief than joy. I had hoped that, after ten years of abstinence, I would be able to achieve the papal restraint and maturity of my friend Alex, with his occasional after-dinner cigarette. But nicotine obviously answers a different need in me, and the slope from dalliance to addiction is as irreversible, and as breathtaking, as a gondola ride to an Alpine crag. The notion that one can flirt with one's demons, I was beginning to fear, might be the hubristic act of a Faustian dandy: all it takes is the end of an affair, a death in the family, or a slide into depression for the flirtation to turn into the beginning of a really nasty relationship.

I still had my Esplendido to smoke. I'd considered pulling it out at the owner-operated Occidental Cigar Bar, but was willing to settle for silencing the deprived locals with a less ostentatious, but no less Cuban, small-caliber Larrañaga. (An architect sitting on the next stool had opined, "Cuba started cranking out cigars to supply the international market back in the nineties. And, personally, I think the quality declined." Well, I thought, he would say that, wouldn't he? He was smoking a Dominican label called Flor de Cuba, a lousy Havana wannabe.) I finally burned my Esplendido on the altar of smirting, at a bar called The Odeon, deep in the Mission. The bartender, Flash, a cyclone with a whitening goatee and a biker's leather vest, whipped me up an oversize whiskey sour. Though he gleefully boasted of having been called the "evilest man in America" by Pat Robertson for his role in corrupting the youth of America at the Burning Man Festival—and told anecdotes about delivering smuggled cigarettes to seniors in Arizona ("I tell ya, I felt like the Good Humor man driving down the street, handing out cartons!")— he was a nonsmoker himself.

"You gotta take it outside!" he said, spotting my cigar. "We've had enough problems with the police."

I'd been talking to a massage therapist named Linda. I mentioned that I had a Cuban cigar in my pocket.

"Really?" Linda said. "I've never smoked one. I'd kind of like to try."

We stepped outside, onto Mission Street. I remembered reading that Freud attributed a lust for smoking to a childhood failure to overcome an obsession with "lip eroticism," an ailment with which he was apparently at peace, since he was known to smoke up to twenty cigars a day. Linda and I puffed away. After about fifteen minutes, with only minimal progress down the shaft, we agreed that the process was feeling like a bit of a chore.

A police car pulled up in front of the crowd. A roof-mounted spotlight scanned the crowd, lingering over the stogie in my mouth. Shit, I thought, busted with a Cuban.

But the cop wasn't interested in my flaming contraband; he strode past Linda and me and tried the door to verify it was locked. It was two A.M., closing time, and San Francisco was shutting down for the night. In one of the cities where the smoking ban had started, prohibition had obviously reached its mature phase: accommodation.

I stubbed out the $65 Esplendido and said to Linda, "You know, what I really want is another cigarette."

"Yeah," she said, as we walked down Mission, continuing our smirtation. "You want to feel that smoke in your lungs, not your mouth." She lit my Nat Sherman for me.

I was definitely hooked.

· DIGESTIF ·

Absinthe: A superpotent poison:
one glass and you're dead. Journalists drink it
while they're writing their articles. Will surely
be the end of the French army. Has killed
off more soldiers than the Bedouins.

—*Gustave Flaubert,*
The Dictionary of Received Ideas

6

ABSINTHE *SUISSE*

One Glass and You're Dead

I'D WANTED TO try absinthe ever since I'd seen its name in print.

The first time must have been in one of the expatriate memoirs I devoured as a teenager. Was it an allusion, already nostalgic, to prewar life in one of Henry Miller's Parisian confessionals? An anecdote about the Green Fairy in a volume of Anaïs Nin's diaries? Probably neither. By the time the Lost Generation made it to Paris and started their serious drinking, the belle époque idyll of *poètes maudits* and decadents had already been ravaged by mustard gas and shell shock, and absinthe had been banned in France for almost a decade. In 1920, the resourceful Ernest Hemingway discovered it was still available in Spain. "One cup of it," the narrator of *For Whom the Bell Tolls* recalls, "took the place of the evening papers, of all the old evenings in cafés, of all the chestnut trees that would be in bloom now this month." But a terse journal entry was more suggestive of debauched youth-hostel antics: "Got tight last night on absinthe and did knife tricks. Great success shooting the knife underhand into the piano."

Absinthe, then, was a symbol of waking dreams and excessive behavior, of a lost era of bohemian community and clandestinity.

Traveling through Europe in the 1990s, I'd had my first glass at the Marsella, an agreeably dilapidated bar in Barcelona's Barrio Chino. There, the drinking was preceded by an elaborate ritual. Sugar cubes soaked in absinthe were poised on a three-tined fork, lit on fire until the alcohol burned off, then dropped, molten and caramelized, into the oily-looking liquid. Topped up with cold water, my brandy glass became the crucible for an irresistible alchemy of opacity, as the liquid clouded and turned an opalescent green. With the burnt sugar leavening the herbal bite, the taste was bitter and sweet, complex and corrupt, suggestive of the lost vices of extinct aristocrats. I congratulated myself on my diligence: I'd tracked down my absinthe; a teenage dream had been fulfilled.

Upon closer examination, though, the bar proved to be filled with hipsters in their twenties, most of them shouting over the music in English, and being served by a burly, surly barman with an Australian accent. It was the kind of ersatz expat scene you could find in Prague, Amsterdam, Reykjavík, or whatever other European city happened to be hip that year. Fortunately, I was soon drunk enough not to quibble about authenticity.

When I wrote an article about the experience, an editor asked the inevitable question: "Are you sure you had authentic absinthe? I mean, the same kind that got Oscar Wilde off his tits?" I launched into a spirited defense of my intoxication: I'd had five glasses, and the experience was neither the sloppy, belly-bloating blottitude of beer nor the full body blow of bourbon. I'd felt quick-witted yet tranquilized, an alert mind observing a plastered body with amused detachment. Even the hangover was remarkable: I'd slept till noon and then taken the metro to the beach, where I lay prone in the sun, oozing toxins, until the jackals stopped chewing out my belly and the larvae had finished tunneling through my brain.

"Authentic absinthe—definitely," I affirmed with full journalistic authority. The piece ran and was later anthologized. My claim to absinthe had been copyrighted. I'd become, in a small way, a possessor of the myth.

That was in 1997. Over the next few years, I watched with the jaundiced eye of the initiate as a full-blown absinthe fad developed. A group called Green Bohemia, made up of musicians and writers from the British magazine *The Idler*, started importing a Czech brand named Hill's to England, a nation where the drink had never been popular enough to be banned. (I tried a bottle of Hill's in Vienna. It looked like Windex, tasted like Listerine, and came on like agricultural rum. Overproof vodka, I concluded, spiked with food coloring.) In the French Quarter and the West End, absinthe was promoted as the cocktail of the new millennium. Johnny Depp, playing a psychic detective, debauched himself on jet-black opium and emerald absinthe as he tracked Jack the Ripper in the movie *From Hell*. Certain brands—Absente, Versinthe, and the Hill's I'd found in Austria—started showing up on North American liquor store shelves. I snickered at the hype: Hill's and the brands being imported were nothing like the absinthe I'd had in Spain, still less like the drink of nineteenth-century boulevardiers and flâneurs. Robbed of its essential herbs, the modern version was just high-test booze with a curlicued label: a trendy and overpriced tipple for a passing novelty market.

Inevitably, though, I began to wonder. Had there been anything authentic about my experience in Barcelona? I started Googling around the Internet. In the past few years, it turned out, an international absinthe underground had sprouted from Uruguay to New Zealand, by way of New Orleans and Manchester, a scene with distinctly gothic undertones. On louchedlounge.com, makers of "hogsmack"—from the German *Hausgemacht*, for "homemade"—traded tips, but even the most enthusiastic partisans wouldn't claim hallucinations or waking dreams. Reading their exchanges, which often degenerated into exchanges of porn, was like being in a rec room full of thinteen-year-olds, gagging on their first joint of loosely rolled homegrown, unable to agree whether they'd really caught a buzz. Meanwhile, mediocre Spanish absinthe—which retails for €16 at the Madrid airport's duty-free shop—was being auctioned off for $75 a bottle on eBay.

When it comes to absinthe, authenticity seems to lie in the presence of a single herb: wormwood (from the Anglo-Saxon *ver mod*, or "man-inspiraring," perhaps a reference to its unsubstantiated aphrodisiac qualities). Its active ingredient, thujone, is a constituent of Chartreuse, Vicks VapoRub, vermouth, and Absorbine Jr. In high doses, some researchers claimed, it was a hallucinogen; medical studies, dating from the 1970s, said it acted on the brain's cannibinoid receptors—suggesting that the fin de siècle decadents were merely tripping on a groovy THC-like high. I downloaded an article from a journal called *Current Drug Discovery*, in which several types of absinthe had been subjected to gas chromatography analyses. According to the author, the products being passed off as authentic in Prague and Barcelona contained virtually no thujone. Surprisingly, even a duly sampled and volatilized bottle of 1900 vintage Pernod absinthe contained only trace amounts of the substance. The highest levels were found in a bottle of moonshine absinthe, purchased in a a little valley in Switzerland, a brand the paper referred to as La Bleue. Other Web sites described it as the "holy grail" of absinthe, adding, on the subject of its availability: "Bootlegged—Good luck!"

A miracle. I'd localized authenticity—a quality, in my experience, whose defining characteristic is that it always lies elsewhere.

The journey would have to start in France. Absinthe, once the country's national aperitif, was suddenly experiencing a revival, which was a distinct change from its status only a few years ago. In the late 1990s, whenever I'd asked barmen and wine shop owners about absinthe, they'd given me the same knee-jerk, spitfire response: "Absinthe? *Non non non. C'est la boisson qui rend fou!*"—"The drink that makes you crazy!'"—which was the exact phrasing of the anti-alcohol slogan temperance campaigners had used in the 1890s. In the collective memory of the French, absinthe turned Paul Verlaine from Parnassian genius to Latin Quarter bum, sent Henri de Toulouse-Lautrec to the sanatorium, and convinced Vincent van Gogh that a severed ear might make a charming keepsake.

An older and shakier van Gogh, already lighter by one lobe, ended his life in Auvers-sur-Oise, a riverside village that now lies within the orbit of Paris's northern suburbs. I parked my rented car in a lane along which he carried his easel to paint in the upper pastures and walked toward a modest building of buff-hued fieldstones and green shutters. An oversize spoon, shaped like the Eiffel Tower and bolted to the house's upper floor, announced I'd found the Musée de l'Absinthe.

After inspecting the exhibits—tapering glasses with boll-shaped protuberances on their stems; metal trowels as sinister as Victorian gynecological instruments—I introduced myself to curator Marie-Claude Delahaye, France's leading historian of absinthe. Clad in an elegant summer dress and a pearl necklace that set off her coppery red hair, Delahaye didn't correspond to my image of a scholar of debauchery. She was petite, precise, pedantic—and intensely possessive of her obsession.

"One day, at the flea market at Clignancourt, I found this strange slotted spoon," she recalled. "The dealer said it was used to drink 'absinthe,' which he explained was an alcohol that had been forbidden because it drove people crazy. There were two words in particular that interested me: *forbidden*, and *crazy*." Her flea market find would become the keystone of the museum's collection, and in 1983 Delahaye published a book-length social history of absinthe.

"I was the first one to start talking about absinthe again," she said. "It's thanks to my research, the connections I made between the artistic and political milieux, that people today say absinthe is mythical." Delahaye, an instructor of university-level cellular biology, did her research well. In 1805, Henri-Louis Pernod, who had inherited a recipe for an extract of wormwood from his father, set up a distillery in Pontarlier, a town in the French Jura. His salesmen spread the new aperitif through France, but it was especially appreciated in hot southern cities such as Marseille. In 1830, the first boats of the African Battalion left to conquer Algeria, with casks of absinthe in their holds: the regimental doctors hoped a strong alcohol would purify the local water and stave off malaria. Once they'd picked up the habit, the officers brought it back to the capital, and in turn the Parisian bourgeoisie took to ordering the alluring emerald tipple they saw the mustachioed conquerors of Africa drinking at cafés.

By the 1860s, absinthe had become the ultimate symbol of sophisticated languor, and *l'heure verte*—the green hour, absinthe time—came to stretch from five to seven o'clock. Much of the appeal lay in the ritual. Spidery-limbed absinthe fountains adorned the circular tables of the sidewalk terraces on the *grands boulevards*. The drinker turned a spigot, and cool water trickled from a cylindrical upper chamber made of glass through one of four drooping spouts. At the rate of one drop a second, the water fell on a sugar cube poised on a pierced and filigreed spoon (an implement usually more spatulate than concave) that spanned the rim of a tapering, short-stemmed glass. As each drop of sugared water hit the shot of clear, 140-proof absinthe at the bottom of the glass, the essential plant oils—soluble in alcohol, but not in water—went opaque, streaking the liquid with meteoric trails of opal or emerald. Gradually, as the ideal proportion of five parts water to one part absinthe was attained, the preparation went completely opaque. (This was the *louche*, or "clouding," a term that in English still describes somebody whose background is a little murky.) Beneath the exhalations of anise, fennel, hyssop, and melissa lay the titillatingly maleficent odor of acrid wormwood, like a toxic toadstool lurking in a pine forest's undergrowth.

"It was an effect of fashion," said Delahaye. "It was the first time women, who didn't consume much liquor until then, really started drinking in public. It was also the first time people had tasted fresh plant flavors in an aperitif; the first time they added cold water to their drink. The whole ritual—the spoons, the fountains, the tall glasses—corresponded to a century of new technologies, of new creativity." In the 1870s, as the phylloxera aphid chewed its way through the nation's grape vines, the price of wine shot up, and absinthe, at only three sous a glass, became the official beverage of bohemia. Toulouse-Lautrec mixed his with cognac, a cocktail he called the *tremblement de terre*—the earthquake—which he hid in a vial in his walking stick. Edmond de Goncourt, the boulevardier and diarist, liked to mix his with tincture of opium. The most extravagant abuser was surely Alfred Jarry, author of *Ubu Roi* and inventor of pataphysics, the science of imaginary solutions. A complete aesthete, Jarry once dyed his face and hands green and boasted of starting the day with a shot of undiluted absinthe and ending it with a dose spiked with vinegar and a single drop of ink. (And died, if one is looking for a moral, at the age of thirty-four, of alcohol-aggravated tuberculosis.)

If unemployed artists could afford absinthe, then so could working people, particularly after the vine pest of the 1870s put the price of wine out of their reach. The real drinkers asked for doubles and gradually reduced the amount of water they added, until, like Jarry, they were drinking the dreaded *purée*: virtually pure, 140-proof absinthe. If it had all been as good as Pernod's version, whose alcohol was distilled from grapes, the consequences might not have been so severe. But popular absinthe was also cheap absinthe, made with industrial alcohol rendered from beets or molasses, and distillers—there were almost a thousand different brands by the 1890s—added toxic adulterants like cupric acetate (to provide the green tint) and antimony chloride (to encourage the *louche*). The worst were made with methanol (the same wood alcohol used, fatally, to spike smuggled liquor in contemporary Norway). Doctors diagnosed a new disease: *absinthisme*, whose symptoms included delusions, tremors, and epileptic fits.

From a modern perspective, their methodology looks a little shaky. In a famous experiment, a guinea pig, injected with the equivalent of seven liters of absinthe in a single shot, went into convulsions and died. (But in another, a frog, given a choice between aquariums filled with distilled water, salt water, and one spiked with absinthe, chose to live in the booze. A natural affinity for the green, perhaps.) A pair of intrepid empiricists ingested a gram of wormwood oil—the equivalent of two hundred shots of pure absinthe—on empty stomachs, without ill effect. Nonetheless, absinthe was fingered by temperance groups as "epilepsy in a bottle." There was no question that in the France of Emile Zola's *L'Assommoir*, alcohol had become a huge social problem: in Paris alone there were thirty-three thousand bars and drink sellers (five times as many as in London or Chicago) versus only seventeen thousand bakeries. By 1914, annual consumption had risen to an astonishing thirty liters of pure alcohol per adult (in contrast, the current world champions, the Irish, seem relatively abstemious with their 14.2 liters per year). But the condemnation of absinthe was summary and unfair: what should really have been on trial were the social conditions—monotonous factory labor, overcrowded and insalubrious homes, a lack of affordable organized leisure activities—that drove people to the cafés and bars in the first place.

The Belgians were the first in Europe to ban absinthe, in 1906. A horrible crime sealed its fate in Switzerland: after drinking two glasses of absinthe, a day laborer killed his pregnant wife, then shot their two infant daughters. (That he had downed a crème de menthe, a cognac, and five liters of homemade wine before he started on the absinthe was ignored by local officials, probably because the crime had occurred in the Vaud, a wine-producing region.) Though hardly consumed outside of Jean Lafitte's Old Absinthe House in New

Orleans, the drink was banned by the U.S. Department of Agriculture in 1912 and remains illegal in the United States to this day.

In France, temperance groups, supported by the wine industry—which by the turn of the century was suffering from overproduction and an inability to move its product—made absinthe the scapegoat for all of the problems of alcoholism. As absinthe made inroads into the south, local agricultural unions started to vote for its suppression. (Though absinthe would never account for more than 3 percent of the alcohol consumed in France, versus wine's 72 percent, overproduction meant that winemakers were desperately seeking to enlarge their internal markets.) In 1907, the largest of them, L'Union centrale des syndicats, representing twelve hundred unions, called for its prohibition. Under the slogan *Tous pour le vin, contre l'absinthe* (All for wine, against absinthe), four thousand people met in Paris to rail against the Green Fairy. The public was largely indifferent, and the government resisted; taxes on absinthe amounted to 45 million francs a year, a revenue source it was loath to lose; it took another seven years for the ban to be implemented. By the time the first posters outlawing absinthe were plastered on the walls of France's prefectures on August 14, 1914, the prohibition almost seemed superfluous. Two weeks before, a far more efficient killer of the working class had come along: France had entered the First World War. In contrast to Scandinavia and the United States, the French had averted the disaster of total alcohol prohibition—and the unthinkable notion of the banning of wine—by making a single beverage, absinthe, the sacrificial lamb for all the sins of alcohol.

"Absinthe doesn't make you crazy," insisted Delahaye, as she sold tickets to a group of elderly, straw-hatted visitors. "I've dug up forty years' worth of medical papers, and none of the serious ones mention any 'hallucinatory effects.' It's true, the plant itself, wormwood, isn't entirely innocent. It was known to produce epileptic-style fits; but that was in extreme cases, of very heavy drinkers." She told me she was shocked when she learned that Green Bohemia was passing off the Czech brand Hill's to the ravers and lads in London as the real thing. "It was pure commerce! That horrible fluorescent green color! I've tried Hill's, it doesn't even *louche* when you add water!" Delahaye had concocted a lower-alcohol version, La Fée Verte, which she was selling in the gift shop of her museum.

Along with many other absinthe-related items. "If you see it here, that means it's for sale," she reminded yet another gaggle of day-trippers. In addition to the six different volumes she'd authored, Delahaye was doing a brisk trade in postcards, absinthe spoons, and reproductions of vintage posters. Before I left, I asked whether, as a connoisseur, she'd noticed that absinthe affected her differently from other alcohols.

"I've never had enough at one time to feel the slightest effect. Apart, maybe, from feeling a little hot behind the ears," she said with a girlish giggle. "I own some nineteenth-century bottles, but there's no question of opening them—they're collector's items. However, one time, this fellow brought me a bottle of vintage Jules Pernod, and there was still a little left in the bottle. We tried it. It was very aromatic, a beautiful color, and there was a very strong aftertaste of plants. I didn't necessarily like the flavor—there was too much anise. The pleasure was mostly intellectual."

Delahaye's definition of authenticity, then, was specific: the only real absinthe was a high-quality absinthe, made following a vintage recipe. It was, after all, a symbol of France's past glory, of an era of elegance and creative fervor. As a vendor and a curator, she was cultivating her own interest in the myth. To settle for a cheap, inferior brand would be a betrayal of the elegant aperitif of the boulevards. And to confess to an interest in its potential for intoxication—well, that would be vulgar sensationalism and thrill-seeking, no better than a backpacker getting baked in a coffee shop in Amsterdam.

*   *   *

After the impeccable asphalt of the Autoroute du soleil, which bores southeast from Paris through Burgundy, the road narrows and wends through the trunks of the larch, spruce, and pine trees of the Jura—an area that, thanks to ongoing rural depopulation, is actually more forested now than it was in the nineteenth century. My Michelin guide noted that the Jura was not only an international center of pipe-carving and wood-toy-making, but also the birthplace of one Charles Sauria, inventor of the wooden matchstick.

What struck me as stranger, though, was that the Jura—the coldest part of the country—was also the French cradle of absinthe and Pernod, drinks more associated with café terraces and summer after-noons than Alpine eaux-de-vie. In 1905, there were twenty-five absinthe distilleries in the town of Pontarlier alone, producing ten million liters a year, and one third of its residents made their living in the manufacture of absinthe. Today, the former Pernod factory is owned by a Swiss multinational and turns out millions of packages of Carnation Instant Breakfast a year.

On this June day, the region was suffering through a heat wave, and I decided an absinthe sipped on one of the terraces of Pontarlier's long, boutique-lined main street would be a civilized way to end a long drive. I glimpsed absinthe fountains in local shop windows, slotted spoons and vintage glasses in the antique stores. At the Brasserie de la Poste, I asked a waiter in a white shirt and a broad black tie for an absinthe, and he curtly replied, "We don't have any absinthe."

I'd forgotten. Strictly speaking, absinthe is not yet legal in most European nations. Hence the euphemistic nomenclature: it is im-ported from the Czech Republic as Absinth, ordered as Absenta in Spain, and sold under brand names such as Oxygénée and Absente in France. Changing tactics, I asked for a François Guy. The waiter showed me a bottle labeled *Spiritueux aux extraits de plantes d'absinthe*, and I nodded my head in assent. The Pontarlier version was made without sugar, which means it qualified as a bitter and could contain—under European law—over three times the amount of thujone as other brands. On the terrace, I was presented with a shot of transparent, yellow-tinged liquid in a tall glass, along with all the requisite paraphernalia: an absinthe spoon, a Perrier glass full of ice cubes, and a bottle of water.

To my left, a pair of Tour de France wannabes were working on plates of *steak-frites*, their thighs and calves burnt the same color as the rosé they were sharing. To my right, the waiter stooped to give a plastic water bowl to a panting terrier at the feet of a well-dressed dame. I unwrapped a sugar cube, poured the water over it, and watched the liquid below *louche* creamy white. The taste was slightly bitter, highly herbal, with a bitter menace lurking beneath the anise. I was pleased; I felt that I was tasting something authentic, and briefly I bathed in the aura of a long-forbidden indulgence. A little detail troubled my anachronistic idyll: reading the label, I noticed François Guy was only 45 percent alcohol—far below the proof of its venerable ancestors.

The next morning, François Guy, the man, defended his product.

"My great grandfather, Armand Guy, started making absinthe in 1890," he began. "And now I'm making absinthe exactly the same way he made his."

Guy grew up in this distillery—a cluster of houses with peaked, tiled roofs and white façades on a quiet residential street—and we were in his office, a slightly intimidating setting, as the wall behind me bristled from floor to ceiling with swords, rifles, and helmets. Guy himself, his head shaved to stubble, six foot three in loafers, with powerful forearms and a prominent chin, exuded the kind of self-assurance that must come from belonging to an industrial dynasty in what was once a one-industry town.

He dismissed Czech absinthe: "*Attention!* Poison. That stuff is pure shit. There isn't a single gram of wormwood or anise in it. You might as well put it in your gas tank."

He mocked the European Union's laws on thujone content: "It's utter hypocrisy. You can only call it absinthe if it has thirty-five milligrams of thujone a liter or more. But if you do call it absinthe, it's illegal."

And he made short work of nineteenth-century claims of toxicity: a conspiracy between doctors and wine merchants. "You'd have to drink six liters a day before you started having problems with thujone. The issue wasn't the wormwood, it was the percentage of alcohol. People were drinking sixty milliliters of absinthe at a go, at sixty-eight percent alcohol! And this was after work, on an empty stomach! It's the equivalent of drinking six modern aperitifs in a single glass. No wonder those artists were completely cracked."

And while singling out thujone as inoffensive and alcohol as the harmful ingredient—hence his brand's modest 45 percent by volume—he also boasted the thujone content of his brand was higher than that of any other on the market. "We're currently at thirty-three milligrams a liter. Any more, we'd be in trouble."

I was given a quick tour of the premises. In one corner, nylon sacks filled with Spanish anise were stacked to the ceiling. Employees in blue overalls sealed crates of cherries preserved in alcohol. We came to the heart of the distillery: a copper still, connected by a swan-necked pipe to a refrigerating unit.

"We load a vat in the center of the still with alcohol, wormwood, anise, and other herbs, heat them, and let them soak overnight," explained Guy. "Then we boil them, and the essential oils evaporate and travel through the pipe with the alcohol, and then pass through water-cooled condenser coils." From a pipe, a clear liquid trickled from the bottom of the cylindrical condenser into an oak cask: pure, high-proof absinthe. "I've already distilled two thousand liters this morning. Most of the Spanish brands don't even bother to distill. They make what we call *absinthe-bâton*." Absinthe, in other words, stirred with a stick. "They add ready-made wormwood extract to alcohol and stir. That's why they taste so bitter—and it's the acidity and impurities that give you a headache the next morning."

Up a flight of stairs, Guy opened a door to a sunlit backyard, where a garden was planted with hundreds of wormwood plants. It was the first time I'd seen the living herb. For all its attendant mythology, it was a dowdy-looking shrub that rose no more than waist-high.

"Rub one of the leaves," insisted Guy. Gray-green on top, whitish below, the intricately lobulated leaf felt silky between my finger and thumb. "Now smell your thumb." A medicinal odor, of the toadstool hidden in the pine forest, emanated from my pores. I touched the tip of my tongue to the leaf and winced; it was as bitter as earwax. "This is just a show garden," said Guy. "I have fifty-five thousand plants in a field not far from here. We use goats to keep the weeds away; they won't touch the wormwood, it's too bitter."

Guy's claim to authenticity lay in his garden. By growing his own wormwood—a fact prominently proclaimed on every label—he was hoping to make Pontarlier's absinthe a veritable product of the Jurassien *terroir* and thus reclaim from Iberian savages and Balkan cossacks a drink that was, for him, quintessentially French. I asked him if he planned to seek out an *appellation d'origine contrôlée* (AOC), the same designation the cheesemakers of Burgundy had obtained for Époisses.

"Strictly speaking, an AOC wouldn't be possible, because some of the ingredients—the anise, in particular—can't be grown in this climate. A year and a half ago, we put in our request for an *appellation d'origine réglementée*, an AOR, which is a guarantee of quality. It's like a business card; it puts a necktie around every bottle."

It would also relegate foreign absinthes—the Spanish and Czech brands that Guy despised—to second rank. Only the absinthe of the French Jura, made according to ancestral recipes with wormwood grown in Pontarlier, would be authentic. All others would be imitators—like a vulgar Polish *méthode champenoise* next to a true Dom Pérignon.

We repaired to a corner of the distillery, where a young couple, part of a prematurely jolly crew of bus tourists, were enjoying a late-morning tasting. Their baby, planted on top of an upended oak barrel, knocked a lump of sugar off a spoon into a glass of absinthe; I was surprised she wasn't reeling from the fumes. François Guy proudly opened a bottle of his eponymous aperitif and showed me how it veered from transparent yellow to milky white with the addition of water. I praised the *louche* and the flavor, but confessed my mission was to seek out a bottle of La Bleue. Which led me to the question I'd been saving: Wasn't absinthe first made in Switzerland? And if so, how could he possibly hope to claim it for France?

"Listen," he said energetically. "The absinthe that was known the world over didn't come from Switzerland. It came from Pontarlier." He went to his office, returning with a book published by the Pernod distillery in 1896, and read aloud, " 'In spite of the name *Swiss absinthe* by which it often goes, the famous liqueur is of French origin. At the end of the last century, a French doctor, Dr. Ordinaire, exiled in Switzerland . . . did not scorn panaceas, [and] employed one in particular, the elixir of wormwood, composed of aromatic plants whose secret only he possessed.' " Guy closed the book with satisfaction. "Even if it was first made in Switzerland, the inventor himself was French." Nonetheless, Guy reached behind a row of bottles of his own *spiritueux* and brought out an unlabeled liter bottle of clear liquid. "I bought this in Switzerland. Look, when you add water, it turns blue. French absinthes, real absinthes, turn green or opal." He was right: when I held the glass to the light, I noticed a captivating bluish tinge.

I also couldn't help noticing that Guy kept his bottle of Swiss absinthe on the top shelf.

A decent creature of myth, by its nature, disappears before it can be grasped. Wood sprites, leprechauns, fairies—they lead a merry chase, then evanesce, leaving the covetous with the echo of a laugh, alone in the middle of a darkening pine forest, to be tracked and slaughtered by more malign ogres. In the Jura, the reigning numen is the *vouivre*, a snake with a seductress's head that haunts secluded torrents. According to legend, the *vouivre* appears in a cloud of mist, tempts unwary hikers to the riverbanks with a bejeweled ring, then sucks them to their death in the icy waters. As a creature born of Celtic forest panic, rather than some talking grasshopper confected for pastoral fable, the *vouivre* illustrates no clear moral point: it is an incarnation of deep-seated fears, unavowed desires, and wisdom that must not be forgotten.

The rivers of the Jura are as elusive as the *vouivre*. They appear dramatically in mist-filled mountain caverns, meander elaborately through narrow valleys, disappear abruptly into the karst—to re-emerge, dozens of kilometers away, often with completely different names. The Doubs (from the Latin *dubius*, or "hesitant"), which arcs through the center of Pontarlier, is one such river. In 1901, the Pernod factory was lashed by lightning, and the bolt cracked in the basement warehouse, igniting a cask of absinthe. A quick-witted employee, fearing an ethanol-fueled inferno, opened the vats, emptying a million liters of Pernod's highest-quality absinthe into the Doubs. As the factory burned, the river took on a distinctly opaline hue, and between turns at the hose, firemen filled their helmets with a premixed dose of the Green Fairy. Two and a half days later, a geologist traveled several kilometers downstream and discovered that what had long been thought to be an entirely different river was redolent of anise—proving definitively that the River Loue was merely a resurgence of the Doubs.

While the Jurassien waters dip into grottoes and slip beneath frontiers easily, crossing the border isn't always so easy for humans. Abruptly, on the road east from Pontarlier, I came to a Swiss border post, and a grim-faced customs agent with the bluest of gimlet glares motioned me to the side of the road and demanded my passport. A

German shepherd on a leash approached, sniffed my tires. The guard had me empty my trunk and carry my bags into a narrow room, where a younger colleague watched as he patted down the legs of my pants and probed the seams of my backpack with practiced fingers. And then, in another bag, he discovered a bottle of absinthe and a spoon, a gift from François Guy.

"Ah!" The slightest of smiles crossed his face. "You're doing the absinthe trail!" The tension evaporated. "Go ahead: you can close your bags." Outside, I waited until a broad-shouldered woman with a utility belt finished reattaching the door panels she'd unscrewed from my car.

"Welcome to Switzerland," I muttered to the customs agent, a little wryly.

"You have to understand," he countered. "You're a young man, in a rented car, with a Paris license plate. We get a lot of drug traffic here."

In Switzerland, then, French absinthe was clearly too weak to qualify as anybody's idea of a drug.

As I pulled back onto the highway, I realized I had left Europe. Switzerland never officially joined the Union and has its own constitution, its own laws, its own currency, its own quirks. I hadn't driven more than half a kilometer before I glimpsed my first mythical creature: a rosy-cheeked gnome.

It was a garden-variety Happy, planted outside a gas station, flanked by the Walt Disney version of Snow White.

I'd finally made it to the birthplace of La Bleue—moonshine country, the Swiss equivalent of the Appalachians or the Trøndelag in Norway. I was in the Val-de-Travers, literally the "valley that lies athwart," since its bottom was carved from east to west, rather than the Alpine standard of north to south, by the eccentric course of the river Areuse. The French-speaking Traversines call the Swiss Germans the *Neinsa-*

gers, or "no-sayers." In 1992, their compatriots said no to joining Europe—which was perhaps their right. A century ago, however, they said no to absinthe—and for this, the Traversines will never forgive them. On the valley's unofficial Web site, Article 7 of the constitution of the République Autonome du Val-de-Travers enshrines both the freedom to complain and the right to distill.

Had I been on this road a century ago, the entire valley bottom would have been colored grayish blue with wormwood. The herb has always grown wild in the valley's upper meadows, and like many rich and intoxicating substances—opium poppies, milk chocolate, LSD, Gruyère—its potential was first developed by the industrious and inventive Swiss. In spite of the spurious evidence of Gallic origins shown me by François Guy, more serious scholarship indicates absinthe probably first trickled from the still of a certain Henriette Henriod, from the village of Couvet, in the mid-eighteenth century. The French-born Dr. Ordinaire was aptly named: he invented nothing more extraordinary than a tonic made of chicory—an ersatz coffee extract.

The first written recipe for absinthe—probably purchased from Mme. Henriod—which dates from 1794, was found in the record books of the Swiss Abram-Louis Perrenod, who changed his name to Pernod when he set up his first distillery in Couvet. (The Pernod factory in Pontarlier was established a decade later, to satisfy French demand and circumvent custom duties.) For over a century, the Val-de-Travers owed its prosperity to the planting, harvesting, and drying of wormwood, and the distilling of some of the world's best absinthe. With the prohibition of 1910, the Swiss government ordered the absinthe fields plowed under, and the more pedestrian industries of dairy farming and watchmaking took over. The blue liquid went underground—yet another Jurassien stream disappearing into the karst—only to burble up again in stills hidden in barns, broom closets, and attics. For 250 years, this has been the one place on earth with an uninterrupted history of absinthe making.

I'd been told that if you spoke a bit of French and didn't look like a cop, tracking down a bottle of La Bleue in the canton wouldn't be too hard. After a dinner of fried lake perch, I headed into the hills north of the village of Couvet. A half dozen cars were parked outside a modest, brown-roofed restaurant that backed onto a lake. The dining room was empty, but a group of sun-pinkened farmers seated at a corner table watched me approach the tall, dark-haired woman behind the bar.

"*Une petite bleue?*" I asked.

The room went silent. The barmaid looked me up and down—seemed to note my longish hair and foreign accent—and made up her mind. Disappearing into a cupboard behind the bar, she returned with an unlabeled liter bottle and poured a shot into a Duralex glass. I took a seat at the table next to the farmers, who watched as I poured chilled water from a ceramic yellow container into the liquid and observed its *louche*. I glimpsed the telltale aura of blue around the edges, the guarantee that I was about to drink the world's most authentic and deadly absinthe.

I lifted the glass to my lips; it was slightly sweet, with a strong flavor of anise, but also an aroma of freshly cut flowers I'd never encountered before. The farmers, who were flipping through a flag catalog, talking tractors, and vaguely following the score of a lackluster Neuchâtel soccer game, watched me as I asked the barmaid for another.

The old guy next to me nodded approval: "It's better for your balance if you have two. After all, you have two legs!"

"Unfortunately," I told him, "I also have four wheels. I have to watch out tonight."

"Absinthe helps you drive better!" another farmer shouted, and there was laughter from the next table.

I asked my neighbor if it was difficult to get your hands on a full bottle in these parts.

"You want one now?" he said, sotto voce. "I can get you some tonight."

But I refused his offer. Before I started filling my trunk with bottles, I planned to do a little shopping around. I bid adieu to the room; and they watched me leave, a little disappointed, I thought, that I didn't lurch into the doorjamb as I left.

The drive back to my hotel along the lonely, winding road was slow and spooky. Thick tufts of fog had descended on the dark mountain meadows; entering one, I felt as if I'd driven straight into a clouded glass of absinthe. Spectral beings lined the roadside. No *vouivres*, though; only sleeping cows, collapsed and folded for the night.

The following afternoon, I had an appointment at the Blackmint Distillery in Môtiers. Yves Kübler, the stocky young scion of a distilling family who was making the only legal form of absinthe in the Val-de-Travers, met me in the garden. Like François Guy, he was at once distracted and explosive; it was as though the minds of distillers were congenitally preoccupied by the potential eruption of a boiling still.

Switzerland had been one of the first nations to suppress absinthe, and its agriculture laws still prohibited the sale of any drink so labeled. The maximum legal limit for thujone in any drink was ten milligrams per liter. For the moment, Kübler was forced to sell his product as an *extrait d'absinthe*. It was essentially a commercial version of moonshine La Bleue. I pointed out that even the legal French absinthe had three times more thujone than his. Kübler responded by promulgating his own definition of authenticity.

"François Guy's absinthe is not absinthe! All he uses is wormwood, fennel, and anise. And a real absinthe has at least seven different ingredients. It's proven historically. I use nine plants in mine!" He poured me a shot from a half-liter bottle; there was indeed a complex herbal bouquet, though it was less heady than the glass of Bleue I had had the night before. Kübler had launched his own attempt to claim the absinthe of the Val-de-Travers as intellectual property, submitting a request for an IGP—an *indication géographique protégée*—the Swiss equivalent of an AOR.

"Our historical dossier is solid as rock. The Pernod family was Swiss; the first distillery was in Couvet. My great-grandfather founded this distillery in 1863. We're going to call our absinthe Fée Verte de Val-de-Travers, Véritable Absinthe."

Kübler leaned back in his chair, satisfied. Not only was the French version inauthentic; there was nothing especially interesting about the legendary, underground Bleue. He was confident that the Swiss authorities—disgusted by the fact that the French had pinched the name *Gruyère* centuries ago—would vote to abrogate the law, allowing absinthe to become a product of the Swiss *terroir*. His final obstacle to selling his *extrait* as "absinthe" would be removed, and authenticity would be his alone.

"Kübler?" said Pierre-André Delachaux with a grimace. "What he makes isn't absinthe. *This*, this is absinthe." He waved his hand toward an antique bleach bottle embossed with a skull and crossbones. We were sitting at a picnic table in his backyard, sipping absinthe from short-stemmed goblets. Tall, blue-eyed, and yellow-bearded, with a balding pate lightly beaded with sweat in the late-afternoon heat, Delachaux stood up, raised a pottery pitcher above his head, and let a long stream of water trickle from a narrow spout sculpted into the shape of a tiny boar's head. This, he explained, was the authentic Traversine method of preparing one's absinthe; it ensured there was more oxygen in the mix.

Delachaux, a teacher of high school French and history, was infamous in the canton. When he was a Socialist deputy in the early 1980s, he had served the late French president François Mitterrand a soufflé glazed with absinthe at a dinner in one of Neuchâtel's leading hotels. A head of state had consumed a forbidden substance at an official function; the uproar was enormous. Delachaux survived the scandal (the next time Mitterrand saw Delachaux, he quipped, "That matter of the absinthe—liquidated?"), but it turned him into a public champion of the Traversine tradition. Delachaux ran the local museum in the town of Môtiers, where a room is devoted to absinthe, and is the author of several books and studies on the subject. When I mentioned all the claimants to authenticity I'd encountered so far, Delachaux was scathing.

On François Guy: "It's absinthe in a hoopskirt. It's as if you decided to prance around in a top hat, with a cane and a cape. That's what the French like: folklore. They're trying to re-create old recipes, whereas here we have an uninterrupted tradition that goes back over two hundred years. And our tastes have evolved; our absinthe has changed over time. That's why we don't use a sugar cube; over the years we've added sugar to the mix."

On Kübler's claims that his was the only authentic brand: "That guy says whatever suits his needs. Sometimes he says his stuff is the real, old-time absinthe; but when the authorities ask, he says it isn't absinthe at all, just a harmless liqueur. I call it decaffeinated absinthe."

Delachaux, it turned out, was opposed to legalization. "If absinthe is legalized, two or three brands—probably Pernod in France, maybe Kübler here—will dominate the market. Right now, there are between sixty and eighty clandestine distillers in the Val-de-Travers, and they all have their own distinct recipes. Everybody here has his favorite. Legalize it, and gradually all that will disappear, and we'll be left with a single standard—the Coca-Cola of absinthe." It was a compelling, if familiar, argument: like the champions of Slow Food and the makers of Époisses, he was defending gastronomic biodiversity against a globalized monoculture.

But what Delachaux really valued in his absinthe was its clandestinity, a trait intertwined with the history and character of the Val-de-Travers. "We are *résistants*," he said, "and our resistance expresses itself in one important form: absinthe. When absinthe was forbidden, this canton had only been part of Switzerland for sixty years. Until then, we had been independent. And all of a sudden, these Swiss Germans, who are still constantly messing with us politically, come along, launch a rigged trial against absinthe, and ban our drink! So quietly, absinthe went underground—and it's this resistance that interests me. For people here, absinthe corresponds to the pleasure of transgressing, the pleasure of offering. I'd be ashamed—and I'm not alone on this—to offer a visitor a glass of legal Kübler."

I suggested to Delachaux that he was being a little elitist. Before the prohibition, absinthe was a popular drink, cheap and widely available—like beer or soft drinks today.

"Perhaps," he said, "there *is* an elitist side to this. But not economically. The clandestine absinthe here is cheaper than the brands that Guy and Kübler are selling. I concede, however, that I'd like it to remain a little mysterious. I think one has to merit one's absinthe."

Apparently I'd merited mine, because Delachaux poured me another long shot. "Frankly," he said, frowning, "I'm a little disappointed they served you absinthe at that bar last night. They should have refused you. Then you would have gone away, still intrigued, with the myth intact." I took his point. I was a tourist, after all, and as such an agent of globalized culture, another potential underminer of local legend.

The myth, as it happened, was getting a little blurry in my mind—Delachaux's Bleue was mounting to my head, and I was starting to lose my command of the French subjunctive mood. I asked if La Bleue affected Delachaux any differently from vodka or gin.

Lowering his voice, Delachaux said, "Nobody will tell you this, but there *is* an effect in absinthe that you don't find in any other drink.

And believe me, I've been drinking it for a long time now. After three whiskeys, I feel stupid. After three absinthes, I feel more intelligent. It's no accident that so many artists were interested in absinthe. It didn't turn anyone into a genius; but it could help stimulate the genius they already had."

Delachaux disappeared into his house to dig up a treatise he'd authored, leaving me alone with the bottle. I found I was feeling, if not more intelligent, then certainly more receptive to the beauty of this pastoral summer afternoon. Shaded by an overhanging tree, I looked over the wildflower-flecked cow pastures, which the sun was painting in hues of fluorescent yellow and absinthine emerald, toward a clifftop castle on one of the low mountains that rose from the valley floor toward the French border.

The vista called to mind the echo of a quote: "If, while resting on a summer afternoon, you follow with your eyes a mountain range on the horizon or a branch which casts its shadow over you, you experience the aura of those mountains, of that branch." These were the words that Walter Benjamin—another mystic intellectual of the left, a collector with a taste for the unique, the rarefied, the hard-to-obtain—used to qualify the concept of aura, which he further defined as "the unique phenomenon of distance, however close an object may be." At that moment, I was basking in the aura of authenticity: of an absinthe made according to a centuries-old tradition, rather than some modern counterfeit created for the nightclub circuit. And though the sought-after object was sitting within reach—and its molecules were currently coursing through my bloodstream, binding to my neurons—I still perceived the phenomenon of distance; there was no way of knowing whether I was experiencing the effect the nineteenth-century poets were seeking. The aura of absinthe remained ungraspable.

When Delachaux returned, I sympathized more with his prickly distaste for those who sought to collect, commercialize, and possess the myth that was born in his valley. He was right: there is a pure pleasure in offering, and the spoon vendors and elixir peddlers who were profiting from the current revival were missing the point, the heart of the attraction. At the core of the myth lies the idea of danger and transgression; and the attraction of the Val-de-Travers is its underground culture of resistance. Speakeasy passwords, sly euphemisms, over-the-bar winks: in clandestinity lies community.

Delachaux poured me a final shot of La Bleue—aka *un lait de Jura*, aka *un thé de Boveresse*, aka *une couèchte* (Swiss absinthe has as many coy nicknames as Californian bud)—repeating the demonstrative ritual of pouring from on high. It was delicious, I told him—the best I'd had yet, more flowery and complex than the shots I'd had in the bar—and I praised his good taste.

He accepted the compliment with a nod. Naturally, though, he wouldn't tell me where I could buy a bottle for myself.

As much as I appreciated Delachaux's hospitality—and his Bleue—there was something dissatisfying about the experience. His absinthe may have been the real thing, but the setting certainly wasn't authentic. Prearranged by telephone, the tasting had felt semiofficial, a grudging initiation to a rite over which the historian had staked intellectual domain.

But I was determined: I wouldn't stop until I'd scored a bottle of my own. I spent a leisurely afternoon driving down narrow dirt roads, with sheepdogs chasing after the tires of my car. At one dairy farm, I tracked down the owner on the threshold of his cheese room.

"Absinthe?" he said. "I have a few bottles, but they're for myself. My wife uses it to glaze her soufflés. If you'd like some Gruyère, though, I can sell you all you want."

After two more similar rebuffs, I stopped in an antique shop. Browsing through the vintage Swiss army knives and crystal vases, I lingered over a shelf of absinthe memorabilia.

"Are you interested in absinthe?" asked the owner, a slender woman with auburn hair, in a sheer, polka-dotted dress.

"Actually," I said, "I'm not that interested in old spoons. What I'd really like is a bottle."

After a glance outside the front door, she said, "Follow me," and led me into the back of the shop. She pulled an opened bottle from the bottom drawer of her desk and poured me a shot, which she filled with water from a glass coffeepot. "Do you like it?" Indeed I did—it was as smooth as Delachaux's, only a little less sugary. "I can sell you a bottle, if you'd like."

She continued, "The inspectors of the Régie des alcools"—the local version of the Appalachian revenue men—"know perfectly well we're making absinthe here. The stills are in abandoned buildings, in the forest; nobody will ever tell you where theirs is hidden. The distillers buy the alcohol directly from the Régie; myself, I can go to a pharmacy and buy several liters of pure alcohol." (Which was good news for consumers: unlike Norwegians, whose *hjemmebrent* was homemade from alcohol and potatoes, the Swiss could be sure they were getting only the purest, government-manufactured alcohol.)

"And if you know the pharmacist, you can even ask him for premixed packages of absinthe herbs: 'Give me a number three, with hyssop and melissa,' for example. The Val-de-Travers consumes as much raw alcohol as the rest of Switzerland combined, so clearly it's going somewhere. It's all a bit of a game." After directing me to a cash machine ("It's right by the police station"), she sold me my first bottle—for fifty francs ($44 U.S.)—and wrapped the unlabeled liter in a newspaper with practiced hands.

Farther along, at a bend in the road, I stopped at a roadside restaurant—empty except for a solitary drinker—and went through the now familiar ritual.

"Une absinthe?" I asked. The waitress started to reach for a bottle of Kübler above the bar, but I protested, "No, a real one. *Une petite bleue."*

"Kübler," she muttered, "nobody wants to drink Kübler." She leaned beneath the bar, pulled out a bottle with a color-photocopied label of a lowing cow above the slogan *Le lait, un produit naturel de chez nous.*

And I was offered another liter of absinthe, this one at only forty-two francs ($37 U.S.).

"My great-aunt was famous around here," the barmaid told me. "She sold absinthe from her kitchen, just down the street." Delachaux had alluded to this legendary figure: as a child, he used to go to the house of the infamous Berthe Zurbuchen, aka La Malotte, where his father liked to knock back a glass in her kitchen. La Malotte made her own absinthe for eighty years, and when an overzealous liquor commissioner decided to crack down on clandestine distillers in the 1960s, she was the victim of a celebrated show trial. After the penalty—a three thousand-franc ($2,645 U.S.) fine—was announced, she famously asked the judge, "Should I pay you right now, or when you come by my house to pick up your weekly bottle?"

The barmaid still recalled La Malotte with admiration. "The trial didn't stop La Malotte from making absinthe. In fact, she painted her house green—like the Green Fairy." And her clients—many local gendarmes among them—continued to bring her bottles of alcohol, which she'd mix with the necessary herbs in her still, serving her visitors the finished absinthe in her kitchen. "It's illegal to distill absinthe, it's illegal to transport it, but not to drink it! So she risked nothing."

I remember the moral of an old French fable in which a canny grasshopper camouflaged among the green blades of grass watches a showy butterfly being netted by schoolchildren: *Pour vivre heureux, vivons cachés.*

"To live happily, we must live in hiding."

★   ★   ★

But forget fables: the myth was what interested me. And June 14, the traditional beginning of wormwood harvesting season, was my last chance. It was the Annual Absinthe Festival in Boveresse, a community of 350, whose chief tourist attraction was the Drying Shed, a three-story wooden barn where bundles of wormwood were once left to desiccate before being sent to the distilleries. The village's main street was lined with stands selling T-shirts, rusty absinthe spoons and piles of reprinted labels, and the potted herbs that go into the making of absinthe. In a tent behind the town hall, a band was playing "Johnny B. Goode" and "Barbara Ann," as the villagers danced stiff versions of *le rock*. A wormwood-macerated rum called Le Décollage—the name meant "blastoff"—offered me a bit of a lift, but the only absinthelike drink on sale was Kübler's. I wandered to the upper floor of the town hall, a basketball court that had been turned into a kind of bazaar for absinthe collectors. Marie-Claude Delahaye was seated at a table, too busy signing books to notice my presence. Another dealer was trying to peddle a vintage fountain for 2,150 francs. Most of the vendors were from France. For all the overpriced memorabilia, there wasn't a drop of real Bleue to be found.

I wandered back to the main stand, where I muttered to an employee, wearing a sprig of just-picked wormwood in his shirt pocket, that I hadn't come all the way from Canada just to drink Kübler.

A slight, mop-topped man with stooped shoulders and hangdog eyes had overheard the frustration in my voice. He walked up and whispered, "Are you looking for a real bottle?" (Speak of the devil, they say, and sometimes he appears.)

I nodded, and we shook hands. Introducing himself as Charlot, he gestured for me to follow him. Along the way, he whispered something to Serge, a broad-shouldered man with a booming voice, and we were joined by the mustachioed Marcel, in a burgundy singlet, one of the French paraphernalia dealers. We walked past a vacant lot planted with a stunted patch of wormwood, into a gabled house with two sculpted cats above the entranceway. At a melamine table, a bottle was uncapped, the absinthe was poured, silence descended. Whispers, passwords, reverence: I was at the heart of the ritual.

Ice water dripped onto the liquid. The flowery bouquet provoked exclamations; exploratory sips were taken. "Ah, *magnifique*," said Serge. "Not too much anise, not too much sugar. What's in your recipe?"

Charlot was evasive: "I've experimented with several mixes; this is my favorite. It's about fifty-four percent alcohol by volume. I'll tell you one of my herbs: hyssop."

Marcel, jocular, blurted, "And where do you keep your still?"

"That," said Charlot gravely, "I'll never tell. In any case, it's not here—it's in a nearby village." It turned out Charlot was a pharmacist—not a bad day job for a moonshiner—and he had his position to think about.

As the glasses were filled, the anecdotes began. Serge, who specialized in obscure absinthe collectibles, was ironic on the subject of Swiss border guards. "Once, I went to visit François Guy's distillery in Pontarlier; but it was closed that day. So, when I was driving back to Bern, I told the Swiss customs man that I'd been trying to buy some French absinthe. And he says, 'Why would you go to France to buy their garbage, when we have the best clandestine absinthe makers in the world here?'"

I asked whether it would be risky to bring a couple of bottles of Bleue over the border. "Well," said Marcel, "they could fine you and seize your car. Just do like I do. Pour your Bleue into a wine bottle and stick the cork halfway in, like you've just come back from a picnic. They never check."

I was halfway through another glass when I repeated the barbarous, reductive question. Apart from the exquisite bouquet, apart from the sublime mixture of herbs, was there any difference between six glasses of Bleue and a half dozen glasses of, say, vodka?

"*Oui!*" came the unanimous response. Marcel said, "After six of them, believe me, you feel euphoric. If you're feeling depressed . . . it's gone. I'm diabetic, and I feel it drives my diabetes away."

Serge was so impressed with Charlot's Bleue that he bought a dozen bottles. Marcel also bought several, then stood and excused himself: "I have to go back to selling my antique glasses and fountains. If I don't come home with enough money, then no *boum-boum* from my wife tonight." He illustrated the *boum-boum* with a couple of pelvic thrusts, as though sodomizing a barnyard animal. I bought a bottle myself; Charlot wrapped it in newspaper, gave me a super-market bag, and asked for only forty francs ($35 U.S.).

By now, Oscar Wilde's famous dictum about absinthe was starting to make sense. "After the first glass," he had written, "you see things as you wish they were. After the second glass, you see things as they are not." After three glasses, I returned to the main street, which was full of happily inebriated village folk, unselfconsciously fêting their be-loved drink. But I made the mistake of pouring myself a shot of Charlot's absinthe under a picnic table in the party tent, and the last part of Wilde's saying came back to me: "Finally, you see things as they really are, and that is the most horrible thing in the world."

I looked around and saw salespeople, mostly from France, all anxiously seeking to stake their claim to a myth; and it was indeed a horrible sight. Every year, the prices of the collectibles go up, the greed increases, and the myth turns to folklore. The mythic *vouivre* seems fated to be transformed into Happy the Harpy, as anodyne as any ceramic Disney garden gnome.

There was nothing for it but to keep on drinking. As dusk fell, menacing clouds moved in from the south, and thunderclaps com-peted with the clashes of cymbals as a marching band described comically exiguous ovals in the main street. I found myself standing unsteadily in the middle of the street, staring as a full moon, louched with mist, yellow as Pernod, rose over the rounded mountains. Charlot's father, catching me wavering, walked by and gave me a wink: "It was good stuff, *non?*"

My grasp of sequence gets shaky at this point—absinthe, for all its stimulating qualities, can play havoc with the memory—but I was apparently coherent enough to make a new friend. I remember being invited to the apartment of Nicolas, who lived across the street from the House of the Cats. He was my age, in his mid-thirties, modest and bespectacled, and eager to chat with somebody who had crossed an ocean to try his favorite aperitif. We sat on his tiny back porch, and he poured glass after glass. "This is the same kind the Baron de Rothschild—at least one of the barons—has sent to him in Geneva," he boasted.

And I remembered Nicolas talked, honestly, about life in the Val-de-Travers. "This is one of the poorest cantons in Switzerland," he said. "Since quartz killed our watchmaking tradition, all of our industries have disappeared. It's impossible to keep young people here."

At one point he pulled out a guitar and sang an ode to absinthe, of his own composition, sandaled feet tapping beneath the kitchen table.

Nicolas, as far as I can recall, didn't try to sell me an antique spoon, a T-shirt, or his favorite brand of absinthe. He vaguely hoped I could set him up with poets and singers in Montreal; perhaps I could find someone to collaborate on a CD on absinthe for next year's festival. That night, in Boveresse, I felt as if I'd gotten to the heart of clandestinity: a wink on the main street beneath a full moon, a wholehearted invitation, the shared flouting of authority, and the bonding ritual of cold water clouding a sacred liquid. It reminded me of buying *hjemmebrent* in Oslo, sharing pungent French cheese in a New York bar, trading the addresses of smoke-easies in San Francisco—in their purest form, the rituals of clandestinity, born of resistance to oppressive prohibitions, can foster connection and camaraderie.

Too bad they're so often centered around potentially addictive intoxicants, ones that can leave you sick, alone, and hungover. Or, in my case, fighting a rising gorge and leaving Nicolas with a too abrupt adieu. Followed by a long stumble down the main street and back to my hotel. No hallucinations, no sudden bursts of poetry, no trans-figuration of the starry night into Vincent van Goghesque swirls. Just a brief brush with the festival mascot: a woman dressed as a green fairy, wearing a pointed cap and carrying a yellow magic wand, skipping through the crowd. Then, the familiar consequences of besottedness: a slow-motion ricochet up a Caligarian staircase, *Lost Weekend* bed spins, and nightmares of blue-eyed water snakes chewing on my liver.

The next day, the echoes of leprechaun laughter had faded, and all that was left were the ogres of hangover stalking my path.

The banning of absinthe was an object lesson in selective interdiction, in which one substance acted as a rod for legislative lightning, thereby preventing the disaster of total prohibition. Used as a scapegoat for all the problems of alcoholism, *la fée verte* was forbidden on trumped-up charges thanks to the machinations of French vintners, who were more than happy to sacrifice a potent competitor in the beverage market if it meant their sacred grapes would be left untouched. What was equally fascinating, however, was the hyperactive fetishization of absinthe as a mythic commodity that had happened since it was banned—a phenomenon born almost entirely of prohibition. If it had been gin and vermouth, rather than absinthe, that had been prohibited since the era of the Volstead Act, people would be paying fortunes for vintage conical glasses, and reverently quoting Dorothy Parker and Dashiell Hammett about the narcotic qualities of the fabled martini.

In the nine decades since absinthe was outlawed, psychopharma-cologists have synthesized amphetamines that can make your neurons spin like pinwheels, psychedelics that will leave you melding with the spirits in the ferns, and ecstasy so strong it will have you believing techno is the classical music of the millennium. In the final analysis, it is perhaps unwise to put too much stock in the rapturous declarations of the unstable, impoverished, undernourished debauchees of the nineteenth century. Baudelaire thought absinthe a harmless tipple, but considered hashish jelly the most sublime shortcut to an artificial paradise. I was jaded about hot-knifing hash before I turned nineteen.

In some versions of the *vouivre* story, the seductive serpent tempts its victims to the water with a diadem that turns out to be a twig. But even when the jewel is authenticated as genuine, as original, as chemically pure, its aura still holds us at a distance. Authenticity, as always, turns out to be the most persistently elusive myth of them all.

After my visit to the Val-de-Travers, the Swiss House of Representatives voted by a massive majority to remove the ban, and on March 1, 2005, absinthe officially became legal in Switzerland. Yves Kübler announced his plan to seek out an IGP, a protected-designation-of-origin label, to make Traversine absinthe the only kind with the right to bear the name. Pierre-André Delachaux, hearing this, announced that rather than drink the legal, "decaffeinated" absinthe, he was going to switch to whiskey. Some feared the clandestine distilling culture, a century-old tradition, would forever disappear, as the valley's moonshiners opted to go legit.

Which made me all the happier that I'd stocked up before I left. I made it through Swiss and French customs with only the most cursory of passport checks, my three bottles of illegal absinthe hidden in a clear plastic garment bag stuffed with fetid socks and underwear. I wasn't exactly sure what the bottles contained. Though they were transparent, I could at least say with confidence that they were not water, "that terrible poison," as Alfred Jarry put it, "so corrosive that out of all substances it has been chosen for washing and scouring, and a drop added to a clear liquid like absinthe troubles it." Perhaps they were just high-proof alcohol charged with a few aromatic mountain herbs. Or maybe these bottles were so laden with thujone I'll wake up in an asylum, my hands trembling, my face dyed green. Short of subjecting them to a gas chromatography analysis, there was no way of knowing.

The truth is, though, I am not by temperament a collector: in the end, I'd rather drink my absinthe than have it. I carefully stowed the bottles in my suitcase. Eventually, they'd make a course in my devil's picnic—as an offering to friends who were also suckers for transgression, ritual, and myth.

· DESSERT ·

However harmless a thing is,
if the law forbids it,
most people will think it wrong.

—*W. Somerset Maugham*

7

CHOCOLAT MOUSSEUX

The Exonerated Buzz

E VERY ERA CHOOSES its poisons. What a society ends up stigmatizing is often more revealing of its own phobias and prejudices than the inherent nefariousness of the substance in question.

Absinthe was prohibited in Europe with the help of the French wine industry, trying to divert attention from the fact that cheap wine, as much as the Green Fairy, was contributing to a wave of poverty-driven alcoholism. Gin was stigmatized by the ruling classes in England when it was too conspicuously consumed by the poor. The impetus for the ban on liquor in Prohibition-era America came from paternalistic industrialists, who claimed to be motivated by concern for the well-being of their workers, and was made possible by skillful manipulation of popular prejudice against German brewers and Catholic vintners. Contemporary bans—on foreign raw-milk cheeses, Cuban cigars, chewing gum—are justified in the name of public health, political righteousness, or moral hygiene. What other eras considered worthy of banning may look comical to us today, but the slogans marshaled to justify past prohibitions can also sound hauntingly familiar. Lurking behind too many bans there is an elite

using scaremongering and scapegoating to justify an arbitrary exten-
sion of its power. Such is the story behind the energetic, though
ultimately unsuccessful, campaigns to ban a substance that is today
considered harmless: caffeine, the main active ingredient in tea, coffee,
and chocolate.

I'd come to Bayonne, a small town in the southwest of France,
because I'd heard that chocolate makers had once been banished from
the town center. Things had clearly changed since the eighteenth
century: today, the small city center has eleven chocolatiers, and at
five o'clock in the afternoon, the air itself became esculent with the
odor of cinnamon, vanilla, and roasting cacao. At a shop called Pariès,
I'd sampled the *kanougas*, foil-wrapped chocolate caramels created for
the palates of visiting Russian dukes in 1905. At Puyodebat, I'd tried
the *pralinés* and ganaches and bars of chocolate spiked with ground
piment d'Espelette, the same pepper that covers the salt-cured hams of
Bayonne, and taken snapshots of the aerodynamic ziggurat in the
window, a fountain with liquid chocolate constantly spilling over its
rounded tiers. At Andrieu's shop, I'd quizzed the workers in green
aprons while they restlessly tossed folds of liquid chocolate with metal
trowels, so it could be cooled and broken into pieces, which clients
then selected and composed into edible, cellophane-wrapped bou-
quets. I was starting to fear the local gendarmes would arrest me, if not
as a vagrant, then at least as an industrial spy.

As I walked into Cazenave, for the third time, the woman with
curly gray hair behind the cash register looked up and said tartly, "You
must know our prices by now, *non*?"

It was true: I'd become a regular. The oldest chocolatier in this
Basque city near the Spanish border was founded in 1854, and they
still made the best cup of hot chocolate in the country. Cacao beans
imported from Venezuela, Costa Rica, and Trinidad were roasted in a
lab, then crushed into powder with a monstrous nineteenth-century
contraption confected from wood, bronze, and grindstones. Mixed

with vanilla or cinnamon from tropical islands, and milk still brought fresh from farms in metal buckets, the resulting liquid was whipped up in a stovetop pot with a ribbed *moussoir*—a kind of long-handled, manual centrifuge—and served in Limoges porcelain speckled with tiny pink roses. The house specialty, the *chocolat mousseux*, had been served to the likes of the king of Morocco, Roland Barthes, and Yehudi Menuhin. Bullfighters used to stop by for a quick cup after the corrida, gamblers hired fiacres for a pick-me-up between spins of the roulette wheel in nearby Biarritz, and wealthy Spaniards arrived on boats that had cruised up the coast from Bilbao.

A waitress in a black satin skirt and a white lace apron (all the employees were middle-aged women, gliding through their dream job with looks of beatific contentment) brought a silver tray with a carafe of water, a bowl of whipped cream, and a little jug filled with leftover chocolate, like the extra milk shake once served in roadside mom-and-pop diners. But the centerpiece was the *mousseux*, a rounded, bone-white cup wearing a mobcap of light brown foam, a meniscus of tiny bubbles so densely packed it would only collapse under lashings of whipped cream from my silver spoon. Sip by sip, the warm milk fat, sugar, and cacao deliquesced over my tongue and trickled in a molten thread down my throat, to sit like a purring cat in my stomach.

Nowhere does the food writer's penchant for sublimated sexual imagery get more coquettish than in the chocolate shop. "Chocolate," they love to purr, "that sinful self-indulgence, my one addiction, *mon doux péché*, my sweet sin." Give. Me. A. Break. More like: ca-ca-o, that too obvious scatological metaphor, first enjoyed by the Aztecs mixed with chili peppers and the sacrificial blood of slaughtered virgins, still made from beans gathered by indentured slaves on the Ivory Coast. In Cazenave I liked to daydream about the Marquis de Sade, who was more than willing to scrawl the hyphen between *cacao* and *caca* in thick, brown ink. Imprisoned after he'd slipped

Spanish fly into chocolate pastilles at a party, where the resulting orgy allowed him to enjoy the favors of his sister-in-law, he demanded a cake be brought to him. "I want it to be chocolate, and black inside from chocolate as the devil's ass is black from smoke. And the icing is to be the same." Personally, I would have enjoyed the spectacle of the syphilitic nobleman leaping onto one of these lace-covered tables and scandalizing the old girls with a couple of cracks of the whip.

Under the dim light of a stained-glass skylight, signed with the Parisian address of some long-defunct glazier, I spied on the good bourgeoises of Bayonne. At the *heure du goûter*—tasting time, five P.M.—the room, with its superannuated gas fixtures and lace table-cloths under glass, was invariably packed. I sat down next to a trio of women caparisoned in Burberry and Chanel. The most animated of them gave me an encomium to chocolate.

"*Oh, oui, chocolat!* It boosts your morale! It restores you!" she said, galvanizing her spine with an expressive shake of her derrière. "It is a drug, I suppose, but it's one you should not abuse every day. Otherwise, with the whipped cream, you risk losing your figure." She puffed out her painted cheeks, in a none-too-convincing impression of obesity.

I asked Marie-Joseph, a tall, slender waitress with only a little gray starting to appear in her jet-black Basque hair, if she had clients who were regulars.

"Oh, yes! I've been working here for twenty-five years, and we have our habitués, who never miss their chocolate. I've seen their children grow up, and now their grandchildren."

Did she think they were actually addicted?

"I do! I myself am addicted. By nibbling all the time, you get hooked. I have to have my dark chocolate, with a little bit of orange peel, every day. We close for three weeks in the summer, and it's terrible! It's like I am going through withdrawal!"

Addiction; hooked; withdrawal. Perhaps the terms used to describe the chocolate habit weren't just coy hyperbole. Chocolate contains twelve hundred chemicals, among them tryptophan, an essential amino acid involved in the production of mood-regulating serotonin, and three distinct N-acylethnanolamines, which in large quantities can mimic the action of marijuana by binding to the brain's cannabinoid receptors. Commercial chocolate, like the kind that goes into Mars and Snickers bars, is so heavily processed that it is stripped of any compounds—apart from sugar and fat—that could help elevate your mood; but high-quality cacao, like the kind used at Cazenave, is rich in the potent stimulants called methylxanthines. The chocolate at Cazenave must have been particularly high in one of these chemicals, theobromine: there is enough of this smooth-muscle relaxant, cardiac stimulator, and vasodilator in a standard-sized bar of chocolate to send a medium-size dog into fatal convulsions. God knows how it interacted with its chemical cousin, caffeine—probably the most potent active ingredient in chocolate—in the bloodstreams of the women of Bayonne. Immediately after one eats high-quality chocolate, blood flow to the brain increases by one third. That might have explained the look of contentment, frankly postorgasmic, that suffused the faces of the women around me. I watched a high-cheekboned beauty in her sixties, impeccably accessorized in Hermès scarf and Tissot watch, tear chunks from her toast and dab at thin lips with an increasingly chocolate-browned serviette. She seemed to be set in a cameo; I imagined her swaddled in imaginary doilies and damasks, a portrait of satiety, suffused with strange chemicals. From this perspective, the city's chocolate shops looked a little more sinister. If Bayonne was the Amsterdam of chocolate, I was bang in the middle of the red-light district, surrounded by hardcore junkies.

One way of recognizing a drug of abuse is if, at some point in history, it has doubled as a currency—in the same way kilos of Afghan heroin and Colombian cocaine are today traded for Kalashnikovs and Mercedes. For the Maya, cacao was more valuable than gold; four beans would buy you a squash, eight would get you a rabbit, and a hundred equaled a slave. Another strong hint that you're dealing with a drug is if it has ever been subject to a ban. In 1761, the good citizens of Bayonne—the ancestors of the women who were so demonstratively enjoying their *mousseux* today—banded together to prohibit the sale and production of chocolate. In eighteenth-century France, the ban was not about *what* was being sold, but about *who* was doing the selling. As always with prohibitions, the real issue was power.

Up until the seventeenth century, if you were awake in northern Europe, there was a good chance you were also drunk. In Germany, people began the day with beer soup, which was made by heating strong beer, then adding salt, bread, whisked eggs, and more strong beer. Medieval drinking bouts typically continued until all participants lost consciousness. In a time when drinking water was slimed with bacilli, and milk tended to be half-rancid by the time it got to city dwellers, English families drank three liters of beer a day per person. (As late as the 1820s, London hospitals wisely refused to serve their patients anything but alcohol.) Much heavy work was done by people who had been drinking alcohol since breakfast, and "blue Mondays" became national institutions. For centuries, only bread provided more calories than beer in the daily diet of northern Europeans.

All this changed with the arrival of caffeine, the first stimulant to hit Europe, and the first product in the history of the West that allowed you to purchase increased attention and concentration on demand. The first caffeine-bearing plants brought to Europe were probably the cacao beans that Columbus presented to Ferdinand of Spain in 1502. The Chinese had known about caffeine, in the form of tea, as far back as 2737 B.C. (when its medicinal uses were detailed in a book-length treatise). It kept them healthy by providing them with boiled, and thus safe, water and later aided Ch'an monks, the forerunners of the Zen Buddhists in Japan, to remain attentive during their meditations.

Coffee, legend has it, was discovered by an Ethiopian goatherd named Kaldi in the sixth or seventh century, who became curious when his charges started leaping around after eating the cherries of a glossy-leafed shrub. Like most creation myths, this one is probably a little too pat: anthropologists believe that as far back as 1,000 B.C. the Oromo of Ethiopia took larded balls studded with ripe coffee beans on war parties for quick energy. Coffee remained a local specialty in the Horn of Africa, however, unknown to the Greeks or Romans, until the Sufis—the touring Deadheads of Islam, lovers of hashish, wine, and tripped-out dancing—brought it to the Arabian Peninsula in the thirteenth century. Like most drugs, coffee was first consumed in a ritual, communal setting. The Shadhili sect of the Sufis stewed unroasted beans in large clay vessels, while intoning, "There is no God, but God, the Master, the Clear Reality." And then, wide-awake and inspired, these dervishes spent all night whirling in ecstatic trances that had them communing directly with Allah.

As the use of coffee spread into the mainstream of Muslim society, the killjoys started to take note. Islamic cultures were tribal, desert-based, and nomadic, and one way of distinguishing themselves from the older, urban civilizations was to proscribe the use of the signature intoxicant of the Mediterranean coast, wine. The Koran specifically states, "Intoxicants and gambling . . . are an abomination of Satan's handiwork: Avoid such that you may prosper." The traditional Islamic definition of intoxication is "when one is incapable of distinguishing man from woman, or heaven from earth." (If you are Jewish, in contrast, you are actually expected to drink heavily on certain occasions: four big cups of wine, or three quarters of a bottle, during the Passover seder, and so much wine during the spring festival of Purim that you don't know "whether you are blessing Mordecai or cursing Haman." Meanwhile, in the Christian heaven, there is no beer, which is why Bavarians drink down here; the situation is reversed in Islam, and Muslims have to wait for paradise to drink the "purest wine, that will neither pain their heads nor take away their reason.") Coffee's first trial as a suspected intoxicant came in 1511 when Kha'ir Beg, Mecca's chief of police, saw a group of Sufis near the Holy Mosque passing a liquid from hand to hand, as the drinkers of wine did. He set up a kangaroo court, and two Persian physicians confirmed that coffee was indeed an intoxicant. Sacks of beans were burned in the streets, and imbibers were publicly beaten. When the sultan of Cairo, the police chief's royal master, heard tell of the prohibition, he had the edict repealed; the sultan, it turned out, was a coffee aficionado. Beg, the ur–Drug Czar, was replaced the next year.

But the controversy wouldn't go away. On one side, the martinets argued that *qahwa*—an Arabic word that could be construed as meaning "wine"—was not only a stimulant, but should also be forbidden because it was roasted like coal, carbonization being another Koranic taboo. Moreover, the Sufi notion of *marqaha*, or "coffee euphoria," which implied privileged communication with Allah, was as challenging to the imams as Bible study would later be to Catholic priests. On the more permissive side, apologists argued that since coffee, like hashish and tobacco, was not mentioned in the Koran, it fell under the genial dictum of Hanafi jurisprudence: *Al-ibaha al-asliya*—"if it is not forbidden, it is permitted." Coffeehouses spread to every major city in the Islamic world, and by 1570 there were more than six hundred in Constantinople alone. Many were luxurious establishments where men played chess and backgammon, listened to poetry and female singers (hidden behind screens, *natürlich*), while drinking *kahveh* mixed with saffron, pepper, and even opium.

Legend has it that the Sultan Murat IV, a paranoid alcoholic, made a surreptitious visit to a tavern, where wine-drinking revelers were singing songs of love; then stopped by a coffeehouse, where the clients were volubly criticizing his regime. He went back to the palace and ordered the banning of coffee itself (and tobacco, for good measure). Wandering the streets with an executioner, he would behead anybody caught smoking or drinking coffee. Coffeehouses were razed, and repeat offenders were sewn into leather bags and thrown into the Bosporus. It was history's first secular War on Drugs, and the death toll was enormous. Before he died in 1640—of alcohol poisoning—Murat IV may have had as many as one hundred thousand people executed for consuming the newly forbidden fruit.

Perhaps the sultan was not as foolish as he seemed. If the reigning aristocracy in Europe had foreseen all the upheavals coffee would bring, they might have blockaded shipments of beans at major ports. With caffeine's arrival early in the seventeenth century, first in Venice and Marseille, then in London and Amsterdam, Europe began its slow transformation from an easily managed depressant culture of beer soup, gin, and wine, to a significantly more uppity stimulant culture of coffee, cacao, and tea. The cultural theorist Michel Foucault dated the "rationalization" of Western civilization to the birth of the coffee-house: a Lebanese Jew opened Europe's first coffee shop in Oxford in 1650, and in 1689 a Florentine expatriate founded Paris's first café, Le Procope, which is still a Left Bank institution. Caffeine seemed to wake the emerging middle classes from a long alcoholic torpor. The Puritans in particular were fond of history's first temperance beverage—suddenly there was an alternative to the inn and the tavern, where the evenings had tended to end in incoherent maundering, brawls, and the gutter.

It may be another case of commodity hyperbole—in which cod, salt, or spices are seen to be the motor force behind civilization—but caffeine's presence at the birth of some of the key institutions of modernity seems more than fortuitous. Stock exchanges, insurance companies, and colossal corporations appeared with caffeine: Lloyd's Coffee-House, in Lombard Street, where shipowners and sea captains met with underwriters over a cup, became Lloyd's of London, eventually the largest insurance company in the world, and across the Atlantic, Wall Street's Tontine Coffeehouse became the New

York Stock Exchange. The Royal Society, one of the world's leading scientific clubs, was founded in the Oxford Coffee Club, where jittery empiricists were known to clear the tables for public dissections of dolphins.

Caffeine also abetted popular revolt. It was at a café in the Palais Royal that Camille Desmoulins leapt on a table to rouse the rabble against the aristocracy during the French Revolution. At New York's Merchant Coffee House, the Sons of Liberty plotted against another caffeinated drink: British tea, and all the colonialism it represented. Not surprisingly, the new stimulants provoked widespread suspicion from the authorities; only marijuana would provide more novel pretexts for a ban. (And tellingly, the only country to forbear from attempting to ban caffeine in modern times was Holland.) Coffee narrowly escaped condemnation by the Vatican in 1600 when conservative Catholic clerics attacked its black color and use by Moorish heathens as being a sure sign it was a demonic perversion of Eucharist wine; fortunately, Pope Clement VIII had a sip, liked the taste, and sent the prohibitionists packing. In a 1675 proclamation, two days before Christmas, Charles II of England banned the retailing of coffee, chocolate, tea, and sherbet, arguing that the establishments where they were served were a fire hazard and attracted tradesmen who misspent time better employed on lawful callings. The real gravamen of the charge was that in such establishments "false, malicious and scandalous reports are devised and spread abroad to the defamation of his Majesty's Government." After protest from proprietors, Charles exercised his "royal compassion," revoking the ban eight days into the New Year.

One of the more robust challengers to caffeine's relentless advance was Frederick the Great of Germany. Convinced that the custom of drinking beer soup led to a more robust and zaftig peasantry, he issued a proclamation in 1777, with typically terse Teutonic rectitude: "It is disgusting to notice the increase in the quantity of coffee used by my subjects, and the amount of money that goes out of the country in consequence. Everybody is using coffee. If possible this must be prevented. My people must drink beer." He created a corps of "coffee sniffers," retired soldiers who roamed the streets smelling the air for the aroma of roasting coffee. Like the informers who terrorized gin sellers in England, they were given a portion of all the fines they collected, and like the informers, they were widely mocked and detested. Finally, Frederick chose the route later followed by nanny states, from Singapore to Norway, confronted with the un-stoppable rise of a popular psychoactive: he gave the government a monopoly on its sale and made a fortune taxing it.

But these were rearguard actions. A newly sober Europe had awakened to smell the coffee. Gone was the debauchery celebrated by Rabelais, Boccaccio, and Villon: the harbinger of the new age was Samuel Johnson, whose dictionary was composed under the influence of up to forty cups a day, and its exemplar was Honoré de Balzac, whose multivolume, broadly stroked social dramas were pure caffeine prose; he even admitted to eating the powdered beans raw. From this perspective, the Romantic poets of England and the Symbolists of France—who doted on dreamy laudanum and befuddling absinthe—were expressing a quasi-aristocratic longing for a vanishing, precaf-feinated age when free souls, unbound by the minute hand, could indulge in rural idylls and lyric poetry.

The serious attacks on caffeine wouldn't end until 1911, when Dr. Harvey Washington Wiley, the founder of the U.S. Bureau of Chemistry (the forerunner of the Food and Drug Administration, which keeps Americans safe from raw-milk cheese), attempted to ban the use of caffeine in soda pop. A "chemical fundamentalist" who had spearheaded the Pure Food and Drug Act of 1906 and fought to have saccharin banned, he brought the issue to federal court in the watershed case *The United States* vs. *Forty Barrels and Twenty Kegs of Coca-Cola*. The company had already removed cocaine from its coca leaves and managed to convince the court that caffeine was a naturally occurring component, as opposed to an additive, in its formula. Perhaps Wiley wasn't as loopy as he seemed: it is rather strange, after all, that an addictive stimulant, one that inhibits the absorption of growth-inducing calcium and iron, is present in beverages marketed to elementary-school students. Coca-Cola, a good loser, voluntarily agreed not to feature children under twelve in its advertising, a restriction it quietly liberated itself from in 1986. Today, caffeine's triumph is complete: the four most widespread words in the world, borrowed with small variations into virtually every language on earth, are also the names of the four most important caffeine-bearing plants: coffee, cacao, cola, and tea.

This reflects a bizarre dichotomy in modern society. While one can be incarcerated for growing cannabis, a relatively harmless plant, powerful, even dangerous stimulants are available with nothing more than a doctor's prescription. Amphetamine, first marketed as a nasal inhaler for asthmatics in 1932, gave an adrenaline-like charge to its users, increasing attention and warding off sleep. The British military handed out amphetamines as "energy tablets" during the Second World War; the United States. issued 180 million pills to bomber pilots and jungle fighters; college students downed "pep pills" before exams; and a course of methedrine was a popular weight-loss cure in the 1950s. On the illegal market, amphetamine—known as speed, crank, crystal meth, and *ya ba* or "crazy medicine" in Thailand—is a major drug of abuse, with thirty million regular users worldwide (over twice the number that use cocaine). Speed, as Frank Zappa warned in the 1960s, really does kill: chronic use of amphetamines leads to emaciation, psychotic delusions, and albums like Lou Reed's *Metal Machine Music*.

Unlike marijuana, though, speed keeps you busy and so is a drug favored by high achievers. In the final months of the Second World War, Adolf Hitler was receiving five amphetamine-charged "vitamin shots" a day. British prime minister Sir Anthony Eden admitted that the only thing that got him through the Suez crisis of 1956 was a constant supply of Benzedrine pills. John F. Kennedy was injected with Dexedrine before his debate with Richard Nixon. (Nixon, meanwhile, was a binge drinker and sleeping-pill addict. In 1968, he illegally self-medicated his depression with Dilantin, an anti-convulsant whose side effects include confusion, slurred speech, and nervousness.) Paul Erdos—the great master of number theory, the most prolific mathematician of the twentieth century, and an extreme motorhead—fueled his calculations with Benzedrine, Ritalin, and strong espresso, sleeping only four hours a night. (When a friend bet him he couldn't swear off stimulants, he won, but completely lost his ability to concentrate. Collecting his money, he told his friend, "You've set mathematics back a month.") There are currently 1.5 million American children taking speed, in the form of Ritalin, every day of the school week, as a treament for attention deficit disorder (some make lunch money by selling the pills, for up to $100 a pop, to weight lifters and college students cramming for exams). In 2002, F-16 pilot William "Psycho" Umbach killed four Canadian soldiers with a laser-guided bomb in Kandahar, later admitting he'd done it under the influence of Air Force–issued "go pills"; during the inquiry, it emerged that the United States legally requires fighter pilots to sign a release saying they will take speed. In England, the Ministry of Defense is buying bulk orders of a new stimulant, modafinil, a treatment for narcolepsy that has lately become a lifestyle drug for overworked executives in the United States. Available by prescription from family doctors, amphetamines are one class of drug whose abuse will do more damage, more quickly, than just about any drug apart from industrial solvents.

We live in stimulating times, the received wisdom goes, and in a culture of productivity drugs that might make you into a dreamy slacker can only be maladaptive. That's why laughing gas, opium, and ether are no longer popular drugs of abuse, and why the most widespread addictive stimulant in the world—so much so that few people consider it a drug—is caffeine.

Coffee, tea, and chocolate survived the spirited attacks of bishops and viziers, kings and physicians, because their pharmacological effects corresponded to the *Zeitgeist* of the rising era of global capitalism. But the arguments mustered against caffeine in the past are strangely reminiscent of those used by modern Drug Czars to demonize marijuana and ecstasy. Illegal drugs are prohibited today, as we are constantly reminded by fundamentalists, socialist politicians, moral entrepreneurs, and doctors, because:

They are immoral. (It is written in the Torah, the Koran, or the Bible that one should not defile oneself, that intoxication is Satan's handiwork, or that one's body is one's temple. For true believers, there is no arguing with "'Cos the Supreme Being said you shouldn't.")

They encourage antisocial behavior and crime. (In the case of illegal drugs, almost by definition: if they are prohibited, then anybody who uses them will be a criminal. However, if there is one drug that seems to provide license for violence, it is alcohol, which is legal. It's the need to buy expensive drugs on the black market that leads to most of the violence associated with drugs: muggings; burglaries; gang warfare; shoot-outs with the DEA and the Mounties—all are by-products of illegality. Opiate addicts are almost utterly pacified when under the influence of their drug of choice; and back in the days when Bayer sold heroin in pill form, there was hardly a wave of spinsters going on rampages. As for marijuana, as P. J. O'Rourke has pointed out, how much can you say against a drug that makes teenage boys drive slowly? It is drug prohibition that leads to crime; drugs lead to excessive television watching.)

They are bad for your health. (Well, yes: intoxicants are toxic, it's true. But it's all a matter of degree. Does one tolerate the liver damage caused by a lifelong infatuation with single-malt Scotch? The shaky nerves and compromised kidneys and insomnia that come from a weakness for Frappuccino? It was a pet theory of Paul Morrissey, the director who worked with Andy Warhol at the Factory, that the adolescents of the 1960s, one of the best-nourished, most disease-free generations in history, were taking drugs to experiment with ill health. The idea isn't too far-fetched: a well-fed but uninvigorating urban existence can lead people to seek toxic stimulation, just as bored, caged animals welcome almost any drugs their captors give them. If, as some authorities claim, the drive to temporary escape is universal, then the current War on Drugs is as vain as the Victorian war on masturbation, and our efforts should go not toward interdiction, but toward minimizing the toxicity of intoxication.)

They are addictive. (Which is the only really convincing argument. Crack cocaine can put you on a treadmill of desire that will have you emptying your savings account in months, or days, or hours. So can an addiction to video poker. But when something is both dependence-inducing and unhealthy—tobacco for nicotine addicts, fatty foods for compulsive eaters—the public health consequences can be very dire indeed. Making a profit from people who have lost control of their behavior, whether you run a casino on a First Nations reserve, a skid-row crack house, or a fast-food joint in Houston, is one nasty way to earn a living.)

Caffeine could stand accused of all the above charges—particularly if it were prohibited by law. Finally, the only really apposite question is, should a society ban solvents, cigarettes, fatty foods, and every other substance with the potential to cause addiction, or are its resources better spent on treating addiction itself?

I know I could use a little help myself. Since my trip to San Francisco to find smoke-easies, I'd been struggling with an on-again, off-again smoking habit, which I'd been interrupting with occasional courses of nicotine gum. And, like 80 percent of North Americans, I use caffeine every day, in the form of tea, chocolate, caffeinated aspirin, soda, and—this is my biggest problem—short espressos. I've been using caffeine since I was fifteen years old, and I've developed a pretty high tolerance for the shit. I try to dignify my habit by buying high-quality, fair-trade beans for home use; but deep down I know I'm just another addict. If there were no other option, I'd eat Folgers crystals straight from the jar.

I tried to quit once. I lasted three days, and after seventy hours of lethargy and depression, in which I completely lost the will to communicate with kith and kin, I developed a crippling withdrawal symptom: a throbbing headache, unlike any I've known before or since. It went away shortly after I limped to the stove, turned on the gas, and resignedly slapped my fully charged Vev Vigano coffeemaker onto the burner.

When I'm in Montreal, I begin almost all my days at an espresso bar called the Social Club, where the local Italian landlords flip through the pink pages of the *Gazzetta dello Sport* between hands of poker, and the latest soccer games are beamed in by satellite from Milan and Rome. The joint is run by six brothers from Calabria, and at least twice a day I am served a *crema*-topped demitasse of the devil's own brew by the practiced hands of a family called Lucifero.

If psychoactive history had gone a little differently—if Kha'ir Beg and Frederick the Great had managed to permanently ban coffee-houses, or Pope Clement VIII had been served a particularly bitter cup of joe that day in 1600—I might be accompanying my afternoon paper not with espresso, but with a pipe of opium, a bowl of hashish jelly, or a shot of laudanum. I'm not sure I wouldn't rather live in a society where the approved intoxicants were more conducive to reverie; it would make jaywalking a riskier proposition, certainly, but I might hear more discussion of poetry at the Social Club, rather than the usual agitated bitching about the performance of Juventus or the Montreal Canadiens. We'd all complain about the aggressive caff-heads, with their telltale trembling hands, who were breaking into our apartments and stealing Velvet Underground CDs to score their next Ziploc bag full of crystal caffeine. The emergency rooms would be clogged with the victims of overdoses, and at Caffeine Anonymous meetings, recovering addicts would soothe their fried nerves with endless cups of poppy tea.

I first met my friend Alain Dagher at the Social Club, where he was reading *In Search of Lost Time* (written by a bedridden Frenchman working under the influence of morphine, syrup of ether, barbiturates, and heroic doses of caffeine). Alain works at the Montreal Neurological Institute, where, to further his research on addiction and nerve diseases, he gives people amphetamines, nicotine, and chocolate and sticks them into scanners to see what their brains are doing, and then publishes the results in such journals as *Nature* and *Neurology*. (In spite of repeated hints, he has yet to recruit me as a subject.)

In our discussions of drugs and addiction at the Social Club, I like to play the devil's advocate, and Alain, as a practicing physician, tends to defend the status quo—up to a point. He agrees that many of the arguments made to justify prohibitions are arbitrary and have little do with a rational weighing of the real costs and benefits of the substances in question. Though he thinks cigarette smoking is a deadly habit, he also believes that the dangers of secondhand smoke are overstated, and that patch-administered nicotine, as an increaser of concentration, will prove to be a valuable drug in treating Alzheimer's and Parkinson's disease.

Before I went to Bayonne, Alain invited me to his apartment for a quick PowerPoint presentation on the current state of neurological research into addiction.

"All addictive substances," Alain explained in his soft but confident cadences, "have at least one single active ingredient that acts on a specific receptor in the brain. And every known addictive drug increases levels of the neurotransmitter dopamine, which is just one of about fifty known neurotransmitters, including serotonin and noradrenaline.

"Now, there's no drug that will make everybody an addict. The most addictive of all drugs in our society is nicotine, and even then only about one quarter who consume it are addicted by any standard definition. Addictive drugs too act on the brain circuitry that originally developed to serve feeding behavior. I believe hunger is an addiction to food. Hunger, like addiction to nicotine, cocaine, and other drugs, is learned behavior. We believe that when a baby is hungry, it's in a state of unrest, and it finds out through trial and error that it can eliminate this state of unrest by eating. It's a lesson we learn very quickly, probably in the first twenty-four hours of life. Hunger is learned when the brain is still evolving; it's hardwired, whereas drug addiction is usually learned when the brain is finished making all its connections. It's striking how similar someone who's trying to quit nicotine or cocaine is to someone who's trying to lose weight. The difference is, when people try to quit drugs, they can stop, cold turkey. But you *have* to keep eating, which is why only two percent of people who try to lose weight are successful.

"We did an interesting study on chocolate. Subjects were given a square of chocolate, they let it melt in the mouth, and then we put them in a PET scanner to measure their brain activity. We compared this to a study of habitual cocaine users, which showed the brain areas activated by the rush were the same ones that are dependent on pleasure in a chocolate eater. The pleasure from eating chocolate, and the rush from cocaine, involve the same brain areas—in this case, the dorsal striatum, which is where we see the conditioned reponse—and likely develop in the same way, through experience, through repeated use. We're all long-standing habitual eaters, and the act of anticipating food, as with anticipating drugs, can release dopamine.

"Now obviously, cocaine and chocolate are different. We all have a conditioned response to food, but drug users have both a conditioned response and a pharmacological effect—the drug molecules are going into your brain and doing something there."

I mentioned all the psychoactive substances in chocolate: theobromine, theophylline, and, perhaps most significantly, caffeine.

"There's more," said Alain. "Phenylethalamine, which is another neurotransmitter that interacts with dopamine, though we're not sure whether, in the case of chocolate, it crosses over into the brain. But caffeine works by binding to a receptor that's intended for a neurotransmitter called adenosine. This was only discovered recently." Adenosine, in fact, is an internally occurring chemical with mood-depressing, hypnotic, and anticonvulsant properties, one that helps us relax and sleep. Caffeine molecules mimic its shape, plugging receptors meant to receive adenosine: hence, increased alertness, and often, insomnia. "Caffeine induces dopamine release in the same area we found was affected by cocaine; this is the hallmark of addictive drugs. The effect is relatively weak, of course, compared to amphetamines or cocaine."

Alain clicked on an icon that brought up the definition of substance dependence from the *DSM-IV*, the reference psychiatrists use to diagnose mental illness.

"Dependence is defined here as a maladaptive pattern of substance use; it implies the key component of addiction is loss of control over your behavior, but also that some harm is being done. So, if in a twelve-month period you meet three or more of these criteria, you're considered dependent."

At this point, I suggested to Alain we try a thought experiment: let's subject a legal drug, caffeine, to the seven criteria of dependence in the *DSM*.

1. Tolerance—in other words, a resistance to the drug, and a need for markedly increased amounts to achieve the desired effect—We

both agreed that this was the case with our espresso. In some users, in fact, tolerance to caffeine increases to the point where it cannot be overcome by any dose.

2. Withdrawal—Definitely, as I'd experienced myself: symptoms include drowsiness, impaired concentration, irritability, decreased sociability, a throbbing headache, and flulike symptoms such as nausea and vomiting, which can last from two days to a week.

3. The substance is taken in larger amounts than intended—Sure: Alain and I agreed we've both been known to remark, of a Saturday morning, that we'd had one espresso too many.

4. Persistent desire to cut down—Of course: I often find that I'm trying to limit myself to a cup a day, and I deliberately stop my intake after about four in the afternoon.

5. A great deal of time spent in activities necessary to obtain, use, or recover from the effects of the substance—You bet: I don't even want to think of how many hours a week I spend going to, sitting in, and coming back from the café.

6. Important social, occupational, or recreational activities are given up or reduced—Perhaps. I mean, we could have been playing soccer. (If caffeine were illegal, and we had to hustle to find a daily dose on the black market, the last two criteria would have been even more easy to meet.)

7. Use is continued despite knowledge of having a persistent or recurrent physical or psychological problem likely to have been caused or exacerbated by the substance—Arguable. Caffeine definitely causes jitteriness and insomnia, but, as addictive drugs go, its adverse effects on health are small.

The last point is hard to corroborate, however, because it's almost impossible to find control subjects who are not addicted to caffeine. The truth is, as a society, we have become blind to caffeine's omnipresence; we no longer know what noncaffeinated health is. After water, coffee is the world's most popular beverage, with four hundred billion cups consumed a year. Eighty percent of newborns have detectable levels of caffeine in their bloodstream at birth. Even if you restricted your drinking to fresh water, you might still get a dose of the stuff: in a recent test, caffeine was found in over three quarters of 139 streams sampled by the U.S. Geological Survey in thirty states.

An illegal drug like ecstasy, in contrast, does not come close to satisfying the *DSM*'s criteria for addiction. Fatal overdoses are almost unheard of (whereas ten grams of caffeine, about one hundred cups of coffee, is enough to kill most people, and caffeine can be linked to five thousand deaths a year in the United States, more than all illegal drugs combined), and there is no evidence that ecstasy promotes physical dependency in humans. The fact is, few people take enough for the phenomena of tolerance and withdrawal to come into play; though some professional DJs may have reached the point where they had to cut down, for most users ecstasy is a weekend party drug. We may yet learn that repeated use leads to depression later in life—the specter of a cohort of prematurely grumpy rave kids lurks—but the salient point is that a generation was exposed to ecstasy, and few, if any, ended up daily users. The same can be said for LSD, magic mushrooms, and, to a lesser extent, marijuana, which is a drug of abuse for only a small minority of committed potheads. All of these drugs are more potent than caffeine— some psychedelic drugs produce psychotic breaks in susceptible users, for example—but none are as risky as alcohol or tobacco; and unlike coffee, few but the most committed stoners take them every day. Nonetheless, being caught with these nonaddictive substances in your possession can ruin your life: six hundred thousand people are arrested for marijuana possession in the United States alone every year.

Alain preferred to reserve judgment on illegal drugs. However, what he had to say next surprised me.

"If something you become very obsessed with doesn't cause you actual physical harm, say, classical music, tea"—and here his over-weight cat leapt into his lap—"or pets, it will never meet the *DSM* criteria. However, food really is one of the strongest examples of addiction. Look at food use by obese people: maladaptive, absolutely; causes impairment or distress, absolutely; significant health risk and loss of control, absolutely. Finally, continued use in spite of knowledge of adverse consequences—also absolutely the case. You have overweight people who are actually suffering, and they can't stop eating."

So, I asked, could chocolate be considered an addictive substance?

Alain paused and thought about it. "Well, it's got caffeine, and several other psychoactive substances. It's got fat and sugar, which are two of the most important sources of calories. I suppose if you were going to make something legal to get addicted to—besides, say, slot machines—then chocolate would be perfect."

Bayonne, from this perspective, was a city in denial. It owed some of its current prosperity, and much of its tourist trade, to the peddling of an addictive psychoactive substance to a dependent populace.

Chocolate, from the start, has shown all the hallmarks of a drug of abuse. Like opium, cannabis, ergot, alcohol, and tobacco, its birth was swaddled in ritual. First cultivated by the Olmecs, precursors to the Maya in Central America, at least six hundred years before Christ, the cacao tree became a sacred plant to the Aztecs. Like the other major drugs, it was the subject of attempted prohibitions: Charles II's ban on coffee also singled out chocolate as another fomenter of loose political talk in Restoration England. In 1616, a committee of Doctors of the Church condemned cacao as "the damnable agent of necromancers and sorcerers," and the Society of Jesus of New Spain tried to prohibit its use among Jesuits. Fortunately, Spanish monks and nuns were such ardent consumers that chocolate was spared by the prohibitionists.

The secret of chocolate making came to Bayonne in 1609, after the Inquisition had chased the Sephardic Jews out of Spain and Portugal. The stuffy Basque town, if it didn't exactly welcome the new arrivals, at least tolerated them. The hotel I was staying in—my room had an inspiring view of the platforms of the neighboring train station—was in an area called St-Esprit, across the Adour River from Bayonne proper, once the ghetto for the Jews, who were banned from the city after sundown.

Every day, I walked across the long stone St-Esprit bridge to take my chocolate at Cazenave. In the seventeenth century, this bridge had been made of wood, and Jewish merchants crossed it to sell their wares to the people of Bayonne. The Jews were forbidden to own businesses or run workshops, to sleep or eat in the city, or shop at the market before noon. Every evening, the town sergeant locked them out of the city walls, and they trudged back home over the bridge. One of the few items they succeeded in retailing was chocolate, which became a chic delicacy among the middle class. A display in the Musée Basque showed how merchants roasted the cacao beans in a small oven and, after cooling them in a canvas bag, crushed the beans into a paste on a heated, concave stone platform on a tripod. It had to be schlepped from house to house, and the chocolatiers knelt in front of the platforms for up to an hour to coax the beans into a form that could be whipped into a proper cup of hot chocolate.

Gradually, the secret of chocolate's manufacture got out. In 1761, Bayonne's Catholic chocolate makers banded together to form a corporation, "with the goal of perfecting the trade, seeing as a plethora of foreigners are inundating the city and infecting the public with the poor quality of the chocolate they sell." The audacity of the guildsmen was staggering: they claimed that chocolate making had been forbidden to Jews "since time immemorial." The city recognized the new corporation, and for the next six years, the trade was closed to Jews, who eventually threw up their hands in dismay and found other ways to make a living.

I met Jean-Michel Barate, the founder of the contemporary Guilde des Chocolatiers, in his shop, Daranatz, just a couple of doors down the arcaded street from Cazenave. A historian by training, Barate had married into a family that had been in the chocolate business since 1870. Daranatz was staffed by women in striped pink robes, who reverently plucked marrons glacés and gold-foil-wrapped bonbons in the shape of Bayonne hams from the display cases with metal tongs.

"I'm a kind of ayatollah of chocolate, a fundamentalist, if you will," Barate told me. "Most of our chocolates come from South America; as a historian, I strive to find the original flavors. Cacao in pre-Columbian America was no ordinary plant. It had a nutritional role, but also a mythical, symbolic, religious value. The planting and harvesting of cacao were always accompanied by a religious ceremony, and in the Aztec mythology, it was God who brought cacao to earth. The first present the Mexican emperor made to Cortés, the Spanish conqueror, was a field of cacao trees. In terms of its importance, it was the equivalent of the grapevine in the Mediterranean."

Looking around the shop, I noticed bottles of yellow Izarra, a cloyingly sweet Basque liqueur flavored with saffron, coffee beans dipped in chocolate, bottles of Laurent-Perrier champagne, and flacons of eau-de-vie with whole pears floating in them. I observed to Barate that we were surrounded by psychoactive substances; he looked a bit taken aback.

"That's it," he said drily. "We're dealers. That could be an interesting tourist campaign: the dealers of Bayonne."

Soldiering on, I asked whether he had any customers he considered addicts.

"We have clients who come every two days to buy their bars of chocolate. Sometimes one feels a need for chocolate. It contains natural antidepressants; I think it's more interesting than Prozac."

Barate acknowledged that he was familiar with the story of the Jewish chocolate makers.

"It was a small episode in the history of Bayonne," he said with a dismissive grimace, "more anecdotal than anything else. The prohibition only lasted a few years before it was overturned by the parliament of Bordeaux. It's true that there are no longer any Jewish families who make chocolate in Bayonne; they've gone into other businesses. But it's not in the Jewish tradition to manufacture; they're more sellers than manufacturers."

(Especially, I thought, when throughout history the local gentiles had banded together in guilds and corporations to prevent them from doing anything more than door-to-door peddling.)

"I think the real hero in all of this was a pope," Barate continued. "There was a long polemic in Spain over whether chocolate was a solid food. If it was liquid, it could be consumed during Lent, and he finally issued a papal bull that declared chocolate to be a drink. A papal prohibition, in such a profoundly religious society, might have meant the disappearance of chocolate altogether." (The pope in question was Alexander VII, whose cardinal Brancaccio pronounced on the question in 1662.)

Barate, the chocolatier-historian, looked out the window dreamily. "I sometimes say that the chocolatiers of Bayonne should take up a collection to have a statue of this pope erected on the Place St-Pierre. We owe everything to him."

It appeared to me that, on the contrary, the contemporary guild owed everything to the Jews their ancestors had driven out of the chocolate business.

Walking back across the St-Esprit bridge, to the ghetto I'd instinctively gravitated toward, I mentally erected a more appropriate statue on the square. It would depict an unknown Sephardic Jew, kneeling over a stone tripod covered with crushed cacao beans destined for a cup of chocolate for one of the gentiles of Bayonne.

It would be a symbolic piece, executed in smooth, chocolate-hued marble, and dedicated to all the other forgotten heroes—coffee-drinking Sufi dervishes, peyote-eating Native Americans, Mexican hemp smokers—who, throughout history, have faced the wrath of all the sultans, drug czars, and Vatican clerics who have resorted to any spurious pretext to squelch one of the most venerable and misunderstood of human drives: the desire to escape, however briefly, everyday consciousness.

· HERBAL TEA ·

You gentlemen who think you have a mission
To purge us of the seven deadly sins
Should first sort out the basic food position
Then start your preaching, that's where it begins

—*Bertolt Brecht, "What Keeps Mankind Alive?"*

· 8 ·

MATÉ DE COCA

Never Say No

I N L A P A Z, the first thing that hits you is that you are high. Too high. As high, probably, as you have ever been before; higher, certainly, than is proper for any human body to come in the course of a single day. Your plane curves in over the low-wattage slumscape of the highest shantytown in the world, you touch down at the highest international airport in the world, and you go through passport control fifteen hundred feet above the highest capital city in the world. Waiting at the luggage carousel for your backpack to drop onto the rubber, you are thirteen thousand feet above sea level, at the same altitude as the mountaineers who summit Eiger after two days of hard climbing.

Heaped atop the other violent dislocations of intercontinental jet travel—latitudinal, cultural, temporal—the change in altitude elicits groans of protest from your body. *Soroche*, or mountain sickness, is a kind of intoxication that afflicts those who come too high, too fast: the Andean bends, if you will. For most people, *soroche* involves a couple of days of tingling fingers, fatigue, faintness, and mild headaches, though in extreme cases fluid can collect in the brain and lead to cerebral edema, coma, and death. The day I flew south, my father called to tell me about the son of a friend, a man younger than I was, who was found dead in his La Paz hotel after retiring to his room complaining of a migraine and shortness of breath. Changing planes in the low-lying eastern Bolivian city of Santa Cruz, I'd met a young woman from the American embassy in Uruguay, who'd offered me a blister pack of acetazolamide pills, which she said would help me metabolize oxygen better. The drug's side effects seemed almost as severe as *soroche* itself: the box recommended you call a doctor if you experienced unusual bleeding or bruising, tremors in your hands, a pain in your groin, fever or rash. It sounded like a typically techno-cratic treatment; I decided to hold out for a more natural remedy.

The Bolivians, not surprisingly, have long since mastered their *soroche*. In the cab from the airport, I watched awestruck from the bubble of my fatigue as barrel-chested men in long-sleeved dress shirts jogged *up* the switchbacks we were driving down, bearing heavy backpacks. The people of the Andes owe their endurance to gen-erations and lifetimes spent adapting to these mountains, but they also have a secret weapon in their folk armamentarium. After dropping my backpack in my hotel room, I went to a lounge in the lobby, picked a tea bag from the basket of chamomile, tutti-frutti, and anise-flavored infusions, and poured hot water over the sachet labeled "maté de coca." After letting the bag steep for five minutes, I had my first sip of coca-leaf tea.

It was mildly herbal, more reminiscent of Sleepytime than grassy-tasting yerba maté, the bitter national infusion of Argentina. More interesting than its flavor was its effect: after my second cup, the tingling in my fingers stopped and a tightness that had been flickering around my temples relaxed; after my third, I was suffused with a perceptible, if subtle, sense of relaxation and clearheadedness. Coca leaves contain fourteen different alkaloids, one of which is cocaine; a single cup of maté contains a little over four milligrams, enough to make a midsize house cat slightly more skittish than usual, though it's no more stimulating than a regular cup of coffee. There is just enough cocaine, however—as there is just enough morphine in two poppy-seed bagels—to produce a positive result on a drug test. Bolivian soccer player Luis Cristaldo got caught in a urine test after a World Cup qualifier, as did a Chicago woman who drank some coca tea she'd brought back after a vacation in Peru in 2001. Cristaldo was subsequently exonerated, but the woman lost her job at the Cook County sheriff's office.

In Bolivia, visiting dignitaries are typically offered a cup of maté de coca when they step off the plane; John Paul II accepted one, as did the king and queen of Spain, and Princess Anne, who reportedly enjoyed Bolivia's leading brand, Windsor. (Perhaps less surprisingly, Fidel Castro pointedly requested a cup on a 1993 visit, provoking cheers across the nation.) In a poor continent's poorest country, where the average income is $72 a month, coca provides a living for tens of thousands of peasant farmers. You can buy coca tea in the duty-free shop at the airport; local markets sell coca biscuits and toothpaste; and the next president of Bolivia may well be a coca grower. Eradicating coca in South America, an anthropologist told me, would be akin to ridding the northern hemisphere of coffee, tobacco, and Communion wafers.

I took my cup of maté de coca to my room, had a few sips as I watched the children in the street below dueling with discarded cardboard tubes, and wondered if the son of my father's friend would have survived his stay in La Paz if he'd drunk enough coca tea. Thanks to decades of American pressure on the United Nations, Bolivia, Argentina, and Peru are now the only places on earth where you can legally enjoy this beverage. Meanwhile, the Drug Enforcement Agency is sworn to a war whose tools include Black Hawk heli-copters, chemical defoliants, and biological arms, and whose goal seems to be the utter elimination of the coca plant from the face of the earth. If there was any way out of the international prohibition of drugs, that nine-decade-long sinkhole of corruption, constantly eroding civil liberties, and wasted lives, I suspected it might lie in the contents of the soggy tea bag at the bottom of my cup.

I turned off the light and fell into a deep and dreamless sleep. Unlike a café au lait or an Earl Grey tea, maté de coca is one stimulant that doesn't keep you awake at night.

"In Bolivia, coca is part of what maintains connections between people," anthropologist Andrew Orta told me, as he soothed his *soroche* with a big bowl of vegetable soup. "It's a part of daily sociability."

We were sitting in a restaurant on Calle Linares; I was working on a llama steak—thinly sliced, none too fatty, delicious. Orta, a soft-spoken man with round glasses and thinning red hair, was an associate professor at the University of Illinois, and he'd agreed to meet me before I'd flown down to Bolivia. By coincidence, we were neighbors in the same hotel; I'd caught him reading a paperback in a patch of sunlight on the landing outside my room. South America, apparently, can be a small continent—especially for gringos carrying the Lonely Planet guide.

Orta's fieldwork involved living with Aymara peasants in Jesús de Machaqa, a town one hundred kilometers west of La Paz. About 60 percent of Bolivians are of indigenous, rather than European, descent. The two leading groups are the Aymara and the Quechua; the latter are directly descended from the Incas, whose empire of twelve million subjects once ran from Ecuador to central Chile. Though coca didn't grow in the high plains where Orta did his research, it was an essential part of daily life, brought to the altiplano through trade with other communities.

"The leadership of these communities is something all adults are expected to participate in," explained Orta, "and the highest level they achieve in this area is called *mallku*, which is a kind of community leadership that married couples undertake. During the time they serve, they're expected to carry coca around with them in a *chuspa*, or coca purse, at all times. People come to them to resolve family problems, and the way they start talking honestly and openly about something is by sharing coca. Typically, during their *mallku*, these extended patrilineal families will build an additional room around the patio, and this is where they'll receive guests. People would be kind of horrified if there was no coca."

In the traditional context, coca was offered freely, with no expectation of payment. Like tobacco, peyote, or Communion wine in other settings, it was a commodity that was excluded from the regular economy—a gift both valueless and invaluable—and meant to be consumed with other members of the community. Apart from its role in divination, coca had been used for its powerful anesthetic qualities well before the Spanish conquered the Incas in 1532.

I asked Orta whether he'd ever accepted coca from his hosts.

"Oh, sure! You know, it's pretty mild. It has a numbing effect on your mouth, but in terms of a buzz, I would say a couple of espressos would do more for you. Even the Catholic Church acknowledges the ritual use of coca now, which is a turnaround from their position in the 1950s." (And an even more radical departure from their stance of 1552, when the First Council of Lima called for a total prohibition. King Philip II of Spain called coca's stimulating effects an "*ilusión del demonio*," only changing his tune, and overturning the ban, when it was pointed out that the Indians wouldn't go down and slave in the Spanish mines without first stuffing a good wad of coca in their cheeks.) "The only people who preach against coca these days are evangelical Protestant groups, like the Mormons or Seventh-Day Adventists. But then again, they don't chew gum or smoke cigarettes."

The waitress cleared away our plates and brought two cups of coca tea, which we accompanied with puffs of another New World psychoactive, tobacco.

"You know, if you were to grow a cash crop," mused Orta, exhaling a plume of Camel smoke, "you would be foolish not to grow coca. It's perfectly suited for the Bolivian market. You never have to worry about your crop rotting; lack of demand is never a problem. And your clients actually come to you to get it."

In La Paz, the newcomer's gaze is torn between the allures of a prodigious distance and the demands of a teeming proximity. If you allow your eyes to skip up the tiers of cubical terra-cotta-toned homes on the sun-bleached hills that enfold the skyscrapers of the city center, you risk being run over by a packed microbus trolling the curb for one last passenger. Should you become obsessed with the lone toddlers holding up boxes of Q-tips and toothpicks and bars of Lux soap, you find yourself sideswiped, at the turn of the corner, by a view of the five peaks of snow-shawled Illimani, as imposingly pyramidal as the fringe-mantled women who squat behind endless piles of mousetraps, alpaca sweaters, and Windows 98 software.

So, as I entered the food market that rambles up Calle Rodriguez, I was glad that I had settled on a single desideratum—if only to shield my already overloaded senses from the surfeit of *chuño*, *oca*, *tunto*, and the two hundred or so other varieties of spotted, elongated, yellow, truffle-shaped, or dehydrated potatoes that are the mainstay of the Andean diet. The task wasn't as easy as it looked: there are many things, it turns out, that the uninitiated shopper could mistake for coca in a Bolivian market. I paused at a metal cart, with its own hand-operated mill, piled with cacao beans and dried leaves, until I realized I was dealing with a spice merchant. Beyond a wheelbarrow of puffed quinoa, I asked a juice seller behind a stack of glasses what the little green blob sunk in clear liquid was.

"*Quisa!*" she said. "It's sweet."

As the stalls crept ever higher up the hillside, I finally went into a butcher's and asked if she knew where I could find coca leaves. She came out from behind the counter and gave me a firm nudge—I was leaning against the dripping cadaver of a cow hanging from a hook.

"Coca, for chewing?" she asked, wiping her hands on a blood-stained smock.

I nodded. She tugged at my sleeve, pulled me into the street, and pointed toward the hills, directing me in the inimitable South American manner. "Go up one block, turn right, then go down one block, then down again one more half block."

Her directions led me to two fifty-kilogram burlap bags slumped on a street corner, overflowing with leaves. The stallkeeper, seated beneath a parasol, eyed me suspiciously. She was a *chola*, the term for the La Paz–born Indian women who follow a strict dress code: a bowler hat straight out of Edwardian London, and fringed shawls draped over pleated, floral-patterned skirts (a hot look, apparently, in seventeenth-century Toledo). The full *chola* is a bizarre confluence of anachronisms; it was Carmen goes to the City, in the Tibet of the Americas.

All business, she was obviously having none of my exoticizing gaze.

"How much do you want?" she asked brusquely. "One boliviano? Two? Five?"

I opted for five bolivianos' worth—the equivalent of sixty-three U.S. cents—and she scooped the leaves into a green plastic bag, which completely filled my shoulder bag.

"Would you like *lejía*?"

Lejía, which means "bleach," is actually a highly alkaline combination of burnt roots and cane sugar that facilitates the extraction of alkaloids from the leaves. The sweet variety, sold between two pieces of plastic wrap, looks like a squashed chunk of very black hashish.

I pulled out some change, among which were some Chilean pesos and Canadian quarters.

"I don't want any of your foreign money!" she said with a grimace.

Her younger colleague leaned over and said, with a giggle. "But *I* would like to come to your country!"

The *chola* in the bowler showed me how to nip off a piece of *lejía* with a thumbnail and fold it into the leaf. She took the opportunity to stuff her cheek with leaves.

Sizing me up, she said, "You should start with ten leaves." There had been at least three times as many in the handful she'd taken.

I told her I had high hopes they'd help with my altitude sickness. In the noontime heat, I was feeling the edges of a migraine looming every time I started walking uphill.

"They're also good for the digestion," she said, patting her round belly. "Very nutritious!"

I thanked her and found a shaded bench outside a shop where I could take the time to properly prepare my quid. The leaves were oval, dark on one side, lighter on the other, and tapered at both ends, but no more remarkable in appearance than the bay leaves that float in a pot of spaghetti sauce. I nipped a nugget of *lejía*, folded the leaf over it, and tucked it between my gums and cheek. Nip, fold, tuck: once I realized the few passersby who noticed me didn't give a rat's ass about what I was doing, I started to enjoy the rhythm of the slow-paced ritual. My fingers were soon stained black and green, my cheeks bulged—I stuffed in twenty, then thirty leaves—until I noticed the tip of my tongue was going numb. Reduced to a pulpy wad by my saliva, the leaves combined with the alkaline *lejía*, raising the pH in my mouth, which in turn broke down the coca's cell walls, finally releasing tiny amounts of cocaine. Though it was time for lunch, my hunger had disappeared. So had the throb in my temples, as the sweaty malaise of mingled jet lag and *soroche* released its grip.

Suddenly, as the coca took hold, there was no better place on earth to be in than La Paz, and I had all the time in the world, and a seemingly bottomless reserve of energy, to explore it. The precipitous sidewalks were no longer to be slogged up, step by step, but taken at a trot. On the Prado I chatted with the shoeshine boys in black Zapatista-style balaclavas, paused with a group of children who stood rapt before a sidewalk black-and-white television on which Jackie Chan's feet flew, and was anointed with holy water by a nun in the portico of the San Francisco Church. Everywhere I marked my path with globs of fluorescent green spit. It was a lot more satisfying than pan, the gum-staining, betel-nut stimulant I'd chewed in India, and a lot less disgusting than chewing tobacco, with which I'd briefly flirted as a teenager. Coca induced a subtle euphoria, longer lasting than the crystalline buzz of eternal dissatisfaction that comes with cocaine. If chemicals are all about the rush, then the plants from which they are derived offer a softer, more salutary version of the same sensation. Chewing coca, which takes a serious investment of time, is akin to pipe or cigar smoking: a habit from before the industrial revolution, ideal for days of contemplation and outdoor activity.

Perhaps too it was the context. In La Paz, there was nothing covert or shameful about chewing coca; on the contrary, it was an expression of solidarity with the people. Graffiti daubed on peeling walls called for the LIBRE CULTIVO DE COCA, the "free cultivation of coca," and T-shirts in the tourist ghettos proclaimed LA HOJA DE COCA NO ES DROGA—"the coca leaf isn't a drug." My happy, afternoon-long buzz didn't seem to corroborate this last assertion: if the coca leaf wasn't a drug, than neither was the coffee bean, *cannabis sativa*, the tobacco plant, or the opium poppy.

But if agreeing meant I could enjoy my coca with impunity, I was willing to play along.

The slum of El Alto, perched on the same treeless plain as the airport, is now a city of seven hundred thousand. It is from here that shoeshine boys, *cholas*, taxi drivers, unemployed miners, and dispossessed farmers swarm into the European-style plazas of La Paz when the protests heat up; it was here that dozens of people were killed by the army in the demonstrations that led to the ousting of the last president.

I took a taxi up precipitous switchbacks to El Callejón de los Yatiris,

also known as Witches' Alley. On one side of the broad, unpaved
street, a statue of Jesus, Dios de Dioses, blessed the flat rooftops of La
Paz; a single-story building ran the length of the other side, with
sheet-metal doors every few yards, each with a number daubed over
it. Save for the colorful signs offering "to cure different illnesses" and
"call up souls," it could have been a brothel strip in a border town—or
a mini-storage warehouse in the American Southwest. I chose door
number three, DOÑA MAXIMA, whose sign claimed she could destroy
curses by reading coca leaves.

Inside, Señora Maxima was sitting on a narrow metal bed. Her skin
was crosshatched with wrinkles as elaborate as the Nazca lines in the
Peruvian desert, but her hair was thick, black, and long, the plaited
tresses flecked with white flower petals and tucked behind a woolen
blanket she'd safety-pinned around her neck. She smiled, showing a
gold tooth, and beckoned for me to sit down on the chair next to the
bed.

"¿Qué quiere, joven?" she asked. Her first language was Aymara; her
Spanish seemed to be as rudimentary as mine.

I told her I wanted to know what the coca leaves could tell me
about my future.

She unfolded a *chuspa*, a patterned square of wool, laid it on the bed,
and asked me for a five-boliviano coin, which she placed in the center.
Around the coin, she arranged six leaves, dark side down, then
sprinkled them with drops of alcohol from a plastic bottle.

"Tell me the name of your fiancée," she said.

I gave her the name of a distant inamorata.

She started tossing leaves from a plastic bag onto the *chuspa*.
Occasionally, she'd tuck a leaf into her mouth.

My taxi driver, who was waiting by the door, explained that if the
leaves fell dark side up, it was a bad sign. They consistently showed
their light side, the leaf ends pointing away from her; but that wasn't
surprising—Señora Maxima seemed to have perfected a flick of the

wrist that ensured positive results. After she'd tossed down about thirty, she contemplated the pattern.

"You are young and strong. You will have good luck in your travels, in your love. But you must make an offering to Pachamama."

She tucked the five bolivianos I'd given her into a pocket of her thick blue dress. I asked her if I could take a photo.

"*Sí*. For twenty more bolivianos."

She posed, po-faced and stoical, hands in her lap.

Outside, I noticed a row of *braseros*, like little hibachis, outside each *yatiri*'s stall. My cabdriver explained they were used to make burnt offerings to Pachamama, the goddess symbolizing earth. The sugary effigies were encrusted with herbs and llama wool, and if there were dark ashes left after they'd burnt, that was bad luck—though he personally didn't believe in such things. They were being sold in a neighboring shop for 120 bolivianos ($15 U.S.). I decided to skip the ritual; for the same price I could have bought an extra night in my hotel, six decent meals, or two months' supply of coca leaves.

Leaving Witches' Alley, I didn't feel too guilty about cheaping out on the burnt offering; there hadn't been too much that was authentic about the experience, after all. In the slum of El Alto, populated by the dispossesed of broken peasant communities, the traditional had been urbanized and commercialized. As a tourist paying an urban fortune-teller for a reading—extra charge for the photo—I was one long step removed from the way coca leaves were used in rural Bolivia, where they were offered free as a token of hospitality.

Besides, I was pretty sure I'd find a way to make it up to Pachamama.

Bolivia, a landlocked nation with a population of only 8.7 million, has experienced 189 coups d'état since it won its independence from Spain in 1825. The latest change in government happened on October 17, 2003, when Gonzalo Sánchez de Lozada, a University of Chicago–trained mining magnate (referred to by Bolivians, none too affectionately, as Goni, or the Gringo) was forced to resign. Lozada, prodded by the International Monetary Fund, had spent much of the 1990s selling off the national railways, airlines, telephone companies, and tin mines in an effort to overcome hyperinflation (which hit a high of 24,000 percent in 1985), and a crippling debt, a legacy of the looting of the state coffers by decades of general-dictators. For the people, the last outrage came when Lozada, who had opened the country's estimated $70 billion in natural gas reserves to such companies as Shell and Enron, proposed to sell liquid gas to California using a pipeline that would pass through Chile, Bolivia's traditional enemy. Huge street protests, in which at least seventy people were killed, forced Lozada to flee the presidential palace in a helicopter, and he went into exile in Miami. His vice president, Carlos Mesa, a former television journalist, has been at the helm of an uneasy regime ever since, with street protests shutting down the capital several times a week.

Behind the usual shifts of power, a deeper force was at work. Indigenous leaders, many of whom grew up with the coca leaf as a marker of identity, were now posing a serious challenge to the status quo. Since independence, Bolivia's rulers had come from an elite, European-descended aristocratic minority, and many had distin-guished themselves as paragons of avarice. (The worst in living memory was General García Meza, who seized power from a democratically elected socialist in 1980. Bankrolled by one of Bolivia's richest narco-traffickers, and aided by a mysterious German named "Klaus Altmann"—who turned out to be former Gestapo leader Klaus Barbie, the Butcher of Lyon—Meza led a bloody revolution, quickly dubbed the Cocaine Coup, in which five hundred union leaders were executed.) Recently, however, indigenous leaders had started challenging the oligarchy. In the last election, only 1.5 percent of the popular vote had separated Aymara-speaking Evo Morales and his party, Movement Toward Socialism (MAS), from Lozada. Aymara and Quechua leaders now controlled one-third of congress. Mesa, sensing the turning tide, declared an end to the Coca Zero policy, a United States–funded project aimed at the eradication of all coca in Bolivia. It was widely believed that Evo Morales, who had begun his career as a coca grower in the impoverished jungle region of Chaparé, would win the presidential elections in 2007. For the first time, a champion of the coca plant stood a good chance of leading a South American nation.

In the meantime, nothing in Bolivia was certain; everything seemed to be up for grabs. In my first week in La Paz, every day had brought a new demonstration. Andrew Orta told me that on the afternoon he'd arrived, the schoolteachers, seeking a pay raise from the near-bankrupt government, were teargassed by the police. I walked down to the Plaza San Francisco one afternoon to find I was flanked by ranks of cops in khaki, skittish as anonymous hands tossed firecrackers beneath their feet. The square was filled with *gremialistas*, members of the street vendors' guild, protesting a government move to tax them every six months instead of once a year. The next day, the *transportistas*—taxi, truck, and bus drivers—paralyzed the entire city in a protest over a three-centavo hike in the price of gas. And on the elegant promenade called the Prado, there seemed to be a permanent sleep-in, as miners milled around the mining-union headquarters, next to the American Airlines office, which was being guarded by a single nervous-looking member of the Policía Nacional. Many of the miners wore shiny oxblood helmets and killed the time by playing cards, watching televised soccer games through the plate-glass windows of the chic Unicornio restaurant, all the while working on quids of coca leaves. I walked past the scene late one night, when the temperature had dropped to near freezing, and saw the miners were sleeping with their families beneath woolen blankets, using cardboard boxes to divide the pavement into little homes: an instant village on the city streets.

Even in the midst of such chaos, La Paz knew how to show a visitor a good time; what it lacked in world-class museums and cathedrals, it made up for in one-of-a-kind tourist attractions. You could spend a morning at the witches' market, comparing the prices of effigies of the dwarf god Ekeko, potions for improving your sex life, or desiccated llama fetuses—spindly-armed, hollow-eyed creatures straight out of a Tim Burton film, which Bolivians buried in the foundations of their homes to bring luck. Some tourists opted to penetrate the fortresslike walls of the San Pedro prison, where cocaine traffickers and former presidents were freely permitted to hobnob with curious visitors. And just about everybody went to the Museo de Coca, a small museum off a cobblestoned courtyard on the Calle Linares.

In three densely packed rooms, the museum told the story of coca and cocaine from a Bolivian perspective. Sucking on one of the sweet coca pastilles sold at the counter, I inspected black-and-white photos of Andean natives on treadmills being monitored by doctors in white lab coats. A mannequin in boxer shorts showed how coca leaves were stomped, like grapes, in plastic-lined pits filled with acid and kerosene to make *pasta básica*, an easily transportable paste that is up to 65 percent cocaine. Most hilarious was the American cokehead diorama, which featured an exophthalmic yuppie in a suit, holding a rolled dollar bill dipped into a bag of powder, his blue eyes bulging toward a Marlboro ad pasted onto a TV screen. In the guest book, visitors had let slip their obsessions: "Nice museum, very informative," Antony from Manchester had written. "But definitely recommend free samples." Ariel, from Tel Aviv, was more direct: "So where the hell do we score man? This is Bolivia for gods sakes!" La Paz was a global hot spot for a small but significant segment of the travel industry: narco-tourism. The going rate for a gram of high-quality cocaine on the streets of La Paz was $3.85 (U.S.). Though gringos could expect to pay twice that, by global standards it was still a hell of a deal.

I lingered over a panel that recounted an Indian story transmitted orally through the generations, before being translated—rather freely, I suspected—into Spanish in 1921. Its verses predicted that the same coca plant that allowed the Indians to withstand cold and hunger would also ruin the invader: "If your torturer, who comes from the north / the white conqueror, the gold seeker, should touch it / he will find in it only poison for his body and madness for his mind . . . / It will only shatter him / as the icy crystals born in the clouds / crack the rocks / demolish mountains." Crystals, crack, poison: it seemed a succinct prophecy of the impact of cocaine on North American and European society.

That night, I met Jorge Hurtado, founder of the museum and the author of a popular treatise on the traditional and medical uses of coca in Bolivia, *The Legend of Coca.* The only doctor on duty in the country's largest psychiatric hospital, the bearded, bushy-browed Hurtado, dressed in a plaid shirt and jeans, was a study in disabused nonchalance. He obviously relished the role of provocateur.

"Coca isn't prohibited because it's *bad*," he told me, as he rested his loafers on a chair in his fluorescent-lit office. "It's prohibited because it's very *good*. A study at Harvard showed that it contains vitamins A, B_2, E, and more calcium than milk, which is important, because there's no other sources of calcium on the altiplano. It also, as you know, contains cocaine—which is one of the only anesthetics that is both cheap and doesn't produce bleeding. Ophthalmologists prefer cocaine to the synthetic equivalents for eye surgery for exactly that reason. And do you know how many teeth are pulled around the planet every second? Bolivia could have its own medical cocaine industry—one that would be very profitable. But the United States has had a monopoly on coca ever since 1962. Article 27 of the Geneva Law allows coca to be planted, transported, and industrialized for one reason only: to make Coca-Cola. You can look it up."

(I did, perfectly aware that, when it comes to cocaine, the most paranoid-sounding conspiracy theories usually turn out to be gross understatements of an even more bizarre truth. The United Nations convention banning cocaine worldwide does indeed make an exception for a "flavoring agent which does not contain any alkaloids, and in the quantity necessary for that use, [the parties may] authorize the production, importation, and possession of the leaves." This is the loophole that allows Coca-Cola to import 175,000 kilograms of the highest-quality South American coca every year. Known as Merchandise Number 5, the coca leaves are treated by Stepan Chemicals in New Jersey. Coca-Cola once tried to dispense with this troublesome flavoring agent altogether. The result was coca-free New Coke, one of the most memorable marketing flops of the 1980s.)

I pointed out the obvious: coca leaves are the raw material for cocaine and crack, powerful, addictive drugs that have ravaged entire communities.

"Look, I'm a psychiatrist," Hurtado replied. "I believe that drugs are a health problem. But here we have a War on Drugs that's using soldiers, helicopters, arms, to fight against a plant. It is stupid. And, really, drugs are not our problem here in Bolivia. I wish we had more drug addicts here! I'd like to study them. There are forty beds in this hospital, and currently eighty percent of my patients are alcoholics— none are drug addicts. Cocaine is expensive for Bolivians, but alcohol is cheap: you can stay drunk all day for one boliviano." (True enough: I'd seen a liter of 92 percent alcohol in the witches' market that day, selling for a mere five bolivianos, or sixty-three cents. I'd asked the *chola* at the stand who bought the stuff. "*Alcohólicos!*" she'd replied cheerily. There were certainly quite a few lying around the streets, passed out in puddles of their own piss. However, I had yet to see anybody, apart from a few red-eyed narco-tourists, talking too loud and twitching in the streets and bars of La Paz.)

"Cocaine is a problem in Argentina, Brazil, in the United States— but not here, even though this is the country where it's the cheapest in the world. The War on Drugs is an ideology of penetration and political control, one that maintains thousands of people in the North American intelligence community, the people who make their living off prohibitions. It's not based on logic. If there was any logic, we would be able to go to Virginia and uproot all of the tobacco plants, on the ground that cigarette companies, which have been known to put ammonia in tobacco to encourage addiction, are poisoning Bolivians."

I'd hear similar arguments again and again. The United States, for example, was currently the world's largest producer of the illegal drug marijuana. Shouldn't the American government be fumigating the state of California? And if it wasn't, what gave it the right to uproot coca from the Andes?

"You know, as a doctor, I sometimes think the only drug that we should maybe consider banning is alcohol. But it wouldn't work! It didn't work! Prohibition only created more mafias. You don't get rid of an addiction by trying to eradicate the addictive substance from the world. You do it by offering assistance to addicts."

Hurtado said it was his dream to treat cocaine addicts with coca leaves. The few opportunities he'd had, with smokers of *pasta básica* in La Paz and Cochabamba, had shown promising results. He saw coca as a natural antidepressant and stimulant, whose alkaloids seemed to obviate the need for refined cocaine.

"I'm always waiting for drug addicts," he sighed. "But they never come. I need patients!"

Hurtado suddenly grinned. "I know! My museum! I should start asking the gringo narco-tourists!"

The curious notion that the drug problems of the north could be solved by eradicating a plant cultivated in the southern hemisphere for forty-five hundred years really got its start in 1950, the year a United Nations commission released its report on the coca leaf. The timing was strange, to say the least: cocaine, which hadn't been popular since the 1920s, had virtually disappeared from Europe and the United States—the real postwar drugs of choice were amphetamines, which had liberally, and legally, been doled out by the armed forces to keep the boys overseas alert and fighting. The U.N. commission was headed by Howard B. Fonda, vice president of the pharmaceutical giant Burroughs Wellcome, and a close friend of Federal Bureau of Narcotics chief Harry Anslinger. Pill pushers are rarely great friends of messy, chlorophyll-dripping plants, and Fonda was no exception: his report blamed coca-chewing for the "mental retardation" of the Andean people and ordered coca production to be limited. A later commission—which produced the same 1962 treaty that gave Coca-Cola the right to import coca leaves—bound Peru and Bolivia to eradicate their traditional crop over the next twenty-five years.

Subsequent governments of the Andean nations tried to pretend they'd never signed the accord, but when another generation of Americans fell in love with cocaine in the 1970s, Ronald Reagan launched the War on Drugs and the Drug Enforcement Agency started to get serious. The revolution of 1952 had allowed Bolivian peasants to choose their own land, launching the colonization of the Chaparé, a formerly deserted region east of La Paz. The Chaparé proved challenging terrain: coffee crops failed, there were no roads to export fruit, and droughts ruined the maize. When the world tin market collapsed, the region was overwhelmed with a further influx of thousands of unemployed miners. Naturally, farmers turned to coca, the one crop that really seemed to thrive in the tropical lowlands; in the decade after 1978, as rich Colombian smugglers started showing up to feed the nostrils of Hollywood and Wall Street, coca production in the Chaparé increased by 1,500 percent. As author Bret Easton Ellis made allusions to "Bolivian Marching Powder" in *Less Than Zero*, and Bolivia became the world's number two producer of cocaine after Colombia, the United States launched its first serious intervention, Operation Blast Furnace. In 1986, the DEA showed up in Bolivia's Beni department with six Black Hawk helicopters and two hundred operatives. They mangaged to destroy a few abandoned labs before they were chased out by a mob brandishing machetes.

Since using the stick had proved so unpopular, proponents of eradication turned to the carrot. Or more precisely, the coffee bean, the palm heart, and the pineapple, which they earnestly suggested the Bolivians grow instead of coca. Farmers were offered the equivalent of between $350 and $2,000 U.S. to switch to legal crops. The United Nations convinced them of the benefits of a new strain of high-yield coffee, but once in the fields, it could only be sustained with tons of expensive fertilizer—and then the international coffee market collapsed. The Bolivian government started forcing farmers to pay for the inspectors who came to check their own fields for coca, offsetting any compensation they might have received to stop growing it. In 1988, the Bolivian government passed Law 1008, whose aim was to completely eradicate coca from the Chaparé and limit growth in the Yungas to twelve thousand hectares, strictly for traditional use. It was an extraordinary law, overthrowing centuries of Western jurisprudence by presuming that everyone apprehended was a drug dealer until he had proven his innocence. Under Hugo Banzer, a military despot who had first ruled Bolivia in 1971 and came back like a bad centavo in 1997, the government destroyed forty thousand hectares of coca. It was an enormous blow to the economy—before eradication, income from coca accounted for more than 8 percent of Bolivia's gross domestic product and 18 percent of exports—and those hardest hit were the peasants, many of whom I'd seen sleeping in the dirt roads of the El Alto slum.

Fortunately, coca is an extremely hardy little bush—the leaves can be harvested every two months, and individual plants remain productive for half a century. Banzer was ousted in 2001, and in the last couple of years new planting has outstripped eradication in the Chaparé. Meanwhile, Bolivia's neighbors Peru and Colombia have taken up the slack. In 2000, the United States launched Plan Colombia, wading into a war-wracked nation with a radical new concept in the War on Drugs: the aerial defoliation of the coca plantations of the Amazon. Of the $1.2 billion Congress initially allocated to the plan, most went to handouts to private corporations in the United States. Fully $354 million was used to buy new Black Hawk helicopters; only $68.5 million went to helping displaced farmers switch to alternative crops. (Half of the allocation ended up in the hands of DynCorp Aerospace Technologies, the Virginia defense company that won the crop-dusting contract.) Plan Colombia used satellites to spot coca plantations, then sent in fixed-wing aircraft, shadowed by helicopters, to spray the coca fields. The favored defoliant was Monsanto's Roundup SL, a combination of glyphosate and a substance called Cosmo-Flux 411F, which is corrosive to the eyes and causes severe skin irritation; Roundup SL is prohibited for use in the United States.

The sticky clouds of toxic chemicals covered everything, including wildlife in a zone that was home to 15 percent of the world's remaining primates. DynCorp planes had already sprayed defoliant on churches, soccer fields, and schoolchildren; peasants complained that their pigs and chickens were dying off, their legal coffee crops were failing, and that they and their children were afflicted by ulcers, headaches, and diarrhea. Nobody had any idea what long-term effect Roundup SL would have on the environment, though it was known that glysophate routs aquatic ecosystems—Monsanto warns American farmers to keep a milder version of the herbicide well away from ponds and lakes. Fully 14 percent of Colombia's surface area had already been sprayed by DynCorp planes. At the same time, the United Nations declared Colombia, riven by four decades of guerrilla warfare, the site of the greatest humanitarian crisis in the western hemisphere. Two million people had been displaced, many of them driven from failing farms to shantytowns outside Bogotá. Dislocation and the severing of community bonds are powerful predictors of addiction. For the first time, cocaine abuse was becoming a problem among the poor of Colombia.

All of this seemed to fly in the face of an obvious fact: you cannot wage—let alone win—a war against a plant. The balloon effect, in which putting the squeeze on one area causes cultivation to swell in a neighboring region, had lately been joined by the phenomenon of atomization. Tiny tracts of coca were now planted in gullies and valleys of the Santa Marta mountain range, in the national parks where the Colombian supreme court had declared the United States could not spray, and growers had developed new strains of coca that were able to thrive in the shade and yield more cocaine with fewer plants. While the United Nations trumpeted statistics that coca cultivation was down by 20 percent in the Andes, to 835 tons a year, the reality was that the entire American market could amply be fed with only 300 tons. In the United States, cocaine and crack use among youth has stayed stable, and heroin use has actually increased (Colombia is now the leading supplier to the United States). The wholesale price of cocaine, $20,000 a kilogram in New York in 2004 (or $20 to $45 a gram retail, depending on the cut), was a fifth of what it had been in 1981, the year the War on Drugs had begun, and purity was higher. What's more, cocaine was finding new markets. Brazil was now the world's number two consumer, and in England cocaine had plummeted to £40 a gram, supplanting ecstasy as the most popular illegal stimulant, adding a nasty edge to the British binge-drinking epidemic. Four years after Plan Colombia had started, and $3.3 billion later, the Office of National Drug Control Policy admitted its goals had not been met: the acreage under cultivation in Peru and Bolivia was beginning to increase. The balloon had been squeezed again, with predictable effect.

Bolivia, to its credit, never signed on to the insanity of aerial spraying. All eradication so far had been manual, and as uprooting coca plants was labor-intensive, real progress had been slow. Meanwhile, support for legal coca had been growing. In Peru, a company introduced a soda called KDrink, laced with cocaine-containing cocaleaf extract, and in La Paz, I visited a shop up the street from Plaza San Francisco that sold Co-Dent toothpaste, coca wine, and several brands of coca skin cream. Congressman Evo Morales had made it clear where he stood: he was for coca, the plant—in all its traditional forms—and against cocaine, the drug, which he considered a problem of the developed world. He recently told an interviewer:

"I challenge the U.S. ambassador . . . to sign an agreement to carry out a real fight against narco-trafficking on all fronts. First the peasant movement would mobilize against all illegal [coca processing]. And the U.S. would make sure that no chemicals needed to process coca leaves into cocaine would be allowed to be sent to Bolivia. Because where do these chemicals come from? From industrial countries . . . The people who process cocaine handle millions and millions of dollars, and they're not in Chaparé. They are white-collar, tie-wearing people, not the people here wearing sandals and ponchos."

The U.S. ambassador, hearing talk like this before the last election, threatened to yank all foreign aid to Bolivia if Evo Morales ever became president.

For some Bolivians, the answer to keeping the *cocaleros* in business, and coca out of the hands of the drug dealers, lay in encouraging the relatively innocuous habit of coca chewing. I met filmmaker and sociologist Silvia Rivera Cusicanqui, whose documentaries dramatized the plight of coca growers, in her rambling home in the embassy district of Sopocachi. Lively and welcoming, bifocals bumping against her chest as she rushed off to look up another figure, Rivera affected a panama hat, into which she tucked long braids of gray hair. Ushering me into a disheveled office, where Karl Marx shared space with Michel Foucault on the bookshelves, and Ani DiFranco filled her iTunes, she proudly explained that her last name was of Aymara provenance, and that she spoke the language fluently. Nonetheless, she had grown up in Bolivia's small European-descended middle class and was currently a professor of sociology at La Paz's San Andrés University.

"There has been a very strong campaign to Indianize coca," Rivera told me, "to stigmatize it and convert it into a habit that's backward, dirty, ugly. The fact is, when you chew the leaves, you are taking them off the illegal market. Drug trafficking has been a corrupting element that's created a total rupture in democracy in Bolivia. The best way to fight it is to encourage the chewing of the leaves. There's an ever-expanding market in Argentina, where even the highest elites chew coca leaves."

In fact, coca chewing was legalized in Argentina in 1989, and today, truck drivers, doctors, and judges alike enjoy the habit; one estimate puts yearly consumption, mostly in the northern provinces, at several hundred tons.

"When people are harvesting for the drug dealers, they just tear all the leaves off the bushes." Rivera mimed hacking at a bush with a machete. "They can gather twenty or thirty kilos of leaves a day. The Aymara word for harvesting coca is *k'ichi*, which means gathering with your fingers; at best they harvest a kilo and a half of leaves a day. It's very labor-intensive—much more so than the bananas, palm hearts, or pineapples that were proposed as alternative crops—so it keeps lots of peasants employed. Chewing coca is also a much more enduring sensation than cocaine. It's slower, a longer pleasure. Coca is a thermal regulator that helps you fight cold and heat and controls the glucose in the blood."

I noticed that we were sitting in a kind of hamster's nest of shredded leaves, our feet planted in coca scraps. I asked her if she could show me how she chewed it. She leapt up, glasses flying, and came back with her *chuspa*, the coca bag that the *yatiri* in witches Alley had used when she was telling my fortune.

"Normally I chew after a meal," she said. "I have gastritis, and coca is a good antacid." She spread the leaves on the red, white, and gray cloth, carefully tearing the ends off each of them; she explained that, in the long term, the hard stems could irritate the gums. Taking three leaves between her fingers, she held them up to her lips and blew on them three times, before tucking them into her cheek. "It's an offering to Pachamama, the earth goddess, and to the mountains. Since I am a mixture of Aymara and Catholic, I've developed my own syncretic ritual. I'm asking that my spirit go to the mountains, to ask for permission to enjoy the coca, to acknowledge that I'm chewing something sacred—not just bubble gum." I asked her what kind of *lejía* she used, and she pulled out a plastic package that looked like powdered cocaine. "This is Chamabico," she said. "They sell it in Santa Cruz; it's an industrialized *lejía*, and the fact that it exists means the urban upper classes are also chewing coca, not just the peasants. It's a mixture of bicarbonate of soda and an Amazonian vine called *chamayo*, which helps you extract the alkaloids.

"One thing that's important is that you don't really chew the leaves," Rivera continued. "You suck on them, softly." Her words from that point on were punctuated by slow slurping sounds. "I'm not in favor of the legalization of coca leaves. I think they should be decriminalized. First, because coca isn't a drug. Second, because if it were in the hands of companies like Monsanto or Enron, we'd be worse off. Multinational companies are even more immoral than drug dealers!"

Rivera gave me a packet of Chamabico as a going-away present, as well as the address of her favorite coca-leaf dealer, a shop called Luly's, on the Calle 3 de Mayo. A silent prepubescent girl sitting in a chair on the pavement sold me two bolivianos' worth of coca, in the now familiar green plastic bag. After lunch, I lay on the bed in my hotel room and turned on the television. I took three leaves and blew on them three times—I felt it was time to make my peace with

Pachamama—and filled my mouth, this time being careful to suck, not chew. The leaves were crisp, light, and seemed slightly sweet. From time to time I packed my cheek with a bit of Chamabico, which had the same consistency as powdered sugar.

Gradually I became enthralled by the movie I was watching. It was *Air Force One*, in which a wooden Harrison Ford plays a president who single-handedly takes out hijackers holding the first family hostage. As a thick-accented Gary Oldman started offing Secret Service men, I began to sweat profusely. This had to be the greatest movie ever made, I thought, as I stuffed another wad of leaves into my mouth, watching Ford stalk the thick-necked Kazakh supernationalists. I couldn't take my eyes off the screen. It was *fan*-fucking-*tastic*. As Ford dangled out the back of the plane at thirty-five thousand feet, I vaguely noticed I was surrounded by leaf stems, and the bedspread was speckled with dots of spilled powder. Jesus Christ, I was becoming that goddam bug-eyed yuppie-cokehead mannequin in the Museo de Coca. But I didn't care. It was a *great goddamn way to be*. Eventually, and with great effort, I tore myself from the screen, left the coca leaves in the hotel room, and went for a long walk around the streets of La Paz, calming myself with a couple of Paceña beers. I felt no depression or guilt following my binge; in fact, it didn't even keep me awake that night. Perhaps, I speculated, the other alkaloids in the leaves mitigated the effects of the naturally occurring cocaine.

I'd always wondered why there was such animus against cocaine in the United States, why the War on Drugs had concentrated so much of its fury and firepower on this particular powder. After all, there was nothing particularly subversive about stockbrokers and PR people chopping up lines with their credit cards and snorting their savings through rolled-up hundred-dollar bills; quite the contrary: they were acting like model consumers. As a stimulant drug of desire, rather than a heightener of pleasure like marijuana or the opiates, cocaine seemed ideally suited for a culture of mindless consumption. (The old stoner riddle summed it up. Q: When's the best time to do some cocaine? A: Right after you've done some cocaine.) According to David Lenson, a professor of comparative literature whose *On Drugs* is one of the more trenchant analyses of the war on psychoactive substances, consumer society's problem with cocaine is that it supplants other acquisitive behavior.

"Cocaine capitalism," Lenson wrote, "is to conventional capitalism as cancerous cell growth is to normal cell growth in the body—the same thing only faster and deadly. Cocaine must be combated on a war footing for precisely this reason." When you are locked in a cycle of cocaine use, the whole engine of desire—want new laptop, want new SUV, want new condo, must work harder—is supplanted by a simple closed loop that consists of want more cocaine, want more cocaine, want more cocaine, don't have time to work. Consumerism can't tolerate such a cancerous, nonproductive parody of its deepest motive forces. From this perspective, the coca eradication going on in South America was radical chemotherapy on the global economy.

By then, there was no question in my mind: *la hoja de coca es* definitely *droga*—particularly if you buy quality leaves and spike them with a bit of Chamabico. It's a singularly pleasant buzz, smoother than caffeine, with no immediate side effects. (Nor, I'd learn later, appreciable medium-term side effects, apart from tender gums. It's especially good for tasks that require acuity and alertness but little insight—such as transcribing the interviews for this chapter.) Rivera's attempt to sacralize coca consumption with her own ritual reminded me of Pierre-André Delachaux's reverent serving of Swiss absinthe in the Val-de-Travers. In spite of all the fancy intellectual justifications, however, these days—and particularly in urban and middle-class settings—both coca and absinthe primarily served to get their users buzzed. Things might have been different in traditional contexts, where intoxicants were used to reinforce community bonds through Dionysian rites or transcendent ceremonies. Grafting a syncretic ritual on to them was an understandable impulse, but I couldn't see how private consumption could be resacralized; you might as well make the sign of the cross over your morning cup of instant coffee. Interestingly, Delachaux too had argued for decriminalization, as opposed to legalization, afraid that his favorite recreational drug would end up in the hands of Coca-Cola.

Though I sympathized with such fears, I was beginning to feel that if prohibition was the most destructive of policies, mere decriminalization—a legal limbo at best—wasn't the answer either.

Everybody I'd met told me that if I wanted to know about coca in Bolivia, I really had to look up Alison Spedding. She was a *cocalera*, a coca grower, and had spent two years in prison for trafficking. We'd set up a meeting at the San Andrés University, but I had trouble finding her classroom. After poking my head into a half dozen lecture halls, I walked into a gloomy pavilion where a dozen students were sprawled on their desks in attitudes of exaggerated languor. I made out a figure in a broad-brimmed, black sombrero, an oversize, overworn, black overcoat, and a long, black, tassled scarf, bending over a table.

"Señor Grescoe!" she boomed, looking up with a long-toothed smile. Spedding was tall, at least five foot ten inches, and impressively sun-baked. She stood over a table of thin paperbacks she'd coauthored or edited, including one called *Filthy Porn*. After I bought a couple of books on coca cultivation, she led me to a deserted basement bar on the Prado. Over a frothy pilsner, she explained that she'd been arrested for marijuana, not coca.

"This dealer I know got busted," she said in her thick Derbyshire accent. "The police said to him, as they always do, 'If you bust somebody else for us, we'll let you go.' So they raided my house, and they found a couple of kilos of this really naff grass, provided to me by this compadre of mine who happened to be at my place.

"They sentenced me to ten years, but I only served two and a half.

They put me in the women's jail in Miraflores. As prisons go, Bolivian ones are pretty okay. To start with, they're all open, the prisoners don't even get locked in their cells. The governor actually used to complain that prisoners would come up to her office and just sit in her armchair. I even taught my university classes there; the students would come on visiting days twice a week, and I'd teach my class in the yard."

Spedding had first come to Bolivia as a backpacker in 1982. After graduating with a degree in anthropology from Cambridge, she returned to live full-time in the Yungas in 1989. The local campesinos offered her some land, and she decided to try her hand at farming.

"They sold it to me really cheaply; it was just a patch of weeds, anyway. And so, I thought, if they think I should have this coca field, why not? I've still got it, in fact. I'll be harvesting there this Saturday."

Spedding had chosen her location well: Law 1008 allowed for the cultivation of coca for traditional purposes in the Yungas, and the eradication program at first focused exclusively on the Chaparé lowlands.

"It was pretty much a farce in the beginning. The eradication really started in 1986, just when the price of coca dropped through the floor. The sharecroppers could no longer live off their harvest, so they just fucked off, leaving the owners with these fields full of weeds. And so, what a gift! The government comes along saying, 'We'll give you money for getting rid of this field,' which nature would have gotten rid of anyway. In other cases, the peasants pruned the coca down to the stump, and since the plants are accustomed to having all their leaves torn off every three months, they just grew back." Gradually, however, the eradication efforts started to work. Spedding, like Rivera and Hurtado, told me there were few coca plantations left in the Chaparé. In the Yungas, Spedding's territory, it was a different story.

"In 2001, the government decided to send in troops to start

eradication in the Yungas. Well, they sent them in in a very disorganized fashion, and unlike the Chaparé, which is flat, the Yungas is perfect guerrilla country. It's just valleys, and though there are roads, they're death traps, even when you don't have people waiting to ambush you around the corner. There are these bloody footpaths all over, and coca fields going up the sides of cliffs, and you get totally lost if you don't have a local guide. So they sent these young conscripts in, and the peasants rose up en masse and surrounded them. The peasants weren't armed; maybe just a few sticks and machetes. The women went to the front, as usual, and started throwing beehives at the soldiers. Basically they just herded them out of the Yungas like they were sheep; they didn't even let them sleep for an entire night. Since then, the government has known that, if the eradication has been somewhat bloody in the Chaparé, it would be like really, *seriously* bloody in the Yungas."

She suggested I go to Chulumani, one of the larger towns in the Yungas, to see the terrain for myself. I told her I'd been trying, but the roads had been blockaded for the last few days. Apparently disorder was becoming the norm in Bolivia.

"Yeah," she said, stubbing out a cigarette, "superficially you might say Bolivia is chaotic and disorderly, but really it isn't. Family structures here are like iron. One of the main reasons there's very few problems with drug addiction is that people don't live on their own enough to get strung out before a family member does something about it. Unlike industrialized societies. I mean, instead of spending all this money on these eradication programs, why don't they try to figure out why life in the United States is so bloody unsatisfactory that half the population has to be boxed out of its head on Ritalin, Prozac, and cocaine all the time?"

It was an interesting question. I was beginning to understand that, from the perspective of the natives of the Andes, the War on Drugs could only look like pure injustice, if not insanity. People have been chewing coca here as far back as the archaeological record stretches—statues with the telltale bulging cheek of the coca chewer date back to 2500 B.C. It was northern industry that really potentiated the coca plant, transforming it from a pleasantly invigorating chew into a powerfully addictive substance. The Spanish set up massive planta-tions, tended by slave labor, to fuel the labors of indigenous miners in the silver mines of Potosí. A German chemist, Albert Niemann, isolated cocaine from coca leaves in 1859, and soon its anesthetic and stimulant properties became widely known and trumpeted by a young Sigmund Freud, who touted it as a cure for morphine addiction. In 1885, explorer and botanist Henry Hurd Rusby was sent to La Paz by the Detroit pharmaceutical company Parke-Davis to expedite the export of coca leaves, which tended to rot on the trip back to Europe or America. Rusby developed the technique for making *pasta básica*—the stable, easily shippable precursor to powdered cocaine that is still used by drug traffickers today.

Like ecstasy, cocaine had initially been billed as being free of side effects; the honeymoon ended when the first users started experienc-ing psychotic breakdowns. On the advice of his friend Freud, Ernst von Fleischl-Marxow substituted cocaine for morphine—a case of driving out one devil with another—and ended up dying an addict with a gram-a-day intravenous habit. The Harrison Act of 1914 punished the sale of cocaine, heroin, and other drugs by sentences of up to ten years in American prisons. Two years later, England's Defence of the Realm Act made such drugs available only by prescription. A century after the first American had come down to Bolivia and extracted cocaine from coca, his compadres returned with Black Hawk helicopters and troops in a vindictive frenzy, to tear up the very plants they'd once been so enamored with.

The Aymara and Quechua peasants could only tuck another quid into their cheeks and sigh: *Son locos*, these gringos. It had all been foretold: according to the legend, those who, rather than respectfully plucking the leaves, tore up the venerated plant by its roots—like the eradicators from the north—would inevitably be punished by Pacha-mama. For his disrespect, the white conqueror would find in coca "only poison for his body and madness for his mind."

As I prepared to go to the Yungas, the area east of La Paz that is the center for legal coca production, all the portents were bad. An image of the defunct space shuttle *Columbia*, with a Bolivian flag on one wing, was airbrushed on the side of the bus I was about to board. Before turning the ignition key, the driver mumbled a prayer, touched his fingers to his lips, and made the sign of the cross. Fortunately, I was seated on the back bench, in the middle seat, so I had to make an effort to crane my neck to glimpse one of the more terrifying roads in the world. Whenever the rear axle really started jumping, I stared straight ahead, trying to focus all my attention on the *Wrestlemania* video flickering on the television screen at the front of the bus.

On the road out of La Paz, teams of workers in yellow overalls were hauling boulders to the side of the road, clearing the remains of recent blockades erected by protesting campesinos. At La Cumbre, we waited for the truck ahead of us, which was piled with apples—and the apples piled with peasants—to be thoroughly checked for drugs. At the dismal roadside stop of Unduari, we were forced off the bus while soldiers in camouflage searched our bags. I ate a sandwich at a chicken shack, next to a huge sign warning that the possession of any precursor to the manufacture of cocaine—ammonia, batteries, ether, acid, tin foil—would be strictly punished. Then the road went narrow, following the contours of a serpentine river valley. The brown hills, stippled with landslides of slate, came to be covered with broad-leafed palms and flowering trees as we lost elevation. Lacy waterfalls poured down the cliffs, occasionally rolling the roof with snare drum rat-a-tats. At every blind corner, the driver sounded a warning honk, but several times we came to a skidding halt in the gravel before an oncoming truck. Then the driver would have to grind into reverse, and everyone would stand up and peer downward as the rear wheels backed ever closer to the cliffside. As the setting sun daubed distant summits with orange, a full moon rose over the jungle, and the tiny baby strapped to the back of the peasant woman next to me fell asleep, his head resting on my biceps.

I got off at the main plaza in Chulumani. It was here that, after the wife and daughter of a local coca farmer were abducted and raped by police, the campesinos had marched on the station and burned it to the ground. They then captured the fleeing officers and castrated them. Tonight, however, all was quiet. Three little girls briefly trotted after me, bearing green bags of leaves and shouting, "*Coca! Coca!*" Soon I left behind the lights of the town and walked for a few minutes beneath the Southern Cross, until I came to the gate of an isolated guesthouse. I rang the bell and waited.

"Well, you're obviously not Israeli," said, in perfect English, the short, bearded man who came to greet me. "They just ignore the sign and let themselves in. I usually find them standing in the lobby."

He introduced himself as Xavier and said he could let me have a nice room, escorting me across a second-story porch decorated with pinned and framed tarantulas, grasshoppers, and bats (a good introduction to the fauna that would feast on me that night). In fact, apart from Klaus, a language teacher from Berlin, I was the only guest there. Itor, the cook, a tall man of mixed Basque and German parentage with a rattling cough and a severe limp, made me spaghetti carbonara, and Xavier joined me as I ate dinner on the porch.

"So you have come to see coca?" he said. "No problem. You'll see plenty when the sun comes up; we're surrounded by it. The first people to come here for coca were the Nazi chemists, who came to make anesthetics. Some of the Nazis stayed on after the war, living the good life; in fact, their children are still living here. Josef Mengele, the Auschwitz doctor, was here too, until people from the Wiesenthal Foundation came and started walking down the Prado in La Paz with pictures of the Nazis they were hunting. Tomorrow, you'll walk past Klaus Barbie's estate—he lived just down the road." Xavier had worked in New York in the 1960s. He'd been to Woodstock, then come back to La Paz to open a bar. "I used to do a lot of coke. Alone, I snorted up half the Chaparé! But I quit when I started to see all the damage it was doing to my clients. People stop making sense; it's terrible for the morality. Chewing coca is okay; it's good for reading, great for working, though I find once you're distracted from your task, you can't think straight."

The next morning, Xavier gave me a tour of the grounds. He insisted I hold a chattering, chained monkey named Martín.

"He won't bite!" said Xavier.

Martín immediately sank his fangs into my forearm.

The parrot, he insisted, was *más tranquilo.* As Xavier took my picture, though, the bird bobbed forward and tore a chunk out of my ear.

"It is because you are too nervous!" said Xavier.

"That's not true," mumbled Itor. "They bite everybody."

After breakfast, Xavier gave us a map, and Klaus and I set off down the road. We'd packed bottles of water, but no food—Xavier assured us we'd find something to eat in a village called Ocobaya. As we walked down the shaded dirt road, Klaus, whose blond hair looked as if it had been cropped with the help of a soup bowl and a razor, made a few lugubrious attempts at humor.

"It is funny that they should have called him Klaus Barbie," he mused as we walked by the Nazi's house at Puente de Tablas. "He was not very much like a children's toy, I would say!"

After we'd come to a bend in the road, bridging the river that had carved the valley bottom, we doubled back, mounting the hillside. Chulumani was visible high on the other side; terraces of coca plants, like tiered rice paddies in the Himalayas, corrugated the steep hillsides down to the river. After an hour, we were joined by a stocky man, in a long-sleeved shirt, a baseball cap, and sandals, carrying a sagging, empty sack over his shoulder. He'd taken a shortcut from Chulumani, fording the river and following footpaths rather than following the main road.

He told us his name was Alberto Chura, he was sixty-four years old, and he'd just come back from the market, where he carried a fifteen-kilogram bag of dried coca leaves every Saturday. He'd got a good price, he told us, thirty-five bolivianos a kilo, which meant a total of $65, enough to buy wheat and other essentials.

Would we like to see his *cocal*, his coca patch?

Leaving the main road, we followed him up a path to the terraces of coca plants. He had three hectares, two planted with coffee and fruit, and one with coca. He picked four oranges, handed them to us, and showed us peanutlike coffee beans drying next to the coca on a concrete platform.

"I get up at five in the morning," he said. "Then I chew my coca, and by six I am picking the leaves." He tied a canvas bag around his waist and bent over an unassuming-looking little bush with light green leaves that came up to his belt, showing how he plucked the leaves with two fingers and dropped them into the bag.

In a drying shed, he showed us a fifty-kilogram sack of leaves. I asked if I could buy some.

"No," he said. "But you may *have* some." He filled my shoulder bag with leaves. "My coca is very organic. I don't use chemicals!"

I gave him the rest of my cigarettes. He smiled a broad smile. Once again, when it was a question of hospitality, coca was not sold: it was given away for free, and the giving was a pleasure.

Back on the road, I offered Klaus some leaves.

"No," he said grimly. "I do not like the taste."

Your loss, I muttered, as I got a good quid going.

We trudged along, and the sun climbed in the sky. Groups of women dotted the terraces, doing their *ayni*, or collective labor, in which campesinos help their neighbors harvest a *cocal* on the understanding that they will do the same for them when their fields are ready. Soon, the coca started to kick in, which was a good thing, because we'd run out of water, and the only shop in Ocobaya turned out to be filled with bags of dried grains and shelves of canned goods, but no empanadas or sandwiches.

Beneath the hot sun, Klaus was clearly starting to suffer. I suggested we try a shortcut, down to the river, and then up the other side of the valley to Chulumani, which we could see perched on the opposite hillcrest. We left the road, descending broad switchbacks that quickly turned into footpaths through forest.

I rounded a corner, and in a clearing I could see a young guy with a thick mustache and a dirty T-shirt, rolling a cigarette. Through the trees, I could just glimpse a half dozen other figures; two of them were pacing back and forth in a what appeared to be a little pit.

The lookout with the cigarette smiled a crooked, worried smile. I explained we were trying to get to Chulumani.

"You can't get there this way," he said. "You have to go back." He took me firmly by the shoulder and turned me toward the road. It was clear he didn't want me to get a closer look at what was going on behind me.

Klaus walked up and demanded to know what was going on.

"We're going to have to go back," I said.

"What do you mean?" he said. "The river is right down there. We have every right to be here!"

The guy with the mustache was studying the red-faced Klaus with sinister amusement. Not a good time, I thought, for Teutonic rectitude.

"*Gracias,*" I said. "We are going back to the road." I caught a last glimpse of the men behind him and immediately wished I hadn't. They were stomping leaves in a plastic-lined pit, exactly like the one I'd seen in the Museo de Coca. Here in the Yungas, the zone where coca was supposed to be produced only for legal, traditional purposes, we'd stumbled on a crew making *pasta básica*, the first step in extracting cocaine from the leaves, for the narcotics trade.

With adrenaline joining the coca alkaloids already coursing through my veins, I strode up the terraces. Klaus struggled behind, spluttering, "Wait! I don't understand!"

"Look, Klaus, they were making *cocaine*. As far as they know, two gringos, we could be DEA agents. We should get out of here, *right now.*"

"But I have, how do you say, burrs, in my socks." While Klaus paused to pick them out, I watched the bushes nervously, all the time expecting to feel a machete slicing into my shoulder. Just then, a rawboned young man noticed us and came striding up the coca terraces at a fearsome pace.

"Do you need help?" he said. We did, I confessed; we were completely lost. Alison Spedding had been right: I could understand how all these footpaths made the Yungas perfect guerrilla country.

He smiled, indicated we should follow him up the hill, and set a grueling pace back to the road. I gave him ten bolivianos for his help, which he accepted with a broad, these-gringos-are-loco smile. It seemed a small price to pay—he might have saved our lives.

A minivan came along and gave us a lift back to the guesthouse. Klaus, hungry, tired, sunburned, and seriously pissed off, was no longer speaking to me.

After we'd cleaned up, I sat down with our hosts over a sandwich and a cup of maté de coca and recounted our adventure. Itor was silent when I described what I'd seen, but after a pause, Xavier burst out:

"Sure, they were making *pasta básica*. But fuck, let them make cocaine! The peasants here have nothing. They can't even buy shoes to put on their kids' feet. The people you saw probably don't snort cocaine themselves. They use the little money they get to fix up their roof, repair their vans, or buy toys for their kids.

"Have you heard the Legend of Coca? How coca is a gift from God, but will fuck up the children from the north who don't know how to use it? Well, it is completely true! There are people in Miami making millions from it. Let the Third World have a little money, for God's sake."

By this point, I wasn't inclined to disagree.

The War on Drugs is a war on plants by another name. Name a major drug of abuse, no matter how artificial or synthetic it may sound, and ultimately you can trace its existence back to a plant. OxyContin, or "hillbilly heroin," the painkiller that got conservative commentator Rush Limbaugh strung out, comes from the poppies that grow in World War I cemeteries and the highlands of Afghanistan. Crystal meth, or speed, is a synthetic modification of ephedrine, derived from the ephedra plant that grows wild throughout Asia and the American West. Nature is the great biochemical genius. In contrast, man is a dogged lab technician, shamelessly plagiarizing the complex molecules that took millions of years to evolve in rain forests and mountain meadows.

Why do plants synthesize substances that induce euphoria, hyperactivity, or even hallucinations in animals? Simple: they can't move, and they are afflicted by mobile pests—insects and herbivores—that bore through their trunks and chew up their leaves. Unable to flee, they have resorted to chemical warfare, relying on mutation and natural selection to innovate bitter alkaloids that repel parasites by killing their appetite or sex drive, disorienting and temporarily paralyzing them. I'd already encountered a few examples in my travels: the poppy, whose seeds go into Marks & Spencer's narcotic crackers, produces morphine and thebaine, which can poison horses, cattle, and other herbivores that browse on them. The tobacco plant makes nicotine, which paralyzes its predators or sends them into convulsions. Wormwood, which is so bitter that even goats won't touch it, produces thujone, a convulsant neurotoxin that, like camphor and other terpenes, repels moths. The coffee bush makes caffeine, which prevents insects from reproducing. More interestingly, plants such as jimsonweed, or datura, produce scopolamine, which stops larger animals from grazing by sending them on a three-day-long dissociative trip of dry mouth and hallucination—overkill indeed.

Drugs, then, are poisons. In large doses, they can kill; in small doses, they intoxicate, a sensation that can be pleasurable, confusing, enlightening, and, in some cases, addictive. Early man probably observed animals—from cats lolling and mewing after gorging on catnip, to cattle overdosing on inebriating locoweed—for tip-offs about which plants to investigate. Elephants like to get drunk on the juice of fallen, fermenting berries, actually ramming the trunks of the marula tree to hasten the process. (In South Africa, the same berries are used to make a cream liqueur called amarula.) Pigeons get uncoordinated and listless when they eat cannabis seeds, which might be how the ancient Scythians figured out hemp was good for more than just rope-making. The urge to alter one's consciousness is so universal that psychopharmacologist Ronald K. Siegel has called it the fourth drive, after hunger, thirst, and sexual desire. Even when drugs aren't available, people find ways to get out of their heads, which explains such diverse phenomena as the self-flagellation of Capuchin monks, the whirling of Sufi dervishes, the meditation of Hindu sadhus, hyperventilation among children, and bungee jumping.

Every known human society has used some kind of plant intoxicant. Tongan fishermen drink endless bowls of relaxing kava kava, Somalian tribesmen while away afternoons in inspired conversation between mouthfuls of the stimulant shrub khat, and even nomads in the bleak tundra of Siberia trip out on hallucinogenic toadstool called fly agaric. (The only historical exception were the Inuit of North America, who had no greenery to speak of.) "That humanity at large will ever be able to dispense with Artificial Paradises seems very unlikely," wrote Aldous Huxley in *The Doors of Perception*. "Most men and women lead lives at the worst so painful, at the best so monotonous, poor and limited that the urge to escape, the longing to transcend themselves if only for a few moments, is and always has been one of the principal appetites of the soul."

As Huxley intuited, drugs are not just a poor, material substitute for religious transcendence, but probably the source of religion itself. Psychoactive substances are nestled too close to the heart of too many faiths for this to be mere coincidence. The Indo-Aryans, whose Rig Veda is the earliest known religious scripture, worshiped soma, the inducer of "bliss-bringing Rightness," which may have been the fly agaric or the harmel plant, a weed that has the same vision-inducing alkaloids as the Amazonian jungle vine yajé. The likes of Plato, Socrates, and Aristotle attended the Mysteries of Eleusis, a harvest festival that involved the consumption of a hallucinogenic potion, probably the ergot fungus that colonizes barley and rye and is also the source of LSD. Anthropologists have theorized that humanity's encounters with intoxicants—particularly magic mushrooms, those chemical inducers of waking dreams and transcendent visions—were the seeds that crystalized early man's capacity for religious sentiment. Name any plant intoxicant, and you will find, even today, a group of humans who use it to worship. Peyote is a sacrament in the Native American church, marijuana is a holy herb for Rastafarians, opium candy and bhang (the pollen of cannabis) are sold in government shops in Varanasi to induce trances in Hindu temples. And during

Mass, Catholics line up to consume wine (an appropriation of the Dionysian and bacchic rites of antiquity), which they believe is transformed into the blood of Jesus Christ as they drink it from the chalice.

Clues to the original role of drugs, as agents of pleasure, transcendence, and strengtheners of community (rather than addiction, impoverishment, and alienation), lie in the way they were used in traditional societies. Even tobacco, now the most banalized of commodities, was once the object of respectful ritual. Before the arrival of Europeans, the Karuk Indians, who lived in what is now California, consumed tobacco in tribal gatherings that were limited to adult males. In large doses, nicotine provokes hallucinations, and Karuk shamans ingested so much that they vomited and went into convulsions and a deathlike trance that they believed put them into direct contact with the spirit world. European traders taught the Karuk to smoke "white man's tobacco," which was less potent, but consumed far more frequently. From occasional communal use, during which treaties were made and the pipe was passed from hand to hand, the Karuk fell into the contemporary pattern of casual private abuse and addiction. An anthropologist who lived with the Karuk noted that, as late as the 1920s, "the old-time Indians never smoked but the merest fraction of the day, disapproved even of the smoking of men as old as in their twenties, and regarded the modern boy and girl cigarette fiend with disgust."

Typically, sacramental use of drugs is also use outside of commerce. There is no charge for Communion wine, nor for the peyote consumed in the Native American church; and in traditional Rastafarian belief, marijuana is a sacred herb that can be given as a gift but not bought or sold. (That's not to say that early civilizations—particularly the more organized kleptocracies—didn't equate psychoactive plants with currency. The Aztec ruler Montezuma I, whose empire was a vast military machine for exacting tribute from subjugated peasants, limited chocolate use to warriors and kept a treasury of a billion cacao beans in his palace.) Traditional use also tended to be occasional use: hunter-gatherer Siberians, for example, had to compete with reindeer foraging for psychedelic mushrooms, and—as I learned in Norway—the Vikings could afford to squander only a little of their precious grain on communal alcoholic binges. I'd seen how coca was offered to guests in traditional contexts in Bolivia. Only with the rise of modern commerce were plant drugs snatched from their sacred roles and turned into items of trade.

The first step was medicalization: in Europe, plant knowledge, once the domain of pagans, was taken over by the doctors. The pharmacopoeia of Paracelsus, considered the Father of Medicine, was a wholesale pilfering of the belladonna, cannabis, mandrake, opium, henbane, and other plants that went into the hallucinogenic flying potions of witches. The second step was industrialization: opium, for example, was refined into morphine, used to spike cheap and widely available patent medicines, and finally synthesized into heroin, which could instantly be administered through the hypodermic syringe. The hour-long tobacco pipe was supplanted by the half-hour cigar, then the five-minute cigarette. The slow, subtle high of coca leaves gave way to the instant rush of cocaine, and eventually the ten-minute buzz of crack. From one perspective, the industrialization of plant drugs was also their democratization: where a fifty-cent Havana had been the indulgence of plutocrats, nickel-a-pack Camels were well within working-class budgets. From another, it was their final debasement. There was wisdom, after all, in the religious instinct that such powerful substances should not be banal items of commerce; once you deliver them to the ingenuity of industry, you give quacks and amoral entrepreneurs a license to profit from the potentially limitless market in addiction.

These days, it is plants—atavistic, smelly, pagan—that stir modern legislators into a frenzy. Opium was probably the first drug systematically cultivated by early man; deposits of poppy seeds have been found in Neolithic Swiss lake villages dating to 6000 B.C. For most of human history, it was regarded as a panacea and served as one of the most useful painkillers and anxiety relievers in the pharmacopoeia of medical men and women. Throughout the nineteenth century, when opiate nostrums could be purchased at drugstores and soda counters in the form of Mrs. Winslow's Soothing Syrup or Battley's Sedative Solution, the typical dope fiend was a middle-aged woman, troubled by nothing more than constipation, drowsiness, and shame. (Doctors too were quiet users. Dr. William Halsted, the father of American surgery and founder of Johns Hopkins Medical Center, took morphine all his adult life and died at the age of seventy, after having performed some of his most brilliant operations as a junkie.)

Opium was first banned in 1875 in San Francisco—the first modern law criminalizing drug users—on the ground that it was a Chinese conspiracy to addict the white youth of California. Cocaine had to be proscribed because it turned the Southern Negro into a crazed rapist. Marijuana presented more of a challenge; it was hard, after all, to demonize a weed that tended to make people giggle and eat too many potato chips. In the absence of any demonstrable nefariousness, the prohibitionists decided to toss every possible accusation at cannabis to see what would stick. When smoking marijuana was nothing more than an obscure habit of Mexicans who came to the Southwest looking for work, scare stories about dope-crazed psychotic killers led to the El Paso ordinance of 1914 that gave local police the perfect pretext for arbitrary body searches of immigrants. Headlines about Negro jazz musicians in Harlem smoking "muggles" gave additional impetus to the passing of the Marijuana Tax Act of 1937, which required anybody growing marijuana to apply for a tax stamp. (It was the prototypical catch-22, well before Joseph Heller: the Treasury Department *didn't give* stamps to hemp farmers.) In the 1950s, the emphasis switched to the fifth column: pot raids netted entertainment types like Robert Mitchum and Gene Krupa, and drug peddlers were accused of being Communists trying to dope up the youth of America.

Eventually, though, the official propaganda about marijuana—that it caused murderous rampages, that it was a steep, slippery slope to heroin—started to backfire as tens of millions tried it without turning into bank-robbing Bolshevik junkies. By the 1960s, the "enemy within"—once a minority of beatniks and Reds—turned out to be anybody curious enough to take a toke at a party, and an unofficial civil war, between turned-on baby boomers and the so-called silent majority, was declared. Richard Nixon abrogated fundamental constitutional principles by empowering the newly created Drug Enforcement Agency to tap phones and spy on private citizens; Ronald Reagan launched the War on Drugs, overturning a law dating to the Civil War that prevented the U.S. military from interfering in civil affairs; and George Bush Sr. built more jails to house the casualties of the Zero Tolerance Program. (The only retreats came during Jimmy Carter's presidency, in which marijuana was actually decriminalized in Oregon, and Bill Clinton's tenure, when some drug war money was diverted into research on addiction.)

Too much has been written about the absurdity of marijuana prohibition for me to dwell on it for long here. The immeasure of the penalties has become a kind of cliché—even conservative legislators sense there's something disproportionate about the fact that a citizen of Oklahoma can be jailed for life for growing a single marijuana plant in his yard. By 2000, the American prison population reached two million—the highest of any nation in the world, including China— and a quarter of them were serving time for drug offenses, mostly possession. Fortunately for the government, the War on Drugs is rather good for the budget. Since the Zero Tolerance Policy was introduced under Ronald Reagan in 1988, the feds have been allowed to seize all assets associated with drug arrest; including, in one incident, a $2.5 million yacht on which a tenth of an ounce of marijuana was found. The U.S. Customs Service is the only government department that regularly turns a profit.

Was there a way to end this institutionalized insanity? Frankly, I wasn't optimistic. The notion of resacralizing traditional drugs, like Delachaux's absinthe and Rivera's coca leaves, struck me as romantic but disingenuous: most users, certainly in North America and Europe, are too removed from traditional communities for this to be anything but a New Age affectation, a kind of bogus Timothy Leary trip. Besides, the genie has been out of the bottle far too long: it would be impossible to unlearn the knowledge of extracting cocaine from the coca shrub or of synthesizing heroin from the poppy. As Ronald K. Siegel has written, "Once the alkaloids are freed from the plant, it is difficult to put them back." His technological solution was to campaign for the invention of new drugs. "The ideal intoxicants," he wrote in an article in the *Washington Post*, "would balance optimal positive effects, such as stimulation or pleasure, with minimal or nonexistent toxic consequences. The drugs would be ingested as fast-acting pills or liquids or breathed in the form of gases. They would have fixed durations of action and built-in antagonists to prevent excessive use or overdoses." Wishful thinking: given the current political climate in the United States, there was no way the National Research Council would in the near future be funding university labs to devise more pleasurable highs for the population.

The solution was perhaps not to go forward, in the hopes of brewing brave, new, and nonaddictive forms of soma, but to stick with the plants that have accompanied humanity since before humans could stand upright. Khat, coca, poppies, kratom, iboga, ergot, psilocybin, ayahuasca, kava, salvia: there are enough substances in the natural world to keep humanity busy for a long time. And, as the growers of Purple Thai and Sweet Skunk (not to mention herbicide-resistant "super-cocas") have shown, a lot can be achieved through traditional plant-breeding techniques. Legislators could start by acknowledging the absurdity of outlawing plants and stop incarcerating people for planting seeds on their own land. Making milder alternatives to addictive drugs available might bring about a slow but subtle change. Under Prohibition, the popularity of hard liquor soared; but given the easy availability and social acceptance that followed repeal, people reverted to milder forms of alcohol, so that most drinkers now get their ethanol in the form of beer and wine. Just as not everybody prefers hashish to marijuana, it's likely that, if plant-derived alternatives to hard drugs were available, many users would opt for the milder forms. (Interestingly, marijuana use by teenagers actually decreased in the decade that followed the introduction of cannabis "coffee shops" in Holland in 1976; to this day, only 8 percent of Dutch teenagers between the age of sixteen and nineteen are users, versus 16 percent in the same age group in the United States, where full prohibition is in effect.) It's a move that could start in the industrialized nations of the developed world—the ones that suffer most from drug addiction. It would keep Bolivian farmers, like Alberto Chura, in business, growing a mild, pleasant stimulant. Meanwhile, the United States could devote some of the up to $40 billion it spends annually on the War on Drugs to supporting treatment programs for addicts, rather than buying new helicopters.

The only thing that encouraged me was my certainty that the War on Drugs was ultimately doomed to failure. Short of defoliating the entire planet and napalming all of the earth's arable land, the total eradication of drug crops is an unattainable goal: the yearly needs of every heroin addict in the United States could be supplied with the poppies grown on a single twenty-square-mile patch of land. An entire year's supply of cocaine for every user in the United State could be stashed in thirteen truck trailers; and all of the thirty tons of heroin consumed in Britain would fit in a single midsize truck. If Armageddon reduced civilization to a handful of farmers, I was positive that one of the first crops they'd harvest would include some kind of psychoactive: coffee or coca bushes, cannabis or tobacco plants, or the grain and grapes to make alcohol. The human drive to intoxication, self-transcendence, or temporary escape—whatever you want to call it—is too strong to be denied.

The people of Bolivia didn't have to be reminded. They had the statues with bulging cheeks, dating back millennia before the arrival of the Spaniards, to prove that they had always coexisted with mama coca. And they had reason to be optimistic: in South America at least, the tide was turning on the war against plants. Xavier too was convinced that former coca grower Evo Morales, or another coca-friendly indigenous leader, was going to be the next president of the nation.

I lifted the soggy tea bag out of my cup and had a sip of maté de coca, anticipating its subtly revivifying lift. Maybe after dinner, I'd treat myself to another quid of coca leaves and spend some time writing in my journal. One thing was pretty certain: I'd better enjoy it while I could, while I was still in the heartland of legal coca production. There would be no smuggling a backpack full of dried coca leaves back home. If there's one thing that customs officers hate—and that their dogs love to sniff out—it's plants.

Besides, my next destination wasn't exactly a haven for narco-tourists. And though there was a forbidden substance waiting for me, it wasn't one I was looking forward to trying.

· NIGHTCAP ·

Tobacco, coffee, alcohol, hashish,
prussic acid, strychnine, are weak dilutions;
the surest poison is time.

—*Ralph Waldo Emerson*

· 9 ·

PENTOBARBITAL SODIUM

The Last Sip

I T I S A S T R E E T of such unrelieved monotony that walking
on it soon leaches out whatever residual ebullience Switzerland
may have left in your system. In the first few blocks, apartments of
modest respectability are fronted by flowering cherry trees, but they
quickly give way to buildings that, if not shabby—nothing is truly
shabby in Zürich—are about as imaginatively ornamented as parking
garages. Cast-off futons and discarded wicker chairs, piled neatly by
the curb for the garbage trucks, suggest this is the kind of neighborhood people pass through, on the way to brighter, grimmer—or
perhaps merely similar—things. Only the rainbow-hued letters of the
Bambi Kinderparadies day-care center turn your thoughts away from
the darker end of life.

At 84 Gertrudstrasse, four marble steps lead to a foyer where plastic
nameplates, next to twenty buzzers, itemize the occupants of the
building. There are a sprinkling of Germanic umlauts over vowels; an
Italian surname, the *i*'s dotted with circles, handwritten on lined paper
and taped to the metal; names of Indian, French, and Central
European provenance; and one plate that simply reads THAI MASSAGE.
In the upper-right-hand corner is a single word: DIGNITAS, Latin for

"merit, worthiness, dignity." In the hall, a pretty young Indian woman with a baby in her arms gives you a look of mild alarm, but she opens the entrance door just the same. The elevator is one of those no-nonsense models without an inner safety door, where the shaft simply unfurls before your eyes. On the fourth floor, last stop, you walk out onto the landing, where a pale green door has been left ajar.

It is a low-ceilinged studio apartment, with a single bedroom and a kitchenette that doubles as an office. Venetian blinds in the main room block the view to the apartment across the street. The décor is part waiting room, part two-star hotel, part funeral parlor. The half-size fridge is filled with champagne and German beer. There are bowls of loose-leaf Japanese Sensia, and Earl Grey in muslin bags—the owner is a connoisseur of fine tea—an espresso machine for those who like their coffee strong, and a glass dish full of individually wrapped Cailler and Guylian chocolates. A single bed is covered with a striped comforter, and next to it is a small stereo and a collection of compact discs: Handel's *Water Music*, Vivaldi's *Four Seasons*, Bach's *Toccata and Fugue in D Minor*. The only really disquieting details are the images on the walls: semi-impressionistic landscapes, naïve psychedelic paintings. One is a colourful line drawing showing a stick figure in a wheelchair. Before her is a pyramid sitting atop a hill. Behind her is a trail of castoffs: a box of Pampers, a kidney, a liver, a human heart. The figure is holding up a vial of green liquid, and she is smiling. The woman who drew this self-portrait, a doctor, was suffering from a terminal illness. Her last moments were spent at the table in the bedroom, listening to music before she sipped a cloudy potion through a straw. Though she was brought to the fourth floor in her wheelchair, she descended in a body bag. Like most of Dignitas's members, she came to Switzerland without any luggage.

I'm glad I can picture this room, where people from all over the world come to die. It is not a bad thing, after all, to note the location of the emergency exits in this world. For those of us who don't believe in reincarnation or afterlifes, for whom all meaning is perforce concentrated in the material sphere, the awareness that many deaths are lonely, pain-wracked, and humiliating can produce the occasional bout of existential vertigo. To philosophize is to learn to die, said Montaigne, and the longing for a good death (*eu*, "good"; *thanatos*, "death"; hence, *euthanasia*) has occupied thinkers throughout the ages. "I shan't cast old age off," wrote the Roman philosopher Seneca the Younger, "if old age keeps me for myself—whole, I mean, on my better side; but if it begins to unseat my reason and pull it piecemeal, if it leaves me not life but mere animation, I shall be out of my crumbling, tumbledown tenement at a bound." The old Stoic's end, it turned out, was neither voluntary nor expeditious: ordered to kill himself by Nero, he cut his veins with a sword, but, proving to be a slow bleeder, he was forced to resort to hemlock. When the poison also turned out to be slow-acting, he suffocated himself in a steam bath.

Had he foreseen the potential for botching his suicide, Seneca might have appreciated knowing that a place like 84 Gertrudstrasse would one day exist. And he would certainly have wanted to know the formula of the elixir—the modern hemlock—that would be drunk there.

It's easy to poke fun at the Swiss. Especially the Swiss-Germans. Zürich offers endless opportunities for those who still experience wry satisfaction at seeing a national cliché perfectly embodied. I'd already watched a driver in a starched white shirt on the bridge in front of the *Rathaus* polishing his navy blue Mercedes with a white handkerchief, blowing invisible specks of dust off the fenders of his taxi with little puffs from *Spätzli*-fattened cheeks. On the creaking #3 tram on Badenstrasse, a pair of grim-faced ticket inspectors, undercover in faded blue jeans and multipocketed vests, did a spot-check for fare dodgers: everybody, even the goth girl with black fingernails and kohl-rimmed suicide eyes, proffered a valid ticket or pass. I'd stopped smirking at the piles of newspapers, impeccably collated, bound with twine, and filed curbside to be picked up by recycling trucks. And I'd gotten used to all the clocks—the golden, steeple-top hands of the largest clockface in Europe, the shopwindows swarming with cuckoos—whose omnipresence seemed to preclude the need to actually possess a wristwatch. *Tempus fugit*, the Swatches of Switzerland screamed. Interest accrues, the banks of Zürich soothed.

Gradually, though, my amusement was turning to admiration. On the pedestrianized Niederdorfstrasse, I'd watched a dignified Frau open her wallet and hand a ten-Swiss-franc note to a barefoot, but healthy-looking, teenage street punk, who accepted it with a smile and walked back to her mutt singing a happy song. I'd come across at least half a dozen bicycles left unattended and unlocked on downtown sidewalks as their owners ran into stores to do errands. Alone in a used-music store while the owner went outside to wash the windows, I'd realized that all the compact discs were still in their cases, a situation that would have incited a feeding frenzy among shoplifters in just about any other city in the world.

I assembled a picnic lunch of Birchermuesli, potato salad, and a fish burger and brought it to the Platzspitz, a talon-shaped park north of the train station. The spot's reputation had preceded it: this was the infamous "Needle Park," a legendary no-man's-land, unpatrolled by the police, typically filled with two thousand hard-core drug addicts shooting up, nodding off, and keeling over from overdoses at the rate of one a day. Throughout the 1990s, it had been a death scene, a civic abcess used by conservative prohibitionists as an object lesson in the apparently inevitable consequences of liberal European drug policies.

Bracing myself for an onslaught of aggressive eye contact and sibilant solicitation, I found a patch of unshaded embankment and sat next to the Limmat River to take in the scene. A pair of young mothers walked past, pushing babies in perambulators. Secretaries and clerks were eating bag lunches. A young executive, his skinny tie swept over his shoulder, pushed past on a foot scooter. This was nothing like the streets around Oslo's train station, where I'd watched skeletal junkies shooting up in the gutters; hell, it wasn't even Amsterdam's red-light district, where drug addicts offer to sell you stolen bicycles for the price of a fix. Zürich's erstwhile "Needle Park" was entirely pleasant, so much so that I soon found myself gazing dreamily at a wonky tic-tac-toe board being formed by the expanding contrails of jets crisscrossing the blue Alpine sky. The only panhandlers who troubled me were the tall white swans and complaining black coots who paddled up to beg for a handout of crumbs; the only overt drug consumption I saw was a college-aged couple sharing a joint in the shade of a weeping willow.

I couldn't quite figure it out. I'd read that there were still thirty thousand heroin addicts in Switzerland. In any other nation, a contingent that large addicted to expensive, illegal drugs would constitute a significant criminal underclass and be a persistent generator of robberies, break-ins, and petty thefts. The Swiss had obviously managed to stow their drug problem somewhere.

It would be a few days before I discovered exactly where. For now, though, heroin wasn't uppermost on my mind. I'd crossed the Alps in search of stronger stuff: namely, pentobarbital sodium, a fast-acting tranquilizer that, in the dose it is conventionally served in Zürich, produces almost instant death.

It was the only forbidden substance I wouldn't be sampling myself.

What, I wondered, does one wear to an interview with Herr Death?

I'd neglected to pack a Kevlar vest, so I put on long sleeves, cuff links, slipped into my sharkskin jacket, and hoped for the best. Outside the Opera House, I boarded a cream-and-red trolley, which climbed the stolid avenues overlooking the eastern shore of the

Zürichsee, until rambling gable-roofed homes gave way to farm properties where dandelions and daffodils dotted green meadows. I descended at a little rural station called Forch and waited by the roadside, vaguely wondering whether I should be scanning the horizon for a black hearse.

It is daunting to meet a person whose vocation it is to dispatch other human beings; given the history of euthanasia, one is rather inclined to wonder about their deeper motivations. There was Jack Kevorkian, the Michigan doctor who, by conservative count, had presided over the deaths of 130 of his patients—only a quarter of them terminally ill—administering his lethal injections and carbon monoxide in the back of a rusty Volkswagen van. After one such "medicide," he removed the kidneys from the corpse, ostensibly for transplant; he is now serving ten to twenty-five years for second-degree murder in the Michigan State prison. There was Philip Nitschke, the Australian doctor who built a prototype coma machine called Final Exit to help people die by carbon dioxide narcosis, and considered launching a "death ship" in international waters to evade domestic anti-euthanasia laws. And of course, there was the memory of the T4 Euthanasia Program, launched by Adolf Hitler in 1939, aimed at purging the Third Reich of "burdensome lives" and "useless eaters." Eventually, two hundred thousand embarrassments to the master race—among them the mentally retarded, the handicapped, and finally, sick children—were put down against their will, with the complicity of the German psychiatric community.

A red Citroën of 1980s vintage pulled up to the curb, and a stout man in his seventies, with a round, lined face, got out of the car and shook my hand. He was wearing a deep blue ascot tucked into the open collar of a well-pressed, baby blue shirt, and sandals over blue socks. It was a two-minute drive from the station to his home; an elevator took us from the garage to a sun-drenched living room, lined with books, including the complete works of Winston Churchill and

George Bernard Shaw. My host returned from the kitchen with a pot full of Chinese white tea and a plate of honeyed almond cookies. He sat on a wicker chair covered with a well-worn sheepskin rug, poured the tea into porcelain cups, turned his blue eyes to me expectantly and said, "*So.*" It was ten o'clock on a Sunday morning. There had been no mention of church.

Since founding Dignitas in May 1998, Ludwig Minelli, a former human rights lawyer and a journalist for the German weekly news-magazine *Der Spiegel*, had helped 274 people from all over the world to end their lives. Thanks to a sixty-year-old loophole in Swiss law, it is legal to help another person to commit suicide, as long as it is not done for selfish gain. Dignitas's membership list now includes four thousand people, from fifty nations, as far away as Peru and Israel. There are 520 members from Britain alone, where helping a loved one to commit suicide is a crime punishable by a long prison sentence.

Minelli had been a member of Exit, Switzerland's largest assisted-suicide organization, until an internal schism had inspired him to strike out on his own.

"There was an awful general assembly in Zürich in 1998," he recalled, "in which there was much shouting, and that same night I decided to found Dignitas, because I think people who are members in an association for last things would prefer if peace was reigning, and not war. There are only two people in the general assembly of Dignitas—the other is an old friend of mine—and this way you will never have power struggles; you will always be unanimous." Another motive for the split was Exit's restrictive membership policies; it was open only to Swiss citizens. "I cannot accept that people with foreign residencies are discriminated against; because they suffer too. If we have the means to help them, I think we should. The same thing with mentally ill people. Exit has this idea not to get into quarrels with the authorities, but, as a lawyer, I brought a lot of cases against my government. I am used to quarreling."

Minelli laughed. He had one of those laughs that begins with a chuckle, gets delighted with itself, and turns into a cascade of guffaws. Rather to my surprise, I often found myself joining in.

"You know, about eighty percent of our members will never make the voyage to Switzerland; but they are relieved to know that they have a side exit, if they need it. We have a lot of members with cancer. Women with breast cancer, because it is very aggressive and very painful, and men with pancreas cancer, which is very quick in progress. Then we have neurological illnesses, motor neurone disease, multiple sclerosis, ALS. They read reports about us in the newspapers or visit our Web site. Sometimes they want to come immediately, but we ask them to pay a membership fee of one hundred Swiss francs [$86 U.S.], and then to send a personal request telling us why they want to go this way." (Dignitas is a nonprofit organization; Minelli says he survives on a state pension.) "Then we ask for medical records, because we work with seven or eight physicians, and to write a prescription the doctor must be persuaded there are really reasons for this person to commit suicide. When they come here, the doctor discusses alternatives. There have been several cases where a physician told a member that pain therapy hasn't been optimal, and I think you should go back to your country and try the highest level of pain therapy. If there are family members, the doctor will also speak with them. After that, he will write a prescription."

I asked whether foreign members ever had trouble getting into Switzerland.

"Nobody will ask you what you are doing in Switzerland. It is a very liberal country, and it has been so for centuries. We are not in America, where they ask if you are homosexual when you apply for a visa. We are a free land, not a police state!"

Again the rollicking guffaws.

"Then we go to the apartment at Gertrudstrasse. I say good-bye to our member, and then I leave the apartment, and the procedure will begin. There are one or two of our accompanying staff who stay, and they discuss with the members whether they are sure they really want to take this step. We tell them we would be happy if they would choose to go back home. Sometimes the talks go on for hours and hours. If the member decides he or she is ready, he takes Dramamine, or another medication against vomiting. And after half an hour, when the stomach is prepared, they take fifteen grams of pentobarbital sodium, dissolved in sixty milliliters of ordinary water. Sometimes they drink with a straw; if they are on a drip, they will open the valve that releases the pentobarbital. But the last act is always the member's. In these six years, we had only one member who was so handicapped we couldn't help him; he went back home and was helped by another person. One member bit the straw sixteen times; she was not ready to die. But then she came back later, and that time she drank.

"Then they eat some chocolate, or drink something sweet, because the liquid is very bitter. After two to five minutes, the person will fall into a deep sleep—sometimes they are talking, and they fall asleep in the middle of a phrase—and then they go into a coma. Soon, between ten minutes and, at the latest, several hours, the pentobarbital will stop them from breathing, and they die. Then comes one of the public prosecutors, a police officer, and a legal physician. They are looking for indications of a crime, but in the last six years we have never had a procedure against us. The body is taken to the Institute of Legal Medicine, and after the prosecutor has given his consent to burial, it is transported either to the crematorium, or back to the country where the member came from." Not all of Dignitas's members were terminally ill. Some were handicapped; some had mental problems; some were simply terribly depressed, and this has proven the most controversial aspect of Minelli's work.

Once, Minelli told me, a twenty-year-old German man had showed up outside his door telling him that he wanted to die immediately. He told Minelli he had cheated on his university exams, felt unfulfilled in his professional life, and had recently spent time in an institution. Minelli discussed methods of suicide with him, all the while trying to show him that he had reasons to live. They went to a fine restaurant together, where they discussed death by starvation; then spent an evening in a bathing resort, where they talked about the risks of dying of exposure on a glacier. Finally, the young man decided to give life another chance and went back home to Germany.

"I saw him a few months ago, and he is doing very well. He has got another diploma, he has finished his professional training, and he is still together with the same girlfriend. For me, though, this was five days of hard work. I'm persuaded if you want to reduce the number of suicides and suicide attempts, you should never try to influence people not to commit suicide. You should always accept these offers and give them the possibility to discuss the idea without any fear. But it's also our duty to show other possibilities. We should accept that every human being has one, two, or three times in his life where he thinks about killing himself. You know, many people are in a deep, deep hole, and they look up, and they just see heaven, and this means death, and they don't see anything else. If you give them the possibility to speak without fear of being placed in a psychiatric institution, and just on a normal level between human beings, I think then you would be able to show them a lot of choices. If I could make a law, I would devote perhaps half of one percent of the public health budget to organizations in order to prevent suicide."

I asked Minelli about one of Dignitas's most controversial cases, a brother and sister from France, twenty-nine and thirty-one years old, who had been suffering from schizophrenia since puberty.

"With mentally ill people, we are never in a hurry. We know that sometimes, time helps. But this case to us was very clear. No doubt at all. I met them at the Central Station, personally, and on the way to the hotel the young lady began to cry. She actually asked, 'Will it really work?' This was her first and only concern. She was eager to die.

The alternative was for them to be found dead on the railway tracks somewhere."

I was beginning to realize that I was not in the presence of a Kevorkian. Minelli wasn't a physician, didn't display any morbid interest in the mechanics of death, and made it a point not to be on hand when the actual deaths occurred. I asked why he had made helping other people die his vocation.

"I only know that from my youngest time I always have helped other people. When I was twelve years old, I remember that we had a substitute teacher who beat one of the pupils across the knuckles with a wooden stick, which I knew was very dangerous. I complained to somebody on the school authority board, and they disciplined the teacher. When I was a little older, I saw my grandmother die of a kidney illness, and I remember her saying, 'Couldn't you do something so that it goes faster?' And the doctor told her, 'No, I am not allowed.'"

He leaned back in his chair, steepling thick, knobby-bolled fingers.

"People often ask me if all of this doesn't have a negative effect on my mind. Well, we will all be dead one day; it is just a question of when and how. But there is something that is bothering me enormously, and that is the fact that our members must leave their beds, their homes, their countries, and come to a foreign nation, a foreign bed, just to die." Minelli told me of John Close, an Englishman suffering from motor neurone disease, who dreamed of dying in the bay window of his own flat, listening to music and watching the sunset; of a cancer victim whose face was so ravaged he had to wear a mask on the long train trip from northern Germany; of Reginald Crew, who had made the intensely uncomfortable voyage by small plane from Liverpool. "This is always nearly heartbreaking for me. So I am struggling to find a way to change the laws in the rest of Europe, so people will not have to make such travels."

One of the fears expressed by opponents of euthanasia and assisted suicide is the potential for abuse. People who are self-effacing, those suffering from dementia, those unable to express themselves, may be coerced into suicide because they are a burden on their family. The ways the Nazis used euthanasia, I pointed out to Minelli, linger in the collective memory.

"Every allusion to the Nazis is false!" he snapped. "Because in that case, there never was any free choice. In Germany today, they are always speaking of killing another person on demand, and this is not the right way to frame the discussion. You have the taboo of killing a third person, and this can be avoided, by helping and abetting suicide. This way, you have the most control against misuse, because a person who does not want to die will not drink the pentobarbital.

"I am going to read you something." Minelli disappeared into his office and returned with the text of a speech. He read aloud, " 'When any is taken with a torturing and lingering pain, so that there is no hope, either of recovery or ease, the priests and magistrates come and exhort them, that since they are now unable to go on with the business of life . . . they should no longer nourish such a rooted distemper, but choose rather to die, since they cannot live but in such misery. Such as are wrought on by these persuasions, either starve themselves of their own accord, or take opium, and by that means die without pain. But no man is forced on this way of ending his life; and if they cannot be persuaded to it, this does not induce them to fail in their attendance and care of them; but as they believe that a voluntary death, when it is chosen upon such an authority, is very honorable.' "

Minelli put aside the paper. The passage was from *Utopia*, the portrait of an ideal island run on humanist principles by Thomas More, lord chancellor to Henry VIII, in 1516. (Strangely, this prototypical euthanasia advocate was canonized in 2000 by Pope John Paul II as patron saint of politicians and statesmen.)

"You know, sometimes I am thinking about problems in the way Thomas More did. Sometimes we should think utopically, how we would manage a problem if we were free of the usual conditions. First, I think I would accept that every human being has the possibility to make his own choice when it comes to life and death. Of course, this shouldn't happen on first demand, only after some discussion where the person has shown his responsibility vis-à-vis other people, his family, and himself. Second, if there is an illness, I would ask physicians whether they could propose alternative treatments. But as soon as the physician tells us there are no more possibilities, or the patient decides to refrain from further therapy, he could go to the cantonal pharmacist with a paper from the doctor to get fifteen grams of pentobarbital sodium. This way, there would be no danger of spreading narcotics, and we would guarantee freedom of choice, but we would also have the possibility to say to people that want to die, 'Come, and we can discuss things, and maybe help you.' "

Rousing himself from his chair, Minelli said, "I want to show you something."

I was instantly apprehensive. I'd noticed a glint in Minelli's eye, and suddenly I imagined a trip to a bomb shelter in the basement, where I would be inducted into the arcana of some sketchy and troubling taxidermy.

But Minelli merely walked a few feet and slid open a glass door that looked out over his backyard.

"Aren't they nice?" He was staring dreamily over the lawn, in the direction of a somewhat kitschy bronze nude on a pedestal. I followed his gaze to a bush of what looked like purplish pink roses.

"They are camellias," he said fondly. "Normally they don't grow north of the Alps."

The War on Drugs and the taboo against suicide intersect in one of the few substances that can bring a rapid and painless death to the terminally ill. Pentobarbital sodium, Dignitas's hemlock of choice, is a barbiturate, one of a potent class of sedatives first marketed by Bayer and Merck as sleeping drafts in 1903. Great reducers of anxiety in small doses, barbiturates have one fatal flaw: when the recommended amount is exceeded, often by only a gram or two, they can provoke coma and death. With barbiturates the gradations between being dead to the world, one of the walking dead, and actually dead are very fine indeed. In the form of Nembutal, Veronal, and Seconal, barbiturates—also known as goofballs, for their propensity to make users drool and slur their speech—were taken in near suicidal doses by the likes of Sarah Bernhardt, Montgomery Clift, and John Kenneth Galbraith. Overdoses of barbiturates actually *did* end the lives of Brian Jones, Jimi Hendrix, and Janis Joplin. In England, by the late 1960s, only coal gas was implicated in more suicides than barbiturates. Gradually replaced by benzodiazepines such as Valium and Xanax, which are almost impossible to fatally overdose on, barbiturates are now strictly controlled and rarely prescribed; these days, pentobarbital sodium is most commonly used as a veterinary anesthetic, and as a means of painlessly killing large barnyard animals.

After the 1997 Death with Dignity Act made Oregon the only American state where assisted suicide was legal, the former U.S. attorney general John Ashcroft, a Pentecostal Christian who abstains from tobacco and alcohol on religious grounds, worked hard to undermine the will of the people of Oregon—and, interestingly for a Republican, the very principle of states' rights—by threatening to use the Drug Enforcement Agency to revoke the licenses of doctors who prescribed lethal doses of barbiturates. Ashcroft, leaving office after George W. Bush's reelection, expressed his fervent wish that two local initiatives that reduced suffering and curtailed agony—California's medical marijuana law and Oregon's assisted suicide law—be fought with all the power available to the federal government.

Suicide is one of humanity's darkest taboos. For Jews, Muslims, Hindus, and many Christians—Catholics, Baptists, Mormons, and Christian Scientists among them—it represents an inexcusable interference with divine intentions for mankind. God owns life, the reasoning goes, and it is His to give and His to take away; thus, it must be lived to its natural end, even if that means crawling to heaven through a tunnel of thorns. Augustine considered suicide the gravest of all sins, since it was the only one that could not be repented of during the lifetime of the sinner, and later Dante consigned the souls of suicides to the Seventh Circle of Hell. In some medieval European nations, the authorities, furious at being cheated of an exemplary body by self-murder, confiscated the property of the defunct and punished their descendants. In his 1783 essay *On Suicide*, the Scottish skeptic David Hume tried to reconcile suicide with Christian tradition, averring that the "life of a man is of no greater importance to the universe than an oyster." And, since this was so, "When I fall upon my sword . . . I receive my death equally from the hands of the Deity as if it had proceeded from a lion, a precipice, or a fever."

For the pagans, suicide had never been such a conundrum. The Stoics, Cynics, and Epicureans all saw self-slaughter as a rational and honorable end to life, and the list of famous suicides in antiquity includes Zeno, Cato, and the aforementioned Seneca. The legacy of the feudal tradition of hara-kiri, or "stomach cutting," still lingers in contemporary Japan, where people kill themselves over bankruptcy, unhappy love affairs, and even bad exam results. In the contemporary West, the consensus in the psychiatric establishment seems to be that suicidal thoughts are a symptom of mental disease, and therefore no suicide attempt can be considered rational. If you judge your life worth ending—no matter how much grief, depression, or physical pain you are experiencing—your sanity is automatically suspect, and paramedics, police officers, and doctors have a duty to protect you from yourself. In every nation, there are horror stories of depressed individuals being incarcerated against their will for idly, but audibly, musing about ending their life.

Euthanasia simply means killing painlessly, usually at a suffering individual's request. As a cultural practice in Western societies, euthanasia faces two deeply entrenched prohibitions: the rather stark Judeo-Christian commandment "Thou shalt not kill," and the Hippocratic injunction against taking life, which has been part of physicians' credos since 400 B.C. For some, no amount of suffering—not even, say, the pain of an intubated woman with a metastatic sarcoma of the uterus whose cancer is slowly spreading to the bones—will ever justify transgressing the taboo against killing. The only permissible recourse for those whose beliefs forbid euthanasia is pharmacological oblivion—doping a patient up with so many painkillers that he is essentially in a coma—the writing of a do-not-resuscitate order, or the withdrawal of treatment (sometimes called passive euthanasia), in which patients finally succumb to dehydration, starvation, or the very disease from which they've been suffering (which is the way the brain-damaged Florida woman Terri Schiavo ultimately died). Assisted suicide, which is what Ludwig Minelli and Dignitas advocate, makes the means to a painless death available to those who want to die, as long as they perform the last act themselves (which generally means swallowing poison or throwing a switch to administer carbon monoxide gas). It's a proviso that not only sidesteps the taboo around killing, but also helps ensure death is an act of free will. With new technology, like software that initiates death with the tapping of a single computer key, self-initiated suicide, as opposed to physician-assisted euthanasia, could easily be available to all but the comatose and the demented.

Though suicide stopped being penalized in most American states early in the twentieth century, has not been a crime in England for fifty years, and was decriminalized in Canada in 1972, abetting suicide is still a crime in most jurisdictions. The laws are far from symbolic: for example, the general secretary of a British voluntary euthanasia organization was sentenced to eighteen months imprisonment in 1983, and the law in both Canada and England provides for up to fourteen years in prison. In Germany, it is legal to assist in a suicide—on the condition that you immediately resuscitate the patient and call for an ambulance. In Switzerland, one of the few nations in the world to tolerate assisted suicide, the 1942 law was passed to allow for such hypothetical cases as providing a bankrupt friend with a pistol. In Holland, euthanasia has been tolerated since 1973 and was formally legalized in 2001. (Belgium followed suit a year later, and Spain is now considering legalizing euthanasia.) The Dutch criteria require unbearable pain or suffering (opening the door to petitions from the depressed and mentally ill), but they also call for a long-standing relationship with a family physician, and two thirds of requests are turned down—which may explain why Dignitas counts so many Dutch citizens among its members.

The laws surrounding euthanasia and assisted suicide have a lot in common with the way societies handle (or fail to handle) forbidden substances. In Prohibition-era America, it was illegal to manufacture, purchase, or transport alcohol, but legal to drink it in one's home (as though the booze appeared magically in the liquor cabinet, like so much manna from heaven). Today, many jurisdictions have decriminalized the consumption of marijuana, while keeping its growth and sale a criminal offense. Likewise, suicide per se is not a crime, but anything that might make it possible—and less susceptible to botching up—most emphatically is, creating a paradoxical status quo: in most countries, it is now illegal to assist somebody to do something that is, of itself, perfectly legal. By entangling issues of individual freedom in a webwork of complex and often contradictory legislation, lawmakers routinely sidestep the political risks of confronting knotty philosophical issues head-on.

While euthanasia and assisted suicide are deeply controversial in most nations, I was surprised to find there was virtually no public debate over the topic in Switzerland. The Catholic Church had, predictably, denounced the practice, but its influence, particularly in the German-speaking parts of Switzerland was minimal. (Minelli, a lapsed Catholic, told me scornfully, "I don't think religion is opium for the masses, as Marx said. It is opium for the intelligence, because it prevents people from thinking.") Objections to Dignitas focused not on morality, but on a particularly Swiss preoccupation: What impact would all these foreigners—whom the press had dubbed "one-way tourists"—have on their stable, homogeneous, and increasingly conservative society?

I met Andreas Brunner, Dignitas's most outspoken critic, at the public prosecutor's office in downtown Zürich. Brunner showed up at the office on a red Vespa, which he parked under the spreading branches of a Japanese cherry tree in full blossom. A handsome middle-aged man, dressed in blue jeans, a striped tie, and a jacket, he used a lighter emblazoned with a white Swiss cross to light a constant succession of Marlboros.

"The big discussion in Switzerland," Brunner told me, "is about foreigners. 'To See Zürich and Die,' one American newspaper wrote." (The local tourist board's slogan was "Zürich: Live It. Love It." They might have added, "And Never Leave It.") "I think you need to follow people who want to commit suicide over a certain length of time. As it is, they come here one day, they have a quick meeting with a Swiss doctor who writes a prescription, and the same day, or the day after, they pass away. The will to commit suicide isn't always a stable one; in a week, you may change your mind.

"If, for example," Brunner continued, "you think you didn't get any good interviews in Zürich today, Mr. Grescoe, you could say, 'Please, Mr. Minelli, give me the drugs, because I know I'm going to be fired, and I want to kill myself.'"

Brunner thought the suicides of the schizophrenic brother and sister from France was a particularly dodgy one; following the case, the doctor involved had temporarily been prevented from writing prescriptions for pentobarbital. "Examinations and medical records from foreign doctors aren't always good. And often they don't answer the most important question: Is this person conscious of the will to commit suicide?" Brunner said he would like to see a minimum six-month residency requirement before candidates were allowed to commit suicide on Swiss soil; this would virtually eliminate the "suicide tourist" phenomenon, and, perhaps not incidentally, a significant amount of the work of the public prosecutor's office.

(Ludwig Minelli had a low opinion of Brunner's motivations. "As public prosectuor," Minelli told me, "Mr. Brunner is responsible for the field of killing people. How many murders do we have in Zürich in a year? I think it is not a dozen. Now arrives an organization like Dignitas, which had about ninety-two accompaniments last year in Zürich. So his workload has increased considerably, and it's in his personal interest to go back to the old situation. Which is why he's pursuing politicians to make a new law. It's quite as simple as that.")

Brunner, for his part, cited the expense to the canton of catering to the suicide tourists. "It costs us about two to three thousand American dollars a case. With all the officers, doctors, police involved, it brings trouble and takes time. If it continues to grow like this, it could be a problem."

But Brunner knew that even if he succeeded in having a law passed in the canton of Zürich, Minelli would just move operations to one of Switzerland's twenty-five other cantons; in fact, Dignitas had just rented a house in the countryside in the neighboring canton of Aargau for future assisted suicides.

Brunner maintained that the expense was not his chief concern. What he really wanted was to see the whole business regulated.

"If tomorrow I decided I didn't want to work anymore, I could start my own suicide organization in Switzerland. Organizations like

Dignitas and Exit happen to be very good, but you have to be sure that the people in charge are the right people. We can imagine people in religious cults who think death is the best way and use the organizations to do their work. As with everything in the world, we need to have some rules, some quality control—they should at least have a license from the state."

It was a good point. In the quasi-utopian Swiss context, where health care is free and human behavior is expected to be rational, little allowance is made for bad intentions. In my perverse, foreign way, I'd already daydreamed plots for detective thrillers in which a young Lothario took advantage of Swiss credulity to do in a rich widow in the early stages of Alzheimer's, or a wheelchair-bound disciple was bullied into sipping the pentobarbital by some Machiavellian nihilist.

Ludwig Minelli had dismissed such scenarios as far-fetched. "I think we can feel whether the person really wants to die or not, because they come and say, 'I am so glad to be here. Since the moment you phoned to tell me I have the green light, I am so happy.' Nobody would use those words if they were under pressure from third persons. Normally when they arrive, the people who want to die are smiling and joking, and the relatives are just the opposite, very sad. If things would be otherwise, we would think about it."

Still, it all came down to Minelli's ability to quickly and correctly ascertain people's true intentions. Ultimately, only two people determined whether a suicide demand was legitimate: Minelli himself and the Swiss doctor who met the patient and wrote the lethal prescription. I found the fleetingness of their face-to-face contact with suicide seekers a little disquieting. Nor was Minelli a completely neutral facilitator of death: he had admitted to energetically discussing alternatives with the twenty-year-old German man who had finally decided to go back home. Minelli could protest his impartiality, but clearly some screening was going on; one could only hope that the gatekeepers at Dignitas—or any other assisted-suicide association—would continue to be both astute and disinterested.

In the rare cases where opposition to euthanasia and assisted suicide isn't based on religious conviction, the concerns typically voiced are of a slippery slope in which not just the terminally ill would be candidates for death, but also the demented, the disabled, the deformed, the hopeless, or even the severely bummed out. What if, the devil's advocates ask, suicide became a popular institution? What if euthanasia became such a cultural norm it was routinely used to end the lives of people who could no longer express their will to live or die? What if over-the-counter death kits—pentobarbital shooters—were sold at every local drugstore? Suddenly, every heart-broken sixteen-year-old could off himself on a gloomy Saturday night. Surely, some kinds of safeguards must be built in. But who should determine who gets to die? A retired lawyer like Ludwig Minelli? A family doctor, as in Holland, Belgium, and Oregon? Or an ethics committee of physicians and hospital administrators, as some have proposed?

One leading, nonreligious opponent of assisted suicide and euthanasia is Not Dead Yet, a grassroots organization founded in the United States in 1996 in the wake of protests against the work of Jack Kevorkian.

"We view legalization of assisted suicide as discriminatory policy," research director Stephen Drake told me from the organization's headquarters in Forest Park, Illinois. "In most countries, there are statutes that require suicide prevention on the part of health-care providers and law enforcement professionals. What legalizing assisted suicide says is that not only are we going to carve out an exception to those prevention policies, but we're also going to make sure there's professional help so that a certain group of people don't screw their suicides up. And who are those people? The old, the ill, the disabled. If you're one of those people and you start examining it in those terms, it doesn't look so much as empowerment of the individual as empowerment of medical professionals."

Many of Not Dead Yet's two thousand members are disabled, and Drake himself was born hydrocephalic, a condition in which fluid collects in the brain. The experience left him with not only mild neurological disabilities, but also an abiding suspicion of the power physicians have over life and death.

"The disabled are *already* victimized by doctors. The doctor who delivered me wanted my parents to leave me in a corner of the nursery to die. A lot of us come out of those kinds of experiences; we're the survivors."

The more Drake expressed his concerns, however, the more specific they seemed to the United States. As the only industrialized democracy without universal health care, it is an anomaly among nations. In a context where treatment is often ruinously expensive, there are indeed compelling reasons to fear abuse and neglect.

"We don't have to worry about a hypothetical slippery slope in the United States," said Drake. "We're already trying to find traction on it. There are ninety-eight thousand deaths a year through medical errors in this country, but there's a culture of silence in American medicine where you don't admit your mistakes and just sweep them under the rug. And these are the same people we're supposed to trust to be aboveboard about what's going on with assisted suicide?

"Legalizing assisted suicide is just a convenient way of getting rid of the problem, when the whole focus should be on cleaning up the medical system. Rather than giving us access to better palliative care, they're telling us we should just get out of the way, so society doesn't have to feel guilty about paying for what we need."

That more Americans would benefit from access to affordable medical care was hardly controversial. The apposite question was whether in jurisdictions where euthanasia and assisted suicide were allowed that long slippery slide had begun, and people were being euthanized against their will. In fact, the situation seemed to be just the opposite. In Oregon, for example, where mentally competent patients must make three separate demands for lethal drugs, twice orally, and once in writing, and then be adjudged by a physician to have only six months to live, only 180 patients had opted for assisted suicide during the first seven years of the Death with Dignity Act. (Nor was there evidence of an influx of people moving to Oregon to die, and studies showed that some aspects of palliative care had actually improved since the act was implemented.) If anything, the safeguards built into legislation were so stringent that fewer people were availing themselves of the opportunity for a painless death than one might expect.

Besides, there were more treacherous slippery slopes to fear. That many jurisdictions empower themselves to judge adult human beings for their conduct and terminate their lives is surely a more hubristic instance of playing God than either abortion or euthanasia. The existence of capital punishment as a routine civic institution—one that in more sinister contexts could be used to eliminate opponents on political, ethnic, or religious grounds—should give pause to anybody genuinely concerned about a slide into tyranny. Drake, unlike some Christian supporters who oppose assisted suicide but support the electric chair and lethal injections, was at least consistent in his views.

"I'm sitting here in Illinois, and I don't know how anybody living in this state can defend the death penalty. A recent study shows we've ended up with at least seventeen innocent people dying. But compare that to conditions like persistent vegetative state, where there's a forty percent misdiagnosis rate. I'd bet a year's salary that there have been people who have been perfectly aware of what's going on in the room while people around them talked about and implemented their starvation."

Interestingly, Drake wasn't against suicide per se. He cited the libertarian thinker Thomas Szasz, who in his book *Fatal Freedom* defends an individual's absolute right to a voluntary death, but also cautions against giving doctors even more power by legalizing physician-assisted suicide.

"We presented a brief to the Supreme Court," said Drake, "saying that assisted suicide should either be available to everyone, or to no one. If you have a policy that says you're going to prevent it for most people, and facilitate it for others, then it is in fact society that is making the decision; and that's a form of discrimination, because the group that qualifies will be predetermined by their physical characteristics and their health status. What Szasz is saying is that the state shouldn't be empowering professionals to either deprive people of their freedom or to assist in suicide."

Szasz, an extreme libertarian, also advocated a completely free market in drugs—even dangerous drugs—which would make committing suicide as easy as going to the local drugstore. But I understood Drake's point. Anything that endangers the norm of preserving and protecting life—measures that would empower doctors to euthanize disabled newborns, for example—should strenuously be opposed. But that doesn't mean the medical norm should be to prolong the agony of a suffering individual against his will.

I asked Drake what should happen to a cancer patient who was seeking a dignified and painless death. In the United States, access to good palliative care is limited, and a quarter of terminally ill patients still die in pain.

"If they want to commit suicide—and thousands of people every day somehow find the means to do it—then I think they have the same opportunities. But we oppose legalized third-party involvement."

Unfortunately, that left the suffering in exactly the social and legal limbo they'd always been in: jumping off buildings, suffocating themselves by taping plastic bags around their head, and overdosing on pills. In many cases, they botch the attempt and remain incapacitated for the rest of their life.

Ludwig Minelli had described the situation in Switzerland: "Every year, we have about 1,350 suicides, and about sixty-seven thousand attempts—the same as the population of a city the size of Luzern, and we estimate it costs our society 2.4 billion Swiss francs a year. What happens to these people who attempt suicide and fail? We don't know. There are no statistics. Sleeping pills no longer work, because doctors don't prescribe barbiturates, and benzodiazepines like Valium won't kill you, though they'll seriously harm your liver and kidneys. Putting your head in the oven also no longer works, because kitchen stoves now use natural gas rather than coal gas. Running your car motor in a garage—there's no longer enough carbon monoxide in the exhaust. Driving into a wall—the car has air bags. Shooting yourself in the head—you might miss and spend the next fifty years in a hospital bed. One of the few methods that succeeds is throwing yourself in front of a train, which is very popular in Switzerland. But you should also remember it causes enormous emotional problems for the locomotive drivers."

By all accounts, the situation was even worse in jurisdictions where assisted suicide and euthanasia were completely illegal. In an ambitious study, *Angels of Death: Exploring the Euthanasia Underground*, the Australian researcher Roger S. Magnusson documented the way the terminally ill attempt to kill themselves in the United States and Australia. Patients jumped from hospital windows, severed their jugular veins, overdosed on insulin, or were smothered with pillows. Nurses described "splatter suicides," leaping from tall buildings; "air embolism," being injected with air bubbles to stop the heart; and the "Ashcroft kit," a plastic bag and a roll of duct tape for auto-asphyxiation. Doctors often provided lethal doses of drugs to the patients, but, fearing litigation, declined to be on the scene, which meant that relatives were left to watch helplessly when their loved ones started vomiting or went into convulsions. When the suicide did work, bodies were cremated immediately to destroy evidence of foul play, often with the complicity of funeral home directors. Many cases involved young men suffering from AIDS, whose hearts were still strong, and they often survived even after the entire contents of the doctor's bag had been emptied into their veins.

In spite of the prohibition, in other words, euthanasia happens all the time. In one survey, 17 percent of American critical-care nurses had received requests for euthanasia, and 4.7 percent of doctors (almost one in twenty) had provided at least one lethal injection. In Britain, one in seven general practitioners admitted to having helped a patient die. Because euthanasia was unregulated, Magnusson showed, it was also messy and surrounded by shame. He turned up evidence of coercion by relatives, rash and hasty involvement by doctors, and an all-pervasive culture of deception. Moreover, the euthanasia underground tended to attract moral mavericks and cowboys.

"In the absence of regulation," Magnusson observed, "they are the high priests and priestesses of the backrooms, mixing an incomplete and hidden body of knowledge with good intentions and periodic restlessness." Tellingly, the very doctors who performed illegal euthanasia tended to oppose regulation, because it would infringe on their clinical judgment—and their power. (And it is well to remember that doctors are no more immune from mental illness than the general population, and rather more prone to substance abuse: it is estimated that 10 percent of doctors are alcoholic, and 7 percent are drug dependent.) "The law's prohibition of assisted suicide and euthanasia inhibits free discussion of end-of-life decision-making generally, and assisted death in particular," Magnusson concluded, as he called for legalization accompanied by regulation. "Euthanasia is practiced in an informal, intuitive, and arbitrary manner. This is dangerous for patients."

Does any of this sound familiar? It should. By demonizing assisted suicide, society drives it underground, and the resulting social harms are enormous. Shady characters operate on the edge of society, with far too much power over people's lives. A black market develops in medications stolen from hospitals. Those involved, ostracized by society at large, find themselves living with shame at exactly the time when they need the most support. Because there are no standards or regulations, botched attempts end with already suffering people crippled until the end of their days.

Criminal traffickers and dealers; an unregulated black market; marginalized victims; serious and costly long-term health consequences—these are also the harms brought on by drug prohibition. The situation is maintained by the cowardice of politicians and legislators. Unwilling to acknowledge and confront the moralistic, dogmatic nature of the opposition—the idea that addiction is a failure of the will, and that acting on a desire to die is a sin—governments follow the safe course of keeping behavior criminalized, rather than confronting a taboo that would allow society to start discussing and imagining new solutions. Whether it's a botched hanging in a San Francisco AIDS hospice, a solitary drug overdose in an Edinburgh housing project, or a poisoning from methanol in an Oslo fleabag hotel, it is precisely these taboos on discussing all that is prohibited—be it alcohol or assisted suicide, coca or crystal meth—that continue to destroy millions of lives around the world every year.

Compared to the situation in other countries, the status quo in Switzerland, where there was almost no stigma attached to assisted suicide, was hearteningly sane. I met Soraya Wernli, a middle-aged woman who was married to Ludwig Minelli's partner, on the sidewalk terrace of a hotel café near Dignitas's apartment on Gertrudstrasse. A nurse who'd worked in hospitals and homes for the handicapped for twenty-five years, Wernli was responsible for liaising with Dignitas's members from the moment they contacted the association to the day they came and drank the pentobarbital. She was, in effect, an angel of death, and as she sipped a tomato juice and streetcars screeched past, she recalled the last moments she'd spent with members who had come from all over the world.

"To start, we sit down, we drink tea or coffee, and I explain to the person how it's going to happen. We tell them at least three times that they can stop everything, that they can return to their country at any time. When they decide it's time to go—and it can take two or three hours—they drink the liquid. And two to five minutes later, they'll be talking, and suddenly they go to sleep. It's very fast. They're not afraid at all.

"Many people bring a compact disc of classical music, or, if they're young, their favorite pop songs. They'll light candles, bring crosses, surround themselves with photos and flowers. Some people want me to take them in their arms; others ask that I sit quietly by the bed. Once I had a French doctor, a woman, and there were fourteen people in the room, including her grandchildren. They played the flute, and they climbed into bed with her and sang as she died. It was beautiful. Another time, there was a married couple, who had lost their son. They were happy because I had brought tulips, and they'd forgotten to buy flowers. She told her husband, 'Don't be sad, because after we will be reunited with our son.'"

Wernli's words dissolved briefly as she was choked by sobs, but she quickly recovered. "I have to say that it takes a little bit out of me every time, because we get to know people very well. They tell me all about their lives, their whole story. I wish I had a magic wand sometimes"—she tapped the table with her nails—"so I could say, 'You're perfectly healthy again, go and live your life.'

"I'm a Protestant; I believe in the good Lord. But I think he's a kind God, and he accepts that people choose their own paths. Working in hospitals, I saw many cases where people tried to commit suicide, failed, and afterwards had to remain hooked up to machines for the rest of their lives. They became prisoners of their own bodies. I suppose what I find saddest is that people have to travel, sometimes twelve hours, when they're in pain, in order to end their lives. They tell me they would prefer to die in their own homes. But it's not possible, because it's not accepted in their own countries."

I was grateful to Ludwig Minelli for reminding me of Thomas More, the sixteenth-century humanist, and with him the whole tradition of thinking utopically. It was easy to forget that, as inevitable as some social outcomes may seem, humanity was constantly engineering its own reality, and sometimes it was enough to change laws, philosophies, or hierarchies to utterly transform the lives of millions. Imagining what the constitution of a republic of reason would look like wasn't an entirely idle activity. Consider Plato. Or Thomas Jefferson. Or Mahatma Gandhi.

After a year of traveling the world, and observing the effects of official prohibitions on individual freedom, I knew exactly the words I'd turn to for inspiration. They'd been published in 1859:

"The only purpose for which power can be rightfully exercised over any member of a civilized community, against his will, is to prevent harm to others. His own good, either physical or moral, is not a sufficient warrant . . . [there] are good reasons for remonstrating with him, or reasoning with him, or persuading him, or entreating him, but not for compelling him, or visiting him with any evil in case he do otherwise . . . The only part of the conduct of anyone, for which he is amenable to society, is that which concerns others. In the part which merely concerns himself, his independence is, of right, absolute. Over himself, over his own body and mind, the individual is sovereign."

This was the credo the English philosopher and economist John Stuart Mill formulated in his essay *On Liberty*. As a succinct expression of the limits on the role society should rightfully play in the life of the individual, it had yet to be beaten. Any civilized community that considers itself secular—that is, unbound by the tenets of religious faith—and free, could do worse than making individual sovereignty one of the first articles in its constitution.

As a founding principle, it is beguilingly simple. Because certain activities are likely to have a harmful impact on the lives of others, a civilized community has every right to insist that its members play by certain rules. Stopping at red lights, for example. Not driving while intoxicated. Not smoking cigars in crowded restaurants. Not discharging automatic weapons in public. Not selling crack, tobacco, or other addictive substances to children. Not auctioning enriched plutonium, thalidomide, or anthrax spores on eBay. In the case of other activities, whose immediate consequences concern no one but the individual, society's right to intervene should be considered highly suspect. Say, growing cannabis in your own garden, and smoking marijuana in your own home. Getting shitfaced drunk. Masturbating. Having consensual oral sex with another adult. Chewing coca leaves. Committing suicide. Helping a competent adult to commit suicide.

In its application, the principle would be open to all the messy legal and philosophical debates that make living in a democracy a dynamic process. For instance, can an individual who has not achieved the age of reason, who is brain-damaged, in a coma, or in the thrall of an addiction, really be said to be sovereign over his mind or body? If society has no right to penalize individuals for behavior that concerns no one but themselves, does it nonetheless have the right to impose standards for commercial transactions? (To ensure that meat and cheese are not tainted, for example, or that fantastically potent drugs are not available to minors.)

For anybody whose reason is not preprogrammed by dogma, the idea that a civilized community can fine, incarcerate, or execute an individual for activities that concern no one but himself should be abhorrent. In the case of suicide, assisted suicide, and euthanasia, society could start with the simple idea that only the individual is in a position to decide whether his life is worth ending. It would be reasonable, since a third party is facilitating the suicide, and therefore taking a professional risk, to make sure the request is being made by an individual in whom reason is still sovereign (for those who anticipate a decline due to Alzheimer's or dementia, making a living will, or signing over power of attorney, would be a safeguard against such loss of autonomy). It would also be reasonable, given that the desire to die can pass, and that death is irrevocable, to ensure the request is serious by demanding it be repeated several times. But the idea that a team of bioethicists, psychiatrists, lawyers, and philanthropists should be allowed to second-guess a suffering individual's intentions should be anathema to anybody who values the notion of individual sovereignty. This is the situation Stephen Drake of Not Dead Yet feared: too much power in the hands of outside parties. A disinterested, nonprofit, nonmedical organization like Dignitas—albeit, I'd argue, one subject to more scrutiny from the community—is not a bad model of how such an institution might look.

Unfortunately, I live in the real world. A few reasonable policies won't do much good if the surrounding society is insane. In a stable community founded on principles of individual sovereignty, a constitutionally enshrined right to opt for a painless death may be a sensible solution. In China, however, where individual rights are sacrificed in the name of state-determined social engineering, nonvoluntary euthanasia could be used to limit an aging population or terminate unwanted newborns. In the United States, where forty-four million people have no medical insurance whatsoever, and a cohort of baby boomers will soon enter an already stressed-out system, the risk of being coerced into assisted suicide and euthanasia for financial reasons cannot be discounted. Oregon seems to be making it work; but, then again, Oregon has always been the most Swiss of American states.

Assisted suicide isn't going to be legalized in the near future for the simple reason that it is dogma, not reason, that underlies most of the ostensibly secular societies of the West. Americans are required to pledge allegiance to the flag with the words "One nation under God, indivisible, with liberty and justice for all." The Canadian Charter of Rights begins, "Whereas Canada is founded on principles that recognize the supremacy of God and the rule of law . . ." (At least the Preamble to the Fundamental Rights Charter of the European Union, adopted in 2000, sidesteps monotheism: "Conscious of its spiritual and moral heritage, the Union is founded on the indivisible, universal values of human dignity, freedom, equality and solidarity." Amen to that.) With a single Christian Supreme Being written into your most fundamental documents—and His Ten Commandments regulating personal morality—individual sovereignty doesn't stand much of a chance. Though it does help to explain some strange anomalies. Why, for example, consensual acts of anal and oral sex between adults are still illegal in thirteen American states, and it is still illegal for unmarried couples to live together in seven.

We like to pretend that we live in nations founded on the separation of church and state. But when it comes to some of the most important issues—assisted suicide, capital punishment, gay marriage, drugs—it's as though the Enlightenment never happened. For all intents and purposes, we are naughty children, still being punished with paternalistic prohibitions for the original sin of reaching for forbidden fruit.

Only after a week in Zürich did I learn why I could walk the streets, surrounded by thousands of drug addicts, without fear of having a knife pressed to my back. One afternoon I saw a thin young man and woman emerging from the back door of a building without a sign on it. Their pupils were the size of pinpricks; they were obviously under the influence of some kind of opiate. In a drugstore down the street, the pharmacist explained the building was one of Switzerland's twenty-one heroin prescription centers. Since 1994, the government had been giving out free, pharmaceutical-grade heroin to those over twenty years of age who have been addicted for more than two years; there are now three thousand people in the program. The state also handed out methadone, a long-lasting, drinkable opiate, and provided safe injection sites, with clean syringes. Though the addicts could buy heroin on the street if they wanted to, few did: Why hustle for expensive, adulterated drugs when you could get the uncut stuff for free? And why steal compact discs, mug tourists for their wallets, or break into cars when you didn't have to pay off your dealer to get your next fix? Three years after the clinical trials started, a study showed that 224 participants, almost a quarter, had opted to give up heroin in favor of abstinence therapy. In a 1997 referendum, 70 percent of Swiss voters cast polls in favor of making the heroin prescription program into official policy. Switzerland may be a conservative country—a year later, 74 percent voted against legalizing marijuana and other drugs—but, after years of failed attempts to grapple with crime and addiction, the Swiss had been able to connect the dots: when addicts need to score expensive drugs from the black market daily, society at large is going to suffer from more crime and less public safety. The Dutch have also made the connection: an even larger study in the Netherlands came to similar conclusions, and heroin prescription is now available to longtime addicts. A similar study was launched in 2005 in Toronto, Montreal, and Vancouver; in the United States, not surprisingly, the Drug Enforcement Agency made sure a similar initiative never saw the light of day.

The radical nature of the Swiss heroin program should not be understated. This was a government handing out illegal narcotics to addicts for free. Not only had the world as the Swiss knew it failed to collapse into amoral anarchy, but many addicts were spontaneously remitting. When the effort needed to score was removed, all that was left was the tediousness of addiction, one that the junkies could now contemplate abandoning with less anxiety, aware that support from health officials they'd gotten to know and trust during their daily visits would be available. Meanwhile, society as a whole was reaping the rewards: in a stroke, the class of hard-core criminal addicts responsible for most property crimes had been eliminated—simply because they were no longer inherently outlaws. By making drugs free—by subtracting their commodity value—the state had also instantly usurped the power of dealers and traffickers. When that most sinister of drugs, heroin, ceased to be forbidden fruit, and obtaining it became as boring as applying for a driver's license (every . . . day . . . of . . . your . . . life), then its dark glamour started to evaporate.

Critics said that such a policy could only work in Switzerland: it is a small, rich country, with relatively little immigration and a dense network of social services, largely unriven by the kind of political polarization that makes middle ground so hard to find in other societies. But the same could be said of Norway, and the contrast on the streets couldn't have been more stark. At the beginning of my travels, I'd seen how Norwegian junkies, hounded from the train-station park by cops, were dying in gutters and abandoned buildings as the city was flooded by cheap heroin, of dangerously variable intensity, from Afghanistan. As their health disintegrated, the addicts congregated in knots on downtown street corners, scaring shoppers away from local businesses. With public policy influenced by their Lutheran legacy of alcohol prohibition and the paradigm of the War on Drugs, the Norwegians were facing the predictible public health disaster that arises whenever prohibitionists get the upper hand.

I could probably never live in Zürich: it is a sensible-shoe kind of city, and I prefer places with more of an edge. With that said, the more I travel, and the more I see societies whose policies are determined by the arcane dogmas of extremists, the more I appreciate the secular oasis of reasonableness that is Switzerland, an entire nation run on the honor system. Not a very exciting place to visit, it's true; but, if the going gets rough, definitely a good place to seek asylum.

And if ever I learn that I'm succumbing to some terminal disease. I suspect that my last purchase will be a one-way ticket aboard Swiss Air, and that my last earthly address will be 84 Gertrudstrasse.

Here is my final point . . . About drugs,
about alcohol, about pornography . . .
What business is it of yours what I do, read,
buy, see, or take into my body as long as I do
not harm another human being on this planet?
And for those of you who are having a little moral
dilemma in your head about how to answer that
question, I'll answer it for you. *None* of your
fucking business. Take that to the bank, cash it,
and go fucking on a vacation out of my life.

—The late American comedian Bill Hicks

EPILOGUE

P ROHIBITIONS, THE LINES that throughout history
have been drawn around bottles and behaviors, powders and
plants, are tools of power. The drive toward sexual pleasure; the
urge to temporarily escape day-to-day consciousness through intoxication; the questioning of the value of one's existence, particularly when it seems too painful to endure—all are part of what it
means to be human. The way we address these powerful and
primary questions of identity defines our individuality. By circum-
scribing them with taboos and prohibitive laws, society denies its
members self-knowledge and allocates itself punitive power over
sexuality, consciousness, and self-determination—the most intimate
domains of individuality.

It was not for nothing that Islam was built on prohibitions against
wine and gambling, and just about every major faith on proscribing
certain types of sexual pleasure. Nor should it be seen as an accident
that in the Judeo-Christian tradition, the archetypal humans were
warned to stay away from forbidden fruit: the absurdity of picking a
harmless apple (though it may well have been a pear, a fig, or a
pomegranate) says a lot about how power likes to assert itself through

arbitrary prohibitions. It was the serpent, the tempter to knowledge, who invited humans to their first picnic. As Mark Twain put it:

"Adam was but human—this explains it all. He did not want the apple for the apple's sake, he wanted it only because it was forbidden. The mistake was in not forbidding the serpent; then he would have eaten the serpent."

Exactly. If the main course in the devil's picnic had been the devil himself—and with him the notion that self-knowledge is a form of transgression—Christians and Jews would have been spared endless centuries of soul-searching over their natural appetites.

Perhaps there was a certain logic in making a fruit the symbol of all that is forbidden. In the old pagan faiths, power resided in the shamans and witches who interpreted knowledge about plants. From Andean *yatiris* with their coca leaves, to the Siberian nomads and their hallucinogenic fly agarics, in every era and clime plants have been used and venerated for their ability to alter consciousness. By roping off the plants themselves, the monotheistic religions usurped the old pagan plant-knowledge, interposing a new God between humanity and nature; and not incidentally, between humanity and the self-knowledge that can be gained from altering one's consciousness.

Humanity's relationship with psychoactive plants and fungi—with cannabis, the poppy, tobacco, the coffee bush, the coca shrub, the cacao tree, the grape and its fermented juice, hallucinogenic mushrooms, and too many others to list—predates all organized religion, and every existing form of government. These psychoactives have seniority; they are sacred. The notion, shared by so many faiths, that psychoactive plants should be placed outside commerce—offered as gifts, as tokens of hospitality, and used in ceremonies to strengthen community—is an interesting clue to intelligent drug policy. Any authority that threatens to penalize, incarcerate, or execute people for growing, gathering, or consuming plants—from the hemp that grows by the roadside to cultivated poppies—is violating a fundamental human right.

Commerce in psychoactive substances is another story entirely. Though growing and consuming poppies, tobacco, or coca should not be a crime, there's a strong case to be made that selling heroin, cigarettes, or crack cocaine to addicts, or those particularly susceptible to addiction—such as minors—should be penalized. (As should dealing in rare and endangered animals, from rhino horn aphrodisiacs to Caspian sturgeon roe. Though the immediate effects derived may concern no one but the consumer, eating the last living examples of a species definitely harms everybody else on the globe.) It's a fact that anybody with a little experience of the black-market drug world finds self-evident. Individual dealers may be tolerable, but in general, as people who profit from addiction, pushers are scum. When the late gonzo journalist Hunter S. Thompson ran for office in Aspen, Colorado, in 1970, he laid out a singularly intelligent party platform: "It will be the general philosophy of the Sheriff's office that no drug worth taking should be sold for money. Nonprofit sales will be viewed as borderline cases, and judged on their merits. But all sales for money-profit will be punished severely." Sadly, Thompson was defeated, the greedheads, profiteers, and speculators held on to power, and a beautiful idea was squashed.

Though a civilized community has no business legislating private behavior whose immediate consequences affect no one but the individual, commerce is emphatically *not* private behavior. We may like to think we are entering into an entirely private, consensual relationship when we buy a product or service, but there is too much potential for fraud and deception on the part of manufacturers and retailers for this to be anything but one of capitalism's most self-serving fictions. That's why most people acknowledge that a civilized community has some right to mess with trade: to demand that soda companies list the caffeine and other additives in their drinks, that tobacco companies warn of potential health hazards of cigarettes, that distilleries not market hard liquor to prepubescents, and that SUV makers put air bags in their death traps.

The republic of reason proposed by libertarians—people like American economist Milton Friedman, and psychiatrist Thomas Szasz, who call for an unregulated free market in drugs—is an absurdity. Anyone who has actually been addicted to cocaine, speed, or heroin possesses wisdom that Nobel Prize laureates will never have: drugs are not just another product on the market, like widgets and MP3 players, subject to the universal laws of supply and demand. As author William S. Burroughs observed, on the subject of heroin, "Junk is the ultimate commodity, the merchandise is not sold to the consumer—the consumer is sold to the merchandise." The idea that users will somehow regulate their consumption and sagely reject harmful products fails to take into account the insidiousness of addiction, or the deferred health consequences of products like tobacco and alcohol, which can kill their consumers after forty or fifty years of use. It also fails to take into account the sophistication of the pharmaceutical and recreational drug industry, which is constantly synthesizing impossibly potent new designer drugs. Should any adult be able to go to the drugstore and buy an over-the-counter bottle of etorphine, an opiate that is ten thousand times stronger than morphine (quite useful when you've got a rhinoceros to tranquilize, or a town reservoir to poison)? Should nineteen-year-olds be able to pick up packs of cocaine or methamphetamine cigarettes at the neighborhood convenience store?

These aren't merely far-fetched, rhetorical questions: corporations have tried to get in the addiction market before. The pharmaceutical company Parke-Davis marketed coca-laced cigars to the general public in 1886. In England, retailers like Harrods and Savory and Moore offered morphine and cocaine gift packs, a "useful present for friends at the front," in the opening years of the First World War. In 1969, a new-products task force assembled by the J. Walter Thompson Company recommended that cigarette company Liggett & Meyers manufacture "betel morsels," reasoning that because millions of Africans and Asians were addicted to the teeth-staining stimulant, there could be a huge profit-making potential in the domestic market.

"When psychoactive drugs are widely available, heavily promoted, and cheap, they become extremely popular, particularly if they are habit-forming," drug historian David Courtwright observed in his book *Forces of Habit*. He offered as proof the fur traders who sold whiskey to Native Americans, the British who peddled Indian opium to the Chinese, and Buck Duke of British American Tobacco, who got the world hooked on the tobacco of North Carolina. Offering major corporations an unfettered market in addictive substances would be tantamount to selling the world into chemical slavery.

As a general principle, humanity's age-old and sacred relationship with psychoactive plants should trump all prohibitions. When it comes to establishing the nefariousness of novel substances, like designer drugs, the burden of proof should always fall on the regulating government, with preference being given to the individual's right to consume them. But while a civilized community has no right to throw its members in jail or fine them for smoking a joint, drinking Communion wine, or obtaining a poison to commit suicide, it actually has a duty to regulate the *commerce* in potentially harmful substances. Cheese with a high potential to carry listeria should probably be labeled, for example, and factories, farms, restaurants, and supermarkets need to be inspected to protect the consumer. It would be wise to make barbiturates, and other drugs that can too easily cause fatal overdoses, available by doctor's prescription only; and we should probably be made aware that there is caffeine in our soda that is liable to put us on the road to a lifelong addiction. If a company is profiting from the sale of a substance whose abuse or use is liable to harm its consumers, a community has every right to intervene in the marketing to protect its members. It is the extent of the intervention that should be open to debate—and in almost every case, we should come down on the side of accommodation, rather than prohibition.

In most instances, informing consumers—by means of labels warning of potential pathogens on ground beef, or the health hazards of cigarettes or marijuana—should be enough. (And when it comes to the public use of tobacco, why not use municipal licensing systems to grant a certain number of permits to smoking bars, well-signposted so all would know what they were getting into before they swung open the saloon door?)

In contrast, use outside of commerce—of peyote by the Native American church, of pentobarbital by nonprofit organizations like Dignitas, of free heroin by the addicts of Zürich—should be in an altogether different category. As long as there's no coercion, and users are aware of what they're doing, a community shouldn't have much say in what people freely choose to put in their bodies. The resolution to the War on Drugs, then, lies not in the legalization of addictive drugs (which has become a synonym for throwing them onto a free market, and letting the government tax the hell out of them), nor in decriminalization (a byword for buck-passing and legal limbo), but in *decommodification*. Psychoactive drugs should not be treated as commodities; because of their sacred history, their potential to improve health, or cause intoxication and addiction, they belong in an entirely different category. In the medical domain, does anybody—apart from the executives of pharmaceutical multinationals—think that AIDS drugs, insulin, and malaria pills should be sold at anything more than cost to the world's poorest and most desperate? Likewise, should anybody profit from peddling substances that have the potential to addict their users and destroy their health?

It is hard, at this point, to do much about the most deadly and addictive of psychoactives, nicotine. Short of going back to cigars, pipes, and Native American tobacco ceremonies, the current social policy of limiting the number of public places where people can smoke seems to be at once an effective approach to reducing addiction, and philosophically defensible. It is impossible, too, to change the status of alcohol. The vintners of Bordeaux and the distillers of the Hebrides have spent a few too many centuries perfecting their wares to ever acquiesce to giving the stuff away for free. But only a small minority of alcohol users get addicted. The same goes for soft drugs—including marijuana, coca, poppy tea, khat, and, I'd argue, hallucinogenic drugs such as LSD and magic mushrooms. Such plant-derived drugs should, then, be put in the same category as alcohol: available for sale to adults at a price close to cost, and taxed like any other item of commerce, as they currently are in Amsterdam.

Subtracting monetary value from the current panoply of prohibited drugs, especially the so-called hard drugs, by offering them to the existing addict population for free—as the Swiss have done with heroin—would also have some interesting side effects. Dealers and traffickers—the Hells Angels, Afghani warlords, Colombian cartels—would have to look for other work. Suddenly, there would be no more gang wars; no more shootings over turf. Supervised injection sites and clean needles would bring an immediate reduction in HIV, hepatitis, and overdoses. The means of distribution might look a little like those used in Switzerland: clinics requiring daily visits, sterile and unglamorous—scoring drugs would be about as unpleasant as visiting a Vinmonopolet in some remote Norwegian town—with the stipulation that injection, smoking, or snorting would have to happen on-site. But apart from that, no conditions. What should be available is lots of support, recognizing that the users are grappling with what might be a transitional problem with addiction: medically trained staff should be on hand, offering references to treatment programs, detoxification clinics, therapists, support groups.

Indeed. All of this would all make a lot of sense. But I'm not holding my breath. Drugs aren't going to be decriminalized, let alone handed out free of charge, anytime soon. In fact, with the worldwide rise of Christian and Islamic fundamentalisms—two monotheistic faiths whose central myths deal with forbidding apples and fermented grapes—a sensible approach to lifting prohibitions is looking more unlikely than ever.

If there were any evidence that prohibitions were effective, that they actually prevented people from using what was dangerous, I might consider defending them. But throughout history, banning things, particularly drugs, has had three major consequences: it makes what is forbidden more potent, and because it is unregulated, more deadly; it artificially inflates prices, creating fortunes in the criminal underworld that can be used to bankroll arms purchases and internecine wars; and it makes prohibition itself into a self-perpetuating institution, so that monopolies and enforcement agencies—whether it's the American DEA, Singapore's Central Narcotics Bureau, or customs departments worldwide—end up having as much interest in maintaining an unhealthy status quo as the Italian Mafia, the Basque ETA, or the Irish Republican Army.

Prohibitionists like to point to the society-wide epidemic of opium addiction that gripped nineteenth-century China as the classic example of what can happen when there's a free market in drugs. In reality, the situation arose while prohibition was in full effect: the Chinese government had completely banned the import, sale, and use of opium; it's just that the British were very, very good at smuggling drugs into the country. (It wasn't until 1917 that the English stopped flooding the Shanghai market with contraband: the pipe and opium were immediately replaced by the syringe and morphine, the latter far more potent and easier to smuggle.) Today, under worldwide prohibition, more drugs are being consumed than at any other time in human history. Since Ronald Reagan declared the War on Drugs in 1981, Washington has spent at least $300 billion on the battle. Meanwhile, heroin production in the 1990s trebled, and cocaine production doubled. The United States in particular is undergoing an unprecedented epidemic of psychoactive drug use. In 1905, when narcotics were still legal in the United States, and available by mail order and over the counter in pharmacies, less than one third of one percent of the population used cocaine or heroin and other opiates. Today, the figure is closer to 1.6 percent—4.3 million users of hard drugs, and that figure excludes prisoners and people abusing such hard-core prescription drugs as the tranquilizer Xanax, the heavy-duty opiate OxyContin, or the powerful amphetamine Ritalin. All told, 77 million Americans—one third of all adults—admit to having used illegal drugs at least once. So much for the effectiveness of the War on Drugs.

None of this is to deny the danger of some drugs, and the tragedy of addiction. Novel-drug epidemics have devastated societies—whether it was gin in eighteenth-century urban England or crystal meth in contemporary rural America—just as episodes of abuse and addiction will continue to ruin individual lives. The question is whether society is willing to reduce the harm associated with the latest craze—and to offer aid to those who succumb to it—or whether society will continue to pursue and punish them, with all the fury of its unavowed fundamentalisms, for their perceived moral weakness.

As for myself, I had been traveling for a little over a year, selectively sampling the world's intoxicants, and I seemed to have survived the experience without succumbing to anything worse than a short-lived addiction to Nat Shermans. In my early twenties, I went through a period of dalliance and addiction, with a predilection for opiates— codeine, morphine, heroin, methadone, paregoric, anything I could get my hands on—though tranquilizers and alcohol would do in a pinch. The episode went on longer than it should have and included a case of mononucleosis, several candida infections, an overdose, and, finally, an epileptic fit. Prohibition, I still believe, almost killed me. None of it would have happened if I'd had access to milder or less adulterated drugs, and it was hard to seek medical help, since, thanks to prohibition, I saw doctors as croakers to be conned into writing scripts for painkillers and downers. (While the doctors undoubtedly saw me as a nuisance to be ejected from their offices as quickly as possible.)

Others in my entourage weren't so lucky: they died of AIDS, contracted hepatitis C, ended up with criminal records, or went missing on the streets. In my case, addiction certainly wouldn't have lasted as long if there hadn't been such glamour attached to crossing the line, and if talking about it hadn't been made impossible by the demonization of drug use. (How many people write off friends, for fear of being robbed or hurt, when they find out they're using drugs? Conversely, how many drug users lie to their loved ones, thereby losing all hope of meaningful support, for fear of being ostracized?) My drug use certainly wouldn't have had such serious health consequences if some milder versions of the hard drugs were around. I remember that when the local supply of heroin dried up, we were quite happy to brew up some poppy tea—though the vacant lots were too quickly picked over for this to be a reliable stopgap. And I'm grateful that at the time of my worst abuse, my city had a needle exchange, which probably saved me from contracting HIV and hepatitis C or getting abcesses through blunt syringes. After ending up in a hospital after going into convulsions, I quit, cold turkey, convinced—partly by the prevailing discourse of the 1990s—that my only hope of salvation lay in complete abstinence. I even attended some Narcotics Anonymous meetings, in which drug use was demonized through constantly repeated horror stories. But I quickly tired of the talk of Higher Powers and the clichés of confession, and on my own I cut out smoking, drinking, drugs—and even red meat—for ten years.

I found, however, I was missing some of the positive sides of intoxication: the time-out offered by a few drinks, or the salutary alteration of consciousness one can find in the occasional use of stronger stuff. It is a good thing to know, of course, if you are actually an alcoholic, a binge eater, bulimic, or someone who's prone to heroin or cocaine addiction. Some people really do have a kind of "on-off" switch—when they start intoxicating themselves, they can't stop—and their dramatic tales of self-degradation and the harm they inflict on friends and family tend to dominate the discourse on intoxication. They are the minority, however: most people find hangovers or withdrawal, fogginess or the jitters, to be natural deterrents to constant intoxication.

There is, after all, a middle ground between abstinence and excess: it's called moderation, and once you're out of the thicket of post-adolescent overdramatization, it becomes a lot more attainable. Getting there requires a certain amount of maturity and self-knowledge; unfortunately, in a context where prohibition is the reigning worldwide paradigm, where paternalistic laws keep us in protracted adolescence by professing to protect us from ourselves, most people are prevented from ever thinking in shades of gray. Since the Harrison Act of 1914 kicked off worldwide drug prohibition, intoxication has become a black-and-white issue. You are either on the righteous side of the line, or in a world of shame, picnicking with the devil.

Where did that leave me? Exasperated. Curious. And a little wary. "It is dangerous," observed Voltaire, "to be right in matters on which the established authorities are wrong." The old humanist settled in Switzerland—Ferney, near Geneva, to be exact—but probably a little prematurely; for he complained of being hounded by fops and milords on their grand tours of Europe, who came and gaped at him like a "wild beast."

For the time being, I was still young enough to be in love with the world, and all the messiness and irrationality of its antiquated and warring ideologies. The day might come when I would be forced to seek asylum. I already knew it wouldn't be in Switzerland—for all its resemblance to a republic of reason, the old democracy of cuckoo clocks and bomb shelters was a trifle boring and paranoid, and more than a little smug. It wouldn't be in Norway or Singapore, either, where paternalistic busybodies use prohibitive policies to infantilize a citizenry that ends up acting out in the most bizarre ways. I'd already lived in France, and as much as I loved their cheese, chocolate, and wine, Gallic culture has lately become so stagnant, stiff, and mired in its past glory that I'd be worried about developing premature arthritis. As for the United States, I might be able to handle San Francisco—if that city is indeed part of America—where, in spite of the ambient West Coast uptightness, they were pretty loose about things like smoking and pursuing pleasure. I doubted I could settle in Manhattan, the new Singapore of the Americas, a gated island-state run by nanny mayors for the benefit of stockbrokers and trust-fund bohemians. I had high hopes for Canada, which seemed to be doing all kinds of reasonable things, such as allowing gay marriage, giving away free drugs to addicts, and enacting a de facto decriminalization of marijuana possession. Frankly, though, my own country gets a little too cold for my liking in the winter.

When, like Voltaire's Candide, I tired of it all, I was pretty sure I'd head straight for sloppy, anachronistic, paradoxical Spain. I could definitely live in a nation where they don't waste their time chewing each other out for smoking in public, don't bother prosecuting their citizens for private drug use or eating *criadillas*, and where the motto, on tapas-bar crawls, as in life, is *Poco, a menudo*: "Have a little, but often."

I would surely find a nice little gabled house in Galicia, where I'd learn to eat preserved citrons and pistachio nuts and teach myself the gentle pleasures of cultivating a garden. It would be a simple kitchen plot, but I'd set aside ample space to grow coca, tobacco, wormwood, cannabis, and poppies. When visitors happened by, they could expect to join me for a picnic, and I'd offer them—but certainly never charge

ACKNOWLEDGMENTS

I couldn't have written this book without all the people who put me up, steered me right, and put up with my strange ways over the last year.

Thanks to: Charles, Stig, and the gang for the midnight tour of the banks of the Akerselva; Marianne and Jonathan for the *smørbrød* and *lettøl*, Kristina and Osa for the party, Alto Braveboy and the genial crew of the *Innvik* for their many kindnesses.

Pam and Kev for the crash course in Singaporean cuisine and customs.

David, Chipi, Mercedes, Alex, and Peio Amiano for the introduction to offal, *setas*, and *gulas*.

Alexandra and Guillaume of the Rue Poulet, Nidhi of Hoboken, Jaspreet of no-fixed-address by way of Banff, and "Zangs" MacSween of Rue St. Dominique for the Nat Shermans and sympathetic ear.

John and Maud of Noe Valley by way of Pokhara, and Amber and Linda in the Mission.

The kind Swiss: Dora of Zürich, Nicolas of Boveresse, Catherine of Montreal, and Sarah, formerly of Lausanne. The patient French, particularly Sophie Lefort in Bayonne.

them for—my homemade absinthe and homegrown-coca tea, as a token of hospitality.

In a dark corner, next to the fly agarics, the observant visitor might notice I'd planted a little patch of deadly nightshade and hemlock, in case I needed to make a quick exit.

After all, even in a personal Eden, one has to give the devil his due.

My shadow companion in La Paz, David Freitag, who ended up taking the high road to Peru, and Alain of the MNI, for years of stimulating, caffeinated conversation on the topic of addiction.

And, as always, thanks, for everything, to Paul and Audrey Grescoe, Lara and Justin Aydein on the wet coast, Scott Chernoff and Jennifer Ménard in Tokyo, and any ineffable inamorata left unmentioned.

I'm looking forward to the day we can all picnic together.

Finally, with love to Erin Churchill, sweet and surprising robot-redeemer for an errant *advocatus diaboli*.

A NOTE ON THE AUTHOR

Taras Grescoe is the author of two books, one of which, *Sacré Blues: An Unsentimental Journey Through Quebec*, was short-listed for the Writers' Trust Award, won the Mavis Gallant Prize for Non-Fiction, and was a national best seller in Canada. He is a frequent contributor to the *New York Times, Salon, Condé Nast Traveler*, the *Independent*, and *National Geographic Traveler* and has written features for *Saveur*, the *New York Times Magazine*, the *Guardian, Wired*, and the *Chicago Tribune Magazine*.

A NOTE ON THE TYPE

The text of this book is set in Bembo. This type was first used in 1495 by the Venetian printer Aldus Manutius for Cardinal Bembo's *De Aetna*, and was cut for Manutius by Francesco Griffo. It was one of the types used by Claude Garamond (1480–1561) as a model for his Romain de L'Université, and so it was the forerunner of what became standard European type for the following two centuries. Its modern form follows the original types and was designed for Monotype in 1929.